The trial by fire that forged one of the most successful cooperative communities in the world today . . .

J. Donald Walters wanted to serve the organization. He believed in it deeply. However, he would not endlessly compromise his belief. And so he found himself in conflict with his superiors. "My institution, right or wrong," was never his motto. Truth, not institutional priorities, was his guide.

This book tells the age-old story of institutional demands versus individual conscience. It will be familiar to anyone who has had dealings with governments and with large corporations of all kinds: economic, educational, religious. In physics, the electron is considered the key to the universe. So also in human affairs: The key to society is the individual. When individuality is respected, society flourishes. When it is ignored, society stagnates and becomes paralyzed.

Walters describes the painful journey that led to his founding of a new concept in living: Ananda, whose guiding motto is, "People are more important than things."

This story is told with courage and with charity—from the years spent under the great spiritual master Paramhansa Yogananda to years in India, to San Francisco during the 'sixties (era of hippies, the drug culture, the "Hare Krishnas" and Bhaktivedanta, the American Zen movement) and his own encounters with some of the leading figures of the day, to the community he gradually evolved.

"*A Place Called Ananda* is truly a book for, and about, the new millennium. It is not merely the story of one man's extraordinary achievements in pioneering a new paradigm for cooperative, spiritual living. More importantly, it is a handbook for those wishing to live guided by the highest principles of truth and inner freedom." —CP

"The story of your life imparts courage and faith. . . . I am filled with renewed hope and faith." —JP

"A masterpiece of clarity, insight, breadth of vision, and understanding." —SJ

"*A Place Called Ananda* is a must read for all truth seekers. Swami Kriyananda demonstrates how to live with the right spiritual attitudes while faced with the most extreme challenges." —DW

"This book is full of fire and LIGHT!" —CS

"A wonderful book. It brings the history of Ananda to life, and puts it in the context of larger world events." —JN

"More gripping than any novel is Walters' account of the establishment of Ananda Village in the face of impossible odds. The reader comes away convinced of the absolute necessity for Ananda's existence at this time in history, and of a conscious, benign Power guiding its destiny." —SR

"From the story of Kriyananda's life I learned that we really can make a difference in this world." —DS

A Place Called Ananda

The author in Bucharest, Romania, age 10. The book he holds is *Scottish Knights,* by Jane Porter. The dreaming look in his eyes is of a life of freedom and justice for everyone. These were to become the central theme of his life. At 15 he began planning the community he founded a quarter of a century later, named Ananda.

A Place Called Ananda

The trial by fire that forged one of the most successful cooperative communities in the world today

J. Donald Walters
(Swami Kriyananda)

Crystal Clarity Publishers
Nevada City, California

First printing 1996

Cover and book design by C. A. Schuppe

Photos by J. Donald Walters, C. A. Schuppe,
Barbara Bingham, and Sara Cryer

Printed in the United States of America

ISBN: 1-56589-735-8

5 7 9 11 13 12 10 8 6

Crystal

Clarity

Crystal Clarity Publishers
14618 Tyler-Foote Road
Nevada City, CA 95959-8599

Phone: 800-424-1055 or 530-478-7600
Fax: 530-478-7610
E-mail: clarity@crystalclarity.com
Website: www.crystalclarity.com

Dedicated to those
who seek inner freedom

Contents

Main Persons in This Story

Babaji. Known as Mahavatar, or great incarnation. Guru of Lahiri Mahasaya.

Lahiri Mahasaya (Shyama Charan Lahiri, 1828–1895). Disciple of Babaji and guru of Sri Yukteswar. Yogananda described him as a *yogavatar,* or "incarnation of yoga."

Sri Yukteswar (Priya Nath Karar, 1855–1936). Disciple of Lahiri Mahasaya and guru of Paramhansa Yogananda. Yogananda described him as a *gyanavatar,* or "incarnation of wisdom."

Paramhansa Yogananda ("Master," 1893–1952). The founder of Self-Realization Fellowship (SRF). A great master of yoga who lived and taught in the West. Rajarsi Janakananda described him as a *premavatar,* or "incarnation of love."

Rajarsi Janakananda (Saint Lynn, James J. Lynn, 1892–1955). Paramhansa Yogananda's foremost disciple. The second President of Self-Realization Fellowship.

Daya Mata (Faye Wright, 1914–). The third President of Self-Realization Fellowship.

Tara Mata (Laurie Pratt, 1900–1970). Second Vice-President and member of the Board of Directors of Self-Realization Fellowship.

Introduction

When I wrote my autobiography, *The Path,* twenty years ago, it was to fill a gap left by Paramhansa Yogananda in his own book, *Autobiography of a Yogi,* which, as his brother Sananda Lal Ghosh pointed out in *Mejda,* described in detail his encounters with other saints but omitted much that he might have said about himself. As Yogananda told a few of us toward the end of his life, "As a boy, I went to those saints for guidance. But what I found, to my dismay, was that they wanted guidance from *me!*"

My purpose in writing *The Path* as an autobiography was to make it easier for the reader, after he'd become somewhat familiar with me, to weed out possible intrusions of my nature into an account that deserved to be understood as objectively as possible. It was not my aim to interest the reader in me as a person. I hoped to attract readers to the spiritual search, that they themselves might feel inspired to embark on the adventure of self-discovery that finds such fulfillment in the teachings of Paramhansa Yogananda.

Yogananda was one of the great spiritual figures of modern times. In *The Path* I tried to give the reader insight into what it was like to live with him as a disciple, and some understanding of his profound, and at the same time profoundly practical, teachings.

Scott Meredith, the well-known literary agent, to whom I sent an early draft of my manuscript, at once noticed the impersonal flavor in the account of my early years. His comment, based on years of experience with more "normal" autobiographies, was, "I kept wanting to ask, 'Will the real Don Walters please stand up?'"

For my purposes, however, he was mistaken. My main misgiving had been that, given the unusual nature of my upbringing, my readers would not easily identify with my story. Probably this absence of normal commonality was what bothered Scott Meredith. I hadn't related the usual account of personal idiosyncrasies and predicaments. How would "normal" readers, then, be able to relate to me?

Well, there was nothing I could do about it. This was my story. I hadn't really another to tell.

It has been deeply gratifying to me to receive hundreds of letters from readers over the years, thanking me for my book. Their thanks have been not only for the insight it gave them into discipleship under my great guru (whom they also, in numerous cases, have subsequently accepted as their guru), but also extend to the first part of the book, in which they see reflected their own spiritual search.

It is not possible for a single book to say everything, even on the subject it purports to cover. Writers who try to do so become impossibly long-winded and tiresome. Really to know another person's life—

particularly in the case of someone like Yogananda, whose consciousness embraced infinity—one would have to accomplish what he accomplished: in Yogananda's case, to know God. When I hear other direct disciples claim to understand him, I can only think they are mistaking candlelight for the light of the sun. Behind everything he said and did was a consciousness too profound for any merely human attempt to comprehend it. To say "He was like this" or "he was like that"; to claim "He liked this" or "he liked that" is to overlook the fact that, in a deeply real sense, he *was everything.* At the same time, he was not identified with or attached to *anything.* Completely human—lovingly, charmingly so—in the highest and fullest possible sense, he was yet forever at rest in the eternal Self within. Nothing could define him, for he had transcended all definitions, and swam blissfully in *satchidananda*—the ocean of perfect, divine immortality.

My own book, *The Path,* didn't complete even the story of his earthly life. Nor could it have; I wouldn't have presumed to make the attempt. There is one aspect of his life, however, that I feel duty-bound to discuss, and that I couldn't touch on more than lightly in *The Path* from considerations of both length and perspective. This is the commission he gave me, specifically, to carry out in the fulfillment of his mission.

I am not blind to the relative unimportance of my own contribution to that mission, even though—no doubt to inspire me to remain upright before the difficulties he foresaw for me—he described it to me as "a great work." Lest anyone think I am being merely modest, I should add that the only work that matters, ultimately, is the one God has given all creatures: the responsibility of attaining oneness with Him.

I must admit that, even now, my perspective is limited compared to what it might be, say, twenty years from now. By then, however, I may well no longer be here to express it. And from an even broader perspective it might be well to wait another century or two even to attempt the telling. Necessarily, then, my account will represent a limited version of events. I may as well make a virtue of necessity, therefore, and write it not with the impersonality of *The Path,* but with full admission that *I* am the character most involved in this story, and acceptance of full responsibility for any blame that accrues to my role. The only thing I ask is that, if any praise is involved, it be given where it is due: to my guru. For, as Rajarsi Janakananda, his chief disciple, told me after Yogananda's passing, "Master has a great work to do through you, Walter, *and he will give you the strength to do it.*"

My particular incentive for writing this story is that certain people have seen fit to attack this work that I've done. In the process, they've attacked me. I am not their enemy; indeed, I sincerely wish them well. It would be foolhardy, however, to pretend that their attack is not intended to harm me and those who have devoted their lives to working with me. For their sake, and for those many who believe in what we are doing, I feel it would be helpful to make known to them the complete story that led up to the creation of Ananda, and the special role Ananda plays in the overall mission of Paramhansa Yogananda.

It is my practice, whenever I write anything, to form a mental image of my audience—to condense it into a single person, neither male nor female, and visualize that person sitting across the desk from me, listening to me as I converse. Gratifyingly, the most frequent comment I receive from my readers has been, "I feel as though you were talking personally *to me.*"

This is a particular, not a common story. Still, I hope it will interest people in many walks of life whose desire is for inner freedom and who have had to struggle with the demands and expectations of others. It is, of course, especially for those interested in founding intentional communities as a solution to humanity's universal need for inner freedom.

Part One

CHAPTER 1

Yogananda's Mission to the West

Jesus told his Pharisee critics, "The Sabbath was made for man, not man for the Sabbath." Every divinely ordained institution is created for the welfare of mankind, and not for the sake of controlling anyone.

Babaji made a similar statement to Lahiri Mahasaya on the occasion of their first meeting. In response to Lahiri's thought that he ought to leave, since he had a duty to fulfill to his office, Babaji said, "The office was brought for you, and not you for the office."

Masters rarely create institutions. When they do so, it is as a means of serving people. Their aim is to inspire, not to control. Usually, they let their disciples bother with such things as founding institutions. Their mission is to promulgate truth and light in a world filled with the darkness of ignorance. It was one mark of Master's greatness that, in addition to spreading truth and light, he also sacrificed himself greatly to bring about the formation of an organization. For a master of his stature, the cost must have been considerable. It went against everything that came most naturally to him.

How often he sighed in longing for the unburdened life: wandering freely by the Ganges, teaching beneath a tree to those who wanted to listen, singing with devotion to the Divine Mother in the enraptured company of a small band of true devotees. Not once, but many times, he spoke of leaving everything behind and just roaming with God. "Divine Mother," he cried, "I will leave this work and never once look back!" But, he said later, "Divine Mother disciplined me. I had to return and finish the work She had given me."

How did those disciples feel who lived with him? Surely they shared his sentiments, expressed often and with so much feeling. They themselves would have greatly preferred a simple monastic life of devotion to God, serving the guru and meditating. Often we give ourselves the more determinedly to an uncongenial duty, as if to demonstrate our heartfelt willingness to do God's will, not our own.

For not one of them came to Master with organizationalism written sternly upon their brows. Few people realize what it took to live with our guru—the courage, the strength of will, the devotion, the willingness resolutely to set self aside in joyful, unresisting service. Master never demanded anything of his disciples that he hadn't found them willing and eager to give. Hundreds—indeed, many thousands—came to him. Few out of all that multitude had that extra bit of good karma to dedicate themselves unhesitatingly to the cause he had brought.

Nor did he make that dedication easy for anyone. He tested them to see if they truly had the fire of divine devotion that burned so brightly in his own heart. You, who know him mainly through his books, cannot easily imagine the challenge he hurled at the world by the sheer fervor of his own dedication. He was loving, yes—sweet, kind, thoughtful, patient, endlessly forgiving and forbearing—all those things, in short, that every reader feels on reading his *Autobiography of a Yogi.* And yet, where principles were concerned he was unbending.

People often took his sternness in such matters for judgment of *them* in their weaknesses. What they could not cope with was the awareness they developed, in his presence, of their own weaknesses. He was kindness itself in his efforts to bring them out of those weaknesses, but if they lacked the courage to face themselves and huddled fearfully, instead, at the bottom of Mount Carmel, clutching to their bosoms weaknesses they hadn't even perceived previously as such, his very kindness sometimes looked to them like cruelty. Often, alas for their own welfare, they ended up hating him for having tried to free them of their shackles.

It was common for such failed devotees to claim in self-justification that the qualities he was encouraging them to correct weren't shackles at all. "See how free we are!" they cried. "We're perfectly normal human beings." Thus, more determined than ever to please the world and satisfy their own egoistic desires, they remained lost in spiritual blindness for at least the rest of this lifetime.

Look at the matter in a broader perspective. For those whose karma it is to be yogis in this incarnation, to have been born an American in the Twentieth Century is an extraordinary spiritual opportunity, but it is also one fraught with spiritual peril. Those who make the most of this opportunity will gain, spiritually, out of all proportion to other lives they lived in mountain caves and in ashrams in India.

I asked Master soon after I first met him, "Have I been a yogi before this lifetime?"

"Many times," he replied. "You would have to have been, even to live here"—that is to say, at Mt. Washington.

I also said to him once at his desert retreat, "I have always wanted to live alone like this." He replied:

"That's because you've done it before. Most of those who are with me have lived alone many times in the past."

These statements mean that not I only, but hundreds who demonstrated their spiritual sincerity to the extent of dedicating their lives to his cause had been yogis "many times in the past." He said that even to be drawn to the path of Kriya Yoga, which countless thousands were during his lifetime and have been in the decades since then, indicates the karma of one who has been a dedicated yogi in former lives.

We see the present scene—the spiritual laziness of some, the moods of others, the worldly desires and attachments of still others—and we think, perhaps, "That's not much of a devotee!" (Shame on us if we judge anyone!) But we don't see the incarnations of hard climbing that it has taken them to get even where they are now. How many people are there in the world with even a fraction of the good karma it takes to be consciously on the spiritual path?

I remember when I had been at Mt. Washington several months. In sudden rebellion one evening against the constant call to service and meditation, I lay down stubbornly on my bed and spent a couple of blissful hours with a volume of Shakespeare's plays. I simply needed a break.

Master, recognizing the rebelliousness of human nature, encouraged occasional diversions. He encouraged me, too, to be less extreme, and more relaxed, in my zeal. As he told me once, "The mind is like a donkey. If you keep on forcing it, it will stand still and refuse to budge another step no matter how hard you beat it. The thing to do, then, is let it stand awhile. Finally, it will start walking again of its own accord."

But can you imagine the vast majority of people in the world—I don't mean the average worldly person; I'm speaking of fundamentally idealistic, good people. Are they interested in meditating at all?

"What?" you've probably heard them say. "Close my eyes and sit there like a statue, doing nothing—thinking of nothing? I can just *see* myself!"

Norman once said to Master, "I don't think I have very good karma, Master."

"Remember this," Master answered with great firmness, "it takes very, *very,* VERY good karma even to want to know God!"

Alas, people don't always want others to be firm even in their own defense. I remember a company at

Ananda that was obviously headed for bankruptcy. I invited the staff to my home and, purely out of a desire to help them, suggested ways they might yet save their enterprise from collapse. All that the staff derived from the meeting was the conviction that I had "called them on the carpet." It was as though they *wanted* to fail. And, of course, that disaster wasn't long in coming.

Yogananda's Mission to the West

Why did Master come to the West?

Well of course, God sent him, but why?

It was in answer to a universal need. It was time for the world to achieve balance between material and spiritual prosperity. Master was born, he told us, in response to a heart-felt desire on the part of countless Westerners—Americans, especially—for a practical approach to spirituality, one that would match the practicality they'd achieved in their material lives. Yankee ingenuity and modern science had awakened in them an awareness of the need for methods and techniques that would help them demonstrate the practicality of the scriptures also.

By the same token, Master said, people in India were becoming aware of the practical benefits of modern life, and had begun to want to balance spiritual faith and inner peace with material efficiency. Many souls were therefore being drawn from America to take birth in India, to help the Indian people learn the divine law as it is expressed in the material world.

Many Indian souls, similarly, were being born here

in the West to help bring about greater spiritual awareness.

In addition to this mass interchange, dictated by world karma, there was also the fact that Master himself was sent here to help in this process of spiritual awakening in the West. He may quite justly be called the *avatar* (divine savior) for this *Dwapara Yuga.* Equally justly may he be called the guru and savior of America, and of countless souls whom destiny may not even call to his particular path.

Many thousands of those who came to him during his lifetime were drawn either to be with him personally, or to encounter him and thus benefit from the great outpouring of spiritual force that he brought with him. He once told Dr. Lewis, "No one's path has crossed mine in this life without a reason."

Perhaps a majority of these people had spent many incarnations in India. They were not accustomed to the intense demands that would be placed upon them in the materialistic West. Spiritually speaking, they were like fish out of water. Though drawn here by their spiritual karma, they yet found themselves out of their natural element, gasping and confused in the fierce sunlight of excessive matter-consciousness.

It was tantamount, in many ways, to an invading army on foreign soil. On D-Day at Normandy Beach many soldiers had to die for the invasion to succeed. Or, if you'd prefer a gentler image, think how many snowflakes fall with the first snowfall, only to melt before the ground grows cool enough to receive them.

I remember Master saying, after Norman left his life of renunciation at Mt. Washington, "This is the first time in many lifetimes that delusion has caught Norman."

I believe that those who tried to follow the path in this life, but failed, will receive many blessings for even having tried. The *Bhagavad Gita* offers the same reassurance to all failed yogis. How much more must the divine compassion extend to fallen aspirants in this lifetime of so many extraordinary spiritual challenges?

Even those who turned against Master deserve at least our understanding, for they surely have God's. I do not mean we should sympathize with them to the extent of seeking them out and consoling them (or trying to convert them). Their negative influence might prove injurious to the devotional magnetism we're working to cultivate. Usually, a brief "there but for the grace of God" will suffice. But we are all fellow warriors in the war against delusion. Let us remember always that our foe is delusion itself, and not those unfortunate souls who, to their own lasting grief, succumb to its lures. Our task, if we love God, is if possible to help the casualties by mentally sending them our blessings, and by praying for them as we pray for all souls.

Consider, too, that Master's self-styled enemies were at least focused, in their hatred, on a Being of Light whose very divinity could yet redeem them. Is that not preferable to focusing all one's attention on those who, steeped in delusion, could only draw one's mind down into deeper darkness? Ravana, it is said, the supreme foe of Lord Rama, achieved salvation at the end of his life through his hatred for Rama. The very fixity of his concentration on that source of universal salvation freed him, in the end, from hatred itself.

Living with Master produced many spiritual casualties. Many came; few remained. Many more would have remained steadfast on the path, I fancy, had they been drawn to it in India, where the soil is rich with the millennial blessings of God-known *rishi*s. But as the stakes during Master's time were high, so also were the rewards. Those who remained loyal drew to themselves enormous blessings.

As Master himself said during the Kriya Initiation at Mt. Washington in December 1949: "Of those present, there will be a few *siddha*s [souls fully liberated from all delusion], and quite a few *jivan mukta*s [souls that have achieved liberation from further egoic involvement in *maya,* though still retaining vestiges of karmas from past lives]."

Seen in this perspective, it must be realized that to have remained loyal to Master and to his path, especially during the early days before his work was truly established, singled the devotee out as a spiritual hero of epic stature.

In reading the life of Durga Mata, for example, one is struck by her extraordinary energy, faith, and devotion. Master, speaking to me about her, said, "When I first met her I said to her, 'You have come.'" He had been waiting for her, as he waited patiently for many others to come. Often he spoke to us monks about Durga Mata's amazing energy in her devotional service to his cause.

It is easy to see things in a broad perspective from

a distance. But how must it have looked to those faithful few who remained with Master while so many, year after year, abandoned Mt. Washington and returned to the worldly life? I know something about those days not only through what I've heard from the older disciples and through what I've read, but also through my own experience living at Mt. Washington during his later years. Yet even my knowledge must pale in comparison to the reality.

For here was this spiritual giant, whose greatness was not even recognized by most people—to most of them a "good" man, or a spiritual teacher like many others, only more eloquent and dynamic than others they'd heard. (One of his detractors, another spiritual teacher, actually remarked once, "Oh, yes, I know Yogananda. He's a very good—cook.") Think of the steady exodus of people who he had hoped would help him to establish his work. How must it have looked to those few souls who remained loyal to him, and to his way of life, themselves defying the lures of a materialistic culture and the terrible depression that then gripped America? (For a time, Master and his disciples kept body and soul together only by growing tomatoes on the arid hillside below the headquarters at Mt. Washington.) There weren't hundreds of devotees living there then. The blessed Master had only a tiny handful.

The devotees coming and going at that time represented little but froth to those few who remained steadfast. The two constants in their lives were Master, and Mt. Washington—the SRF organization he was trying with so much hardship to hold together.

Centralization vs. Outreach

Nowadays it is relatively easy to see the need to reach out to a spiritually starving public. In those days however, the very people most eager to reach out in this way were also those most ready to forsake him. His worst self-styled enemies were those who, on his behalf, were sent out to lecture and give classes. These false representatives grew to envy him his success with the public. In their zeal for personal recognition, they forsook him. Some of them betrayed him.

The "in" people at Mt. Washington (if I may use this expression without appearing frivolous) came gradually to be, not the teachers (most of whom were men), but the humble workers behind the scenes (women, usually), and those especially who worked in the office, handling the correspondence and sending out the weekly lessons.

The heart of Master's work was not at its ever-changing periphery, but at its changeless core. Even the people living and working at Mt. Washington were not the true heart of the work. Most of these, too, varied from year to year. What remained was Mt. Washington itself.

The loyalty of those "in" people became increasingly focused on Mt. Washington, and on the organization it represented. That, naturally, became their definition of what Master's work was all about.

I will never forget the day a brush fire threatened the headquarters at Mt. Washington. Daya Mata was out on the hillside with the rest of us, fighting the flames. What impressed me about her on that occasion was the extraordinary fierceness in her expression as she fought to put out the flames. Like a mother bear she seemed to me, defending her cubs even before the threat to her own life. I myself was determined, too, to do what I could in the building's defense, but I didn't experience that defensive fierceness Daya displayed. For I hadn't lived through the years of opposition and betrayal to her guru that she'd experienced.

Her loyalty and dedication were centered in Master, in Mt. Washington, and in the life she had known there with him. She said recently in reference to her many years with Master, "I live in those days." Even in her presidency I cannot imagine that he wanted from her anything different. The attitude those years engendered in her was a focus on his organization, primarily, rather than on those who were spiritually starved for the understanding and inner peace that Master's teachings could give them. Even in her efforts to develop the work, her primary interest has always been, quite naturally, in the growth of the organization itself: in its function as an instrument for good, rather than on the recipients of that good.

Could Master have wanted more from Daya Mata? Surely not. To have done so would have been to want her to depart from her own training, experience, and inner nature. His very duty to her, as her guru, was to guide her along her own line of natural development.

I see now that I have been wrong in trying to persuade Daya Mata to direct her energies differently.

The Need for Outreach

On the other hand, does this mean that the organization was Master's ideal for the work? Could he have wanted the organization to be defined so much by its outward form? Surely not, if his work was meant, as he said it was, to bring millions to God.

Could he have wanted his organization to become a powerful institution—a second Roman Catholic Church, let us say? That, indeed, is another story. The entire emphasis of his life and teaching was centered in helping people. To him, the organization was a means, only, to that end. He had, in other words, a further wish for the work than its power as an institution.

Even God-realized masters must work with what God gives them. As Master himself said once to Dr. Lewis (his first Kriya Yoga disciple in America), "Remember, Doctor, no matter what you or I do, this work will follow a certain pattern, ordained by God."

Based on what seems to me self-evident, and supported by the training and instructions Master gave me personally, I have looked upon SRF as a missionary work intended to guide and help humanity. When I say that I have been wrong in trying to persuade Daya Mata to embrace a more expansive path, I do not at all mean that an expansive path is not needed. That, I am convinced, is the direction in which the work must develop. It is a good thing, no doubt, that Daya Mata is focused on the organization itself. That is the charge our Guru gave her. But there is also a need for concentration on the broader purpose behind his work. For his very reason for starting an organization was to reach out with his message to spiritually suffering humanity.

CHAPTER 2

Master's Commission to Me

"The Sabbath was made for man, not man for the Sabbath." Similar sentiments have been stated by masters down through the ages. Institutions of any kind are a means to an end, never an end in themselves. I cannot think of a single statement by any great master who ever lived that contradicts this view, whether in regard to a social convention like the Sabbath or an organization divinely instituted.

Master, in his autobiography, makes clear his disinclination for organized religion. His distaste was based on the fact that, to find God, one must go *within.* He often stressed the importance of loving others outwardly, too, of expressing concern for *their* needs—above all for their spiritual needs, but also for their physical and psychological needs. He came to the West not with the primary purpose of starting an organization, but to help souls. The organization he founded was only a means to that end.

It was an important means, for it helped anchor the work and give it a solid foundation without which the influence of his presence on the West might have been like snow—beautiful for a season, but only a memory by summertime. Still, the organization itself was not his message; it was a means, only, by which his spiritual message could be spread.

It is strange, how many of those who he hoped would teach on his behalf ended up teaching on their own behalf. Strange, too, how many of these ended up betraying him, turning against him to bolster their own need for self-importance.

Yet Master wanted his message to spread. He couldn't be out touring the country, teaching, and at the same time train the disciples at Mt. Washington who would carry on his work after he left. And the disciples who came and stayed were those humble few who came seeking only God. He accepted gratefully what God sent him. It was in the fitness of things that he gave the responsibility for carrying on his work to these loyal ones who had served him with unconditional devotion for so many years.

"Feed My Sheep"

He still needed others, however, who would think not so much of the needs of the organization as of the needs of the people whom the organization was created to serve. It was to men, primarily, that he looked for the manifestation of this kind of energy. As he put it once, "Men's energy has a more outward thrust; women's is more inward. Even their bodies reveal these differences."

In May 1950, while I was walking with him at his retreat at Twenty-Nine Palms, he said to me, "Apart from Saint Lynn (Rajarsi Janakananda), *every man* has disappointed me." He added with intense earnestness, *"And you mustn't disappoint me!"*

Yet he had other good men disciples, and had, in the past, had many more: Mr. Black (Yogacharya Oliver), Dr. Lewis, Michael (Brother Bhaktananda), Mr. Dickinson, Mr. Cuaron—numerous others. What did he mean by saying that "every man" had disappointed him? His disappointment, obviously, wasn't on spiritual grounds. Surely his meaning was, rather, that none of those men had shown an interest in *spreading* his message. None had shown the understanding that his teachings were *for the world.*

Dr. Lewis often scoffed at teachers who, as he put it, "just get up and blow." I sympathized with his attitude. I myself was not interested in lecturing. I had come to Master to find God. In fact, I subscribed wholly to the prevalent thinking at Mt. Washington that public speaking and teaching were for those who liked personal recognition. Such recognition meant nothing to me.

Yet I did want to help people. And helping people meant, in the context of Master's work, not giving food to the poor so much as inspiration and guidance to truth-hungry souls. Master, seeing my interest, encouraged me in that direction.

Once, on seeing me recovered from a mood, Master said to me, "No more moods, now. Otherwise, how will you be able to help people?"

I'd been with him five months when he looked at me concentratedly one day and said, "I have plans for you, Walter." Because he had been speaking at the time to a young monk, Harvey Allen, about sending him to India, I thought he was thinking of sending me there also. But it appears his plans were somewhat different.

I had been with him only eight months, and was still twenty-two, when he had me speak in his stead at the San Diego church. Even more frightening to me was his instruction that I give Kriya Yoga initiation to a member of the congregation. I'd never spoken in public before. And I'd only attended one Kriya initiation—three months after my arrival. When I emerged on the platform to speak, I found the church packed beyond capacity. People were standing outdoors, leaning in at the windows. Even worse than the crowd, from my point of view, was the test of that one member at the initiation afterward staring at me intently for the two hours that it took to complete the ceremony.

I've heard it said that high on the list of people's greatest fears is the dread of speaking in public. Fortunately for me, I've never experienced fear or even nervousness before an audience. The reason is not that I've been puffed-up, happy to be the center of attention, or eager to display to others my powers of persuasion. Quite the opposite. The audience's response has been, to me, a matter of indifference. My feeling, simply, has always been, "Whatever is, is." If people perceive me as a fool, or if in fact I *am* a fool, what does it matter? I want to please God, not human beings. And if lecturing is my Guru-given service to Him, then I will lecture for Him. Nothing matters except that He be pleased.

For many years I held that thought too exclusively. But then in meditation one day I understood that I must please Him *through* others, for it was His presence in them, their own superconscious Self, that I needed to reach. Since then, I have thought of my Guru as residing in the souls of the people I speak to.

Ananda Mata objected to me once in India, "How can you think of yourself as teaching your guru?" I explained, first, that I never teach, for teaching, to me, is an act of *sharing.* And second, I said, by seeing Master as residing in each member of an audience I can ask him to bless that person, through my words and the vibrations I channel from him, that he awaken him or her in divine love.

I didn't want to lecture, at first, but I didn't want to be unwilling, either. I once said to Master, "I don't want to have to lecture."

"You'd better learn to like it, then," he replied. "That is what you will have to do."

Thus, for quite a few years I simply took it as my bad karma that I had to help keep the churches full by taking my turn speaking in them, while others, more spiritual than I, could remain quietly serving behind the scenes.

One time Master was lamenting to the monks about the numbers of ministers in the work who had allowed praise to go to their heads, and as a result had fallen spiritually.

"Sir," I said, "that is why I don't want to be a minister."

I was surprised at the gravity with which he sought to reassure me: "You will *never* fall due to ego!"

This was a consolation, certainly, but it didn't

release any pent-up desire in myself to "get out there and wow the public." It was only after I'd been lecturing almost weekly for seven years that I was brought to recognize that my lectures actually did do some good. One day, someone told me that a talk of mine had persuaded him, after many years of atheism, that God exists. Another day, someone else told me he'd been contemplating suicide, but after hearing me lecture he felt renewed faith in life.

Lecturing

"If even one or two people are really helped," I began to think, "then what does it matter what unspiritual karma I have that keeps me in the public eye? At least I'm doing what I really want to do, which is help people." From then on I took the job of lecturing very seriously—even to the extent (this may seem strange to you) of preparing my talks. In time I learned, much to my surprise, that the talks people liked best were one or two that I hadn't had time to prepare at all.

My focus was not inward, on people's impression of me, but outward—on their need for spiritual insight. What Master's work meant to me was its power to help others. But it went against my nature to think small. If a thing was good, it must be good for everyone. Why limit the benefits to a handful of people? Thus, I universalized every idea. To me, Master has always been for the world.

A friend of mine met an ex-SRF monk recently who had been with Master during those years. The man told my friend, "I once heard Yogananda say,

'If Walter had come sooner, we would have reached millions!'"

Organizing the Monks

Master always encouraged me in my enthusiasm for sharing his teachings with others. To train me, perhaps, he put me in charge of the other monks. Though I'd been with him less than a year, I took this charge seriously. It pained me to see how many monks came and went, and how few realized what they had in Master! Those who had held this position before me had thought in terms of their own dignity and importance. They never saw their job in terms of the needs of the monks. I remember Dr. Lewis in Encinitas once, on finding me seated on a box in the back of a van that was leaving Encinitas for Mt. Washington. "You should be sitting in front," he remarked.

"Why?" I inquired.

"Because," he said, stating what seemed to him the obvious, "you're in charge."

"For that very reason I belong in back," I replied. What mattered to me was the job I had to do; its trappings were to me a matter of indifference.

I was determined to do what I could to organize the monks and develop in them a group spirit, which had been sadly lacking before. My youth was against me, unfortunately. So also was the fact that the monks had never been organized until then. A number of the older monks, especially, were determined to boycott my efforts. I could only ignore their efforts and concentrate on those who saw the need for being organized, as I did. Gradually, over a few years, the "hold-outs" joined us—or, alternatively, left.

Perhaps it was after Master saw my firm commitment to his teachings and to placing his will above all other considerations, that he said to me one day, "You have a great work to do." He had been addressing Herbert Freed, a minister who was about to leave to be in charge of our church in Phoenix, Arizona. I assumed his last remark was addressed also to Herbert, and turned to him with a smile that said, "Good luck!"

"It's you I'm talking to, Walter," Master corrected me.

From then on he told me many times, "Walter, you have a great work to do."

Because the primary need of the organization at the time seemed to me to be consolidation, whereas lecturing was something that others were doing far more competently than I, my assumption for many years was that the work he wanted me to do was organizing.

Organization had never been "my thing." My ambition before coming to Master had been to be a playwright and a poet. I had looked upon writing as a means of inspiring people with new insights into the truth of things.

I remember my cousin Bet writing to me from Wellesley College when I was a student at Brown University. She was thinking, she said, of studying to become a doctor. In reply I wrote, "That certainly is a laudable ideal. Now that you raise this point, however, it leads me to ask myself, What do I want to do with my life? I realize, in thinking it over, that I don't want to take sick people and make them well. I want to take well people and help them to become better. For I find that even after sickness is removed, very few people are happy."

After some time I had given up writing, persuaded at last that I didn't know enough truth, so how could I help anyone? I wound up as a disciple of a great guru. When I came to Master, I was indifferent to religious organizations of any kind. It hadn't even penetrated my mind, as I read *Autobiography of a Yogi,* that he *had* an organization. For Master's sake now, however, and in the belief that he wanted me to help build his work, I set my own disaffection with institutionalism aside and dived enthusiastically into the task of organizing one aspect after another of Self-Realization Fellowship.

My first job was organizing the monks, inasmuch as he'd put me in charge of them.

It might have dawned on me from a few signs he gave me that organizing SRF wasn't the direction he intended for me. The first hint came while I was suffering a period of poor health. I suggested to him that he relieve me of my responsibility for the monks. He'd seemed pleased with what I'd accomplished with them already, though he did scold me once for accepting applicants too readily. Actually, I assumed he would answer as he had when I'd told him I didn't want to lecture: "You'd better accept that that is your duty in life."

To my surprise—and, I admit, some dismay in the

thought that perhaps I'd displeased him after all—he replied simply, "I have been thinking about it."

In the end, he didn't relieve me of that responsibility, but the fact that he'd even considered doing so should have been my clue that this wasn't the destiny he'd intended for me.

He also didn't tell the other leaders of the work about his plans for me. Had he done so, my life might have turned out very differently. (But that account must be reserved for later telling.) Instead, after his passing, my superiors in the work, except for Rajarsi, never thought of me in terms of any work that didn't take its definition from them. (Once, I mentioned to Daya Mata that Master had said I had a great work to do. Her reply, after a pause, was, "Yes, all of us have a great work to do." This thought was one with which I also, of course, agreed wholeheartedly.)

Master told me many of his ideas for the work, but never, as I look back, with the suggestion, "This is what I want you to do in your efforts to build SRF." Rather, he told me specifically, "Your work is writing and lecturing."

On the occasion I just mentioned I asked him, "But Master, hasn't everything been written that needs saying?" I was thinking of his own books, many of which had yet to be published (and some of which are still waiting to be published).

At my question he looked almost shocked. "Don't say that!" he exclaimed. "*Much* yet remains to be written."

One day at Twenty-Nine Palms he looked at me

and, out of the blue (I thought), said, "I predict you will make a good editor someday, Walter."

It was his *ideas* he wanted me to present to people. That was the "great work" he had in mind for me. I see it clearly now.

Expansion from Outside

What I couldn't imagine at the time, but understand now at last, was that he knew I would have to work outside the framework of his organization to work effectively. Any such thought would have been, to me, an abomination. SRF, to my mind, *was* his work. To serve him meant, to me, serving SRF.

And yet, I recall one evening at the Lake Shrine, when Master was walking back to his car with a group of us monks after a concert "under the stars," as it had been advertised. Master turned to me and said, "Someday those who leave here will have their own groups: Jan, David, et cetera, et cetera." I don't know what became of Jan and David, having lost touch with them since they left. I believe now, however, that Master was hinting to me to continue working for him even after I was no longer a part of SRF.

That he saw the work in broader terms than the organization itself I understood also from something he told Debi Mukherjee, a Bengali disciple living then at Mt. Washington. "Someday," Master said, "lion-like swamis will come from India and spread this message all over."

Many years later, in India, I repeated his words to Daya Mata, who was by then the president of SRF.

"Well," she replied dismissively, "he never said that to *me!*"—as if he therefore could never have said it at all. Her reaction to Master's statement to Debi helped me to understand that what Master had revealed to each one of us was a segment, only, of an infinitely larger picture.

I might also have suspected that his plans for me were different from what I imagined from the fact that he never put me in charge of a church (as he did several of my peers), but had me lead the service one Sunday a month at three of our main churches. Thus, apparently, he didn't want me to become entangled in the affairs of one particular congregation or of one particular aspect of the organization.

Meera Mata, a close disciple of Master's, told me once, "I've always felt that the work would spread from outside SRF." I wondered how such a thing could come to pass, but her words lingered in my memory.

Master accepted the help God gave him for the spread of his mission. But he had a larger mission to fulfill. If the means of fulfillment were not to come in one way, they would have to come in another.

CHAPTER 3

Organizing the Work

"You all must work hard to organize the work after I am gone," Master had said. "Otherwise you won't be able to handle all those who will be coming to you."

It was never Master's task to organize the work in the sense here implied. His spirit was too free to be tied down to earthly systems. But what he offered as a general exhortation I took as a personal summons also.

Once I put my mind to it, I discovered that I had a natural flair for organizing. I was able to see instantly what was needed, and what consequences, whether good or bad, would accrue even years later from any decisions taken today. People, I realized, were important to any working system. The highest priority was to enlist their willing cooperation and support.

I had already done much in the way of organizing through my work with the monks. Most of them were now attending the morning and evening meditations. We kept silence together at the dining table in accordance with Master's wishes. Also in accordance with his wishes, I had organized a series of classes in discipleship, and had written elaborate notes for them so that others would be able to cover the same subjects in future, benefiting from the preparation I'd done for them.

I accepted frankly that, whereas monks on fire for God might find it onerous to have to attend relatively short daily meditations with the others, at least the others' meditations would become regular. Even race-horses, I reasoned, could be slowed down by reluctant nags in the community who hardly meditated at all. And the overall morale, I felt, would greatly improve if fewer novices left the monastery to return to a worldly life.

For it caused me deep anguish to see so many promising young men leave the monastery, all because we lacked a sufficiently strong group magnetism to hold them. Master himself was too seldom with the men to give them a sense of abiding reality in their way of life there. He was busy finishing his writings.

The classes in discipleship I now held regularly would also, I felt, be a strong factor in strengthening the group magnetism. Another factor would be faithfulness to our few rules. How often, just to ensure that silence was kept, I had to give up my own meditations and come early to the dining room, to sit there until everyone had finished eating and left. Even so, to get the monks to maintain silence proved impossible at first. Their old habit of talking at the table was deeply entrenched.

Finally, I hit on the idea of keeping silence only at breakfast, which immediately followed the morning meditation. This practice proved relatively easy for people to abide by. After some time, I suggested we keep silence at the table in the evening also, after the evening meditation. Having grown accustomed to not speaking at breakfast, the monks found little difficulty in adjusting themselves to this extension of the rule. I was pleased, finally, to see that they had come to enjoy the silence so much that there was no need to propose we all keep it at lunchtime as well. By then, lunch was already being eaten in silence.

Another problem we had concerned the monks' accommodations. So many were coming that there was no place to put them except in a single crowded room in what was known as the monks' cottage. These were new monks, remember, entering a monastery that had never been organized before, and for which no real models existed. The newcomers who slept in the large room, strangers to group discipline, talked, argued, and joked half the night, their exuberance preventing even those who wanted to meditate from pursuing their spiritual practices.

My room was in another cottage, with a basement that I'd converted into a meditation room. To keep the cottage discipline from breaking down, however, I moved into the large dormitory room with the new monks. There I lived for a year and a half, until the situation became stabilized.

By this time I had the satisfaction of seeing monks come, and not, for the most part, leave. From our prior resemblance to a loosely organized camp, we began to become a true monastery.

The women, meanwhile, growingly aware of my efforts with the men, began to organize themselves also, following more or less closely the system I'd started. Sister Shraddha borrowed my class notes and used them in classes she developed for the nuns. My notes finally became known as Shraddha's notes—a point that wouldn't even deserve mention were it not for the subsequent effort to discredit everything I did, actually to the point of Tara's insisting that I was never even a disciple.

Master's words to me, "You have a great work to do," meant to me only one thing: that I must apply myself energetically to whatever that work was. I had no interest in drawing credit to myself, but only in getting the work done. But I was confident that if I put forth good energy and enthusiasm, the path to accomplishment would open before me. Enthusiastically I set forth to organize whatever needed organizing, since organizing was evidently what was needed, and since I found I did have a certain flair for it.

Still, I wondered why Master hadn't mentioned organizing among the things he wanted me to do.

Office Reorganization

Two weeks after Master's *mahasamadhi,* I was taking seclusion with Andrew Selz, a fellow monk, at the monks' retreat at Twenty-Nine Palms. Andy, who normally worked with me in answering letters, remarked one day, "Our correspondents aren't getting the prompt attention they have a right to expect. Two months sometimes pass before they get our replies! Their letters get routed through department after department—for book orders, for lessons requests, and so on—before we even get to see them.

There should be a system for getting the letters to us first so we can answer them immediately."

I at once recognized the truth of what he was saying. Daily thereafter we discussed enthusiastically how the system might be improved. On our return to Mt. Washington, we were confident that our suggestions would be met with kindred enthusiasm.

They weren't. Habit conspired against me as much here as it had in my first efforts to organize the monks. Fortunately, Faye (Daya Mata now) saw the merit in our arguments. Ever one to pacify opposing sides, however, she felt constrained to heed the objections of certain office old-timers. Finally she requested me to take the matter to Rajarsi Janakananda, our new president. Rajarsi listened calmly to the arguments, then concluded, "These changes are necessary. Please implement them."

And so began a project that took, not the two weeks I'd expected, but a year and a half of intensive effort. For I discovered that the proposed changes in the Correspondence Department required commensurate changes in other departments, and that those changes required changes in still other departments. I ended up having to reorganize virtually the entire office.

The Center Department

A concern of mine continued to be for the future of the monks. Obviously, the work was destined to be guided more and more from the main office. But all the workers in that office except for Andy and me, who worked in another building, were women. The men did the manual labor: building, carpentry, and maintenance. I myself did much of this kind of work also, though not very effectively; I lacked both training and talent. It seemed obvious to me that to have the work run primarily by women was a one-sided arrangement that would keep the men forever subordinate to the women, and their job of teaching forever viewed with that kind of mild disfavor which does little to foster group morale.

In my work of reorganizing the main office I realized that there was one department that might legitimately come under the supervision of the monks: the Center Department.

Our centers constituted our main outreach. Viola Como, who was in charge of the Center Department at that time, had never lectured, and had little or no contact with the public except through the occasional visits to Mt. Washington by the center leaders. Surely the disciples most personally involved with the public—that is to say, the monks—were properly the ones to direct center activities.

I made this proposal to the Board of Directors, who, after consultation with Rajarsi, approved the idea. To implement this change, I wrote a set of rules intended to tie together our centers throughout the world into one coherent system. The year I wrote those rules was 1953. By 1962, when my separation from SRF occurred, the Board of Directors had not yet met to consider the merits of the rules.

It was frustrating to try to develop the Center Department without this minimal guideline for the centers' activities. Meanwhile, sweeping changes were taking place in Self-Realization Fellowship. In 1953 Rajarsi Janakananda became seriously ill with a tumor of the brain, which incapacitated him from addressing the problems of the work. No one felt competent, meanwhile, to make major decisions regarding any department. I tried to persuade the Board that *any* set of rules for the centers would at least enable us to develop some provisional system for their guidance, but my plea fell, not on deaf ears so much as on heads too bowed down with unexpected responsibility even to consider the needs of the Center Department.

Meanwhile, I toured some of our centers. In 1954 I went to Mexico City and Mérida, Yucatán. In 1955 I visited our centers in North America and in Europe, where Mme. Helen Erba-Tissot was doing a wonderful job of spreading Master's teachings in France, Switzerland, Germany, Austria, and Italy.

I also developed a new system that would enable the center leaders, if they so desired, to follow a standard outline for their talks on Sunday mornings. Apart from proposing to them an idea Master had liked, that they all have the same topic every Sunday, the outline I developed was not intended to force anyone into a mold, but only to offer guidelines that some of them might find helpful. In time, this loose system of guidelines became hardened into one of fixed readings that the centers were required to follow verbatim every Sunday. This new system, which became the rule after my departure from SRF, deprived the centers of spontaneity and discouraged them from making any personal contribution to the development of their activities.

Formalization

Indeed, a trend gradually developed to formalize everything. At first, at Mt. Washington there was resistance to change. Then came the thought, generally embraced, "How wonderful that we're getting organized at last!" Finally, organizing was embraced for organizing's sake. Hardly a week passed, it seemed to me, that some new rule wasn't posted on the bulletin boards. My own plan had been only to simplify matters, that we might give optimum service to our members. The new wave of energy, however, which had (to my subsequent regret) been started by me, held that rules represented discipline, that discipline demonstrated our spiritual sincerity, and that rules therefore were in themselves a *good* thing.

When Master put me in charge of the monks he told me, "Don't make too many rules. It destroys the spirit." As years passed, I couldn't help feeling that a plethora of rules was suffocating the earlier spirit of spontaneity, freedom, and devotion. There began a conscious effort to model our way of life on the Roman Catholic monastic rule, and our work on the efficiency of big business. The effort went beyond both these models, however, in the pride that certain disciples took in rules for rules' sake. Because this pride was uncongenial to most of us, it became a proof of our loyalty to embrace them unquestioningly. To protest against them came to be seen as evidence of disloyalty. The newer monks mostly accepted the system as the established order of things—indeed, as "the way Master wanted them." I, with my resistance to too many rules, found myself being looked upon with certain reservations by some of these monks. For me, their disfavor seemed almost an omen—like the blowing of a conch shell to announce the approach of twilight, then nightfall.

A Lay Disciple Order

As an extension of my work in the Center Department, I also organized a lay disciple order, and developed certain ceremonies, notably for the birthdays and *mahasamadhi*s (a great yogi's final exit from the body) of the gurus.

In 1955 I was put in charge of the SRF church in Hollywood. An important way to deepen people's commitment to the teachings, I realized, was to give as many of them as possible an opportunity to serve. More could be accomplished, moreover, by many willing coworkers. We have a song at Ananda that expresses this point: "Many Hands Make a Miracle." There had been, I realized, too much emphasis on presenting the teachings to people, too little on people's actual involvement with the teachings. The best thing for everyone, in terms also of the work accomplished, would be to get people not only meditating together, but working together. Thus, I developed a church committee to greet newcomers and answer their questions. I worked with the committee members to help them with the questions. New members, I had already discovered, were often the ones most eager to approach the latest comers. Finding a constructive outlet for their energies, they were less likely to fragment into little carping cliques. While wrong answers were sometimes given to newcomers, on the whole much good resulted from the committee's activities, and even those wrong answers provided an opportunity for learning the right ones. One's failures are necessary steppingstones to ultimate success. For myself, there was no diminution in my ability to work responsibly. Rather, by delegating authority I found my own ability to serve effectively greatly enhanced. For there is only so much that one person can do.

The Central Committee

There was a committee at Mt. Washington that functioned under the Board of Directors. It was empowered to make many day-to-day decisions. There were several directors on this committee. I also was a member.

As I sat at the meetings, it gradually dawned on me that a vast amount of time was being spent in discussing the pros and cons of every issue. The less personally involved in a particular matter a committee member was, the greater the need, it seemed, to demonstrate a sense of responsibility by talking about it.

It occurred to me that the best way to shorten the meetings and make them more effective would be to assign to each member the responsibility for one aspect of the work. Thus, if a matter was to be brought to the attention of the committee, it would be submitted first to the relevant member. That member would be expected to study the matter in depth, perhaps with outside help, and then submit it to the other members. He or she (actually, I was the only male member) would answer questions, give recommendations, but leave it up to the committee as a whole to consider the matter and decide. Decisions could be reached, this way, in a fraction of the time. My suggestion was never followed, but I always believed it would have spared us endless unnecessary talk.

One summer we were preparing for the annual SRF convocation. The discussion, for and against every suggestion, seemed interminable. When the subject turned to the final garden party and public activities at our Lake Shrine in Pacific Palisades, I could see weeks of discussion ahead of us.

"May I make a suggestion?" I asked. "I have formed a committee at Hollywood Church. They'd love to take on a project like this. Why don't you all let me organize it with their help?" Relief was apparent as all agreed to let me give it a try.

During my service the following Sunday, I invited participation in organizing the garden party, and asked anyone interested to remain after service. To those who stayed later, I read a list of the things we'd need: tables, chairs, water bottles, drinks, food for a potluck picnic, and so on. I asked for volunteers for each area of responsibility, and got the hoped-for response. Later, I phoned everyone to see how things were progressing.

The garden party went like clockwork. Delicious food was brought, in sufficient quantity. Chairs were put out for people to sit on. When the time came for the chairs to be removed and carried over for the public function, I walked around and casually asked a few of the men to help with the job under the direction of the man whose duty it was to see that the process was carried out efficiently. It seemed to me unnecessary to intrude on the way this part of the proceedings was handled. By *expecting* competence, one is more apt to get it. At the end of the day, a clean-up crew removed chairs and tables and left everything spotless.

"How wonderfully everything went!" exclaimed Sister Shraddha afterward.

"And you know," I replied, "it took almost no work." I was trying to make a point.

"No work for you, no doubt," she retorted. "But plenty of work for those who organized it."

"But I organized the whole thing myself!"

My point was not taken, because it was not believed. The assumption, I suppose, was that I was trying to deny a team of willing workers the credit they deserved.

I'd given free rein to their suggestions, however. My main contribution had been to keep clearly in mind where each discussion needed to go. In this way I acted the part, in a sense, of the single committee member of my earlier proposal, responsible for a certain activity. Such a person needs to be in command of his own information, and then to listen openly to counter-arguments and alternate suggestions, changing his opinion where necessary, but never relinquishing the reins of the discussion.

This was the way, as we shall see, that I developed Ananda.

Organizations and organizing were to me then, and have been ever since, necessary evils. They *are* necessary, for without them nothing could function in this world. Our very bodies are supreme examples of efficient organization. Organizations are also an evil, however, in the sense that they too easily become ends in themselves.

For me, the only justification for getting involved in organizing was the conviction that it would enable us to help people more effectively, spiritually.

CHAPTER 4

The Third Presidency

Rajarsi's untimely death in 1955 came as a sad disappointment to all of us—to me particularly so, for one special reason. I had hoped that the monks, in close association with him, would be able to deepen their spiritual life.

Daya Mata was elected president shortly afterward. She was the natural and obvious choice. Durga Mata states in her book that the presidency was offered first to her, and that she declined it. This offer can only have been made out of respect for her seniority. All of us, including Durga herself, knew Daya to be the natural successor to Rajarsi. Daya had, for one thing, the necessary tact for that position. She also had the best grasp of the overall needs of the work. There were people who thought Dr. Lewis would be made president after Rajarsi, but Doctor, who had been a dentist all his working years, had little experience in leadership, and none in the actual running of SRF even though he was in charge at Encinitas.

Daya had been in effect running things already during Rajarsi's illness. Some years earlier, Master had placed her in charge of the main office. Since the office was the main activity at Mt. Washington, this meant in effect that she was responsible for Mt. Washington itself. And since Mt. Washington was the headquarters from which directives went to the other colonies and centers, Daya was also the person de facto directing everything, under Master's supervision. In addition, she was already SRF's treasurer.

I will never forget how pleased Master was by a Christmas card Daya received one year from the staff in the main office: "To our boss who never bosses."

People have recently asked me if I didn't want to change the things I wrote about Daya Mata in my book, *The Path,* considering the harsh stand she has taken against me, in recent years especially. My answer is, "No. I meant every word I wrote there, and still mean it. Daya Mata's recent actions against me introduce a new chapter into the story, but they don't change my friendship for her, nor my appreciation for those early years. I cannot support everything she has said and done; nor did I fully support everything she said and did even then. But I knew she did her sincere best always, and what she has done more recently God surely sees in a broader light than we can, with our limited comprehension. That she loves God and Guru unconditionally I have always been completely convinced."

I consider Daya Mata still, in fact, one of my dearest friends of this lifetime. And in my heart I believe that she holds the same feelings toward me. It is our paths that are, not diverse only, but in her opinion at least irreconcilable. As she said to me in 1985, "It isn't the good people of Ananda I'm against. It's

Kriyananda." I'm sorry for it. And I hope that someday, if only after both of us have left this world, the division between the two of us, and between Ananda and SRF, will end, and that there will be harmony once again. For indeed I have never felt that I was serving any other work than Master's mission. His work has simply taken on for me a much broader scope than the buildings and the structure he established.

My relation with Daya always seemed to both of us based on mutually shared ideals. We served the work with kindred zeal, both of us convinced that in so doing we served the same goal. But our goals were not the same. Each of us came later to believe that the other had betrayed the true goal. The truth is, our ideals had never been identical. We served the same guru. We served his work. But we held different concepts of the purpose his work was intended to serve.

What right had I to hold a different view of the work than the president had? None, surely. I see that now. As Tara Mata said to me years later at the time that she engineered my dismissal, "You have no right to come in and change other people's organizations." Of course, I considered SRF *my* organization, too. My presumption, if such it was, was due to my intense zeal for SRF's growth. I didn't realize that growth was not my fellow Board members' priority. (By then I was also on the Board of Directors, and was the SRF first vice president as well.)

Daya Mata came to Mt. Washington in 1931, long before me. She lived through the years of repeated betrayal by false representatives, of defections more numerous than even she could count, of members who subscribed to the lessons and then casually dropped them, as though dropping stitches in a sweater. She was one of the few who had remained firmly loyal to Master, proving her steadfastness through innumerable tests, both institutional and personal. She had, moreover, worked always behind the scenes, and not, as it were, on the front lines teaching and lecturing to the public. Her job now, as she saw it, was to buttress Mt. Washington and the colonies against further betrayals, and to make SRF financially strong enough to weather future storms. As president she still kept also the position that she'd held already as treasurer, remembering how Master had praised her for her tight-fisted way of handling the finances. (Smiling, she would tell us, "Master used to say, 'Faye is a Scotchman!'") Her job, as she now saw it, was to "run a tight ship," to hold the reins of every aspect of the work in her own hands, and to control matters in such a way that nothing was done anywhere in the work without her knowledge and direction. ("Keep the reins in your hands," Master had told her.)

When, in my position as head of the Center Department, I said to her, referring to the utter lack of direction heretofore among our centers around the world, "I would like to see a strong Center Department," she agreed with me completely. But my view of the Center Dept. was as a strong fountainhead of inspiration for the centers; her view of it was as a center of strong control. Each thought he was agreeing with the other. Neither saw how different our premises really were.

For though I wanted to do only what she wanted, it was always with the conviction that our mutual goal was to *expand* the work. Her goal, obvious to her, was consolidation. To me, consolidation was only a necessary means to an end: It was the end that fired my imagination. To her, consolidation was virtually an end in itself. She saw the conversion of as many as came in terms of an extension of Self-Realization Fellowship.

In any differences that surfaced on these issues I had, as I saw it, to be guided by Master's instructions to me, personally. He, after all, not Daya Mata, was my guru. I tried constantly to bring what looked like two opposite priorities into alignment with one another.

Daya herself never understood my predicament. Increasingly, she demonstrated an attitude of frustration over my unceasing enthusiasm for expansion.

For some years we had a good working relationship. My ideas for office reorganization met with her approval once Rajarsi himself had given his consent to them. She liked my enthusiasm for the work, and saw me, as indeed I saw myself, as her trusty lieutenant, creative in tasks that others so far had carried out perhaps willingly enough, but with more-or-less automatic obedience. Daya was glad to see the monks being organized at last. Later, she approved my work with the centers. Most of all, I think, she treasured our friendship, and the sense that we were fellow warriors for Master. The few occasions when the two of us meditated together, we both went deep into the inner silence. There was a soul bond between us.

We both felt that we had been brother and sister in a past life. Master had told Daya that she was one of his daughters when he was William the Conqueror. One couldn't help feeling that there was a certain regal quality about Daya Mata, as also about Virginia, her sister, who now bears the name Ananda Mata, and who also was closely related to Master during that lifetime. I came to believe, though Master had never told me so, that I was Daya's youngest brother, Master's son, in that incarnation. Many other disciples had asked Master if they were with him then, and what role they had played. He was pleased to answer them. But even during the time when many monks were asking him this question, it never occurred to me to do so, though I felt I must have been close to him, and had always felt an affinity with that period of English history. In retrospect I wonder whether he didn't prevent the question from arising in my mind. At any rate, once the thought of having been his youngest son entered my mind, I went to the Los Angeles public library and did a little research. That library contains a vast amount of information that is of insufficient general interest to appear in books sold in the retail market. I discovered there many facts that went far towards supporting my theory—characteristics and episodes that were subtly reminiscent of similar ones in my present life.

Dayá as Peacemaker

Daya was by nature a peacemaker, a trait for which Master praised her. One example may suffice:

In 1955 I visited our centers in Europe. Alice Bryan, a lady who worked in the office, expressed deep concern to Daya Mata regarding my visit. Miss Bryan had been carefully—far too carefully, in my opinion—babying the European members along, explaining to them at extraordinary length, in letters that took her days to write, the need for certain policy changes and for accepting Mt. Washington's guidance regarding them. (This has always been the weak point in the separation of the Center Dept. from the Correspondence Dept., which is concerned with the individual members. The strength of this arrangement, on the other hand, lies in the balance it provides.) Miss Bryan's distress over the dangers inherent in my impending visit impelled her to request Daya earnestly to cancel the trip.

Daya replied, as she later told me, "Do you think his going there will do more harm than good?"

Well, given this perspective, Miss Bryan had no alternative but to agree that of course my visit wouldn't be *that* harmful.

I've always remembered Daya's answer to Miss Bryan as a classic example of tact. Yet in that case Daya hadn't come to my defense. She had left open the question of my possibly doing harm, even though I don't imagine she saw that as a likelihood. In her very tact, in other words, there was a tendency also to appease both sides, if possible. Anyone with this tendency would be resistant to startling innovations.

Unfortunately I was nothing if not prone by nature to proposing innovations, some of them probably startling. Daya Mata's answer to Miss Bryan, memorable though it was, foreshadowed her answer to mounting objections on the part of others to my innovative ways. Her way of defending me was never to declare boldly, "He's right," but to say instead, "You're both right, but don't you think we ought to give him a chance?" Hostility to my ideas, which had begun during my efforts to reorganize the monks and, later, the office, increased in intensity until it began to appear that what threatened the fulfillment of Master's mission was not adherence to old and familiar ways, but my efforts to find new and better ways of doing things. Many times I would find Daya Mata withdrawing her support for an idea after objections to it had been raised. Finally, I found her actually withholding her support.

"It just isn't *practical!*" she responded repeatedly to my enthusiastically expressed ideas. Gradually I began to experience a deep sense of frustration. Didn't she *want* my help in building the work? Didn't she *want* to see the work itself expand? I simply couldn't understand. I very much wanted to work in cooperation with her. At the same time, I knew in my bones that my ideas were good. I recall writing to her once from India, "I guess I'm going to have to resign myself to living with ulcers the rest of my life." Was that tactless of me? Of course it was. But then, tact was something I needed to learn from her. Her example was invaluable to me, and has proved so many times during later years, especially in the founding and development of Ananda.

My fantasy, which I believe she shared, was that I, as her right-hand man, would bring Master's message out to the world, while she deepened and broadened the wellspring to which souls came to slake their spiritual thirst. I was trying, you see, to bring into harmony Master's instructions to me with her belief, and with what appear to have been his instructions to her, in consolidating the work.

But there were other influences at work at Mt. Washington, and these were growing steadily stronger. I represented the outgoing, progressive element in the work. Others in the monastery argued, not expansively for the needs of truth-seekers everywhere, but more narrowly for protecting the teachings from dilution. Dilution, moreover, somehow became equated in many minds with any but the tamest innovations in the organizational structure. Increasingly, these other disciples—nuns, all—began viewing me as a threat to the work, which, they believed, needed careful supervision and control. Daya came to feel that, in the name of peace and harmony, she had a duty to give this swelling chorus of voices top consideration.

"It isn't practical!" This dismissal of my ideas came with increasing frequency. Yet she appreciated my enthusiasm. She couldn't see why I didn't simply submit to her guidance; more and more the thought grew in her mind that I really ought to do nothing that I wasn't asked to do in the first place.

The point came when she actually proposed that I

go to work in the print shop. I, reflecting that this was very far from what Master had told me to do, cautioned her quite seriously, "If I do go to work there, the machinery will almost certainly break down! I'm afraid my relationship with machines is not what might be described as compatible."

Daya's exasperation found expression one day in these words: "Let's face it, you have *no* taste!" I had been proposing alterations at the monks' desert retreat—which was architecturally unprepossessing anyway—that would make it possible for more monks to stay there. Her words brought to the surface my own frustration, particularly since good taste was important to me, personally, though secondary to more spiritual qualities such as devotion.

As part of Daya's endeavor to carry out Master's instructions to her to "keep the reins in your hands," she decided to give more time to the monks. I approved heartily, and was glad when she encouraged them also to come to her for counseling. More and more, however, I found my own position with the monks being ignored by her. Consequently, it began to be ignored also by some of the newer monks.

I tried to suggest to Daya Mata that, were it possible for her to be with us all the time, my position would become superfluous, but as long as I remained the continuous presence there, whereas her presence was sporadic, group discipline would diminish. Things might even revert to the haphazard situation we had had before Master put me in charge. Daya's focus, however, was on strengthening her own position as president. It was a post in which she never felt secure. It seemed too exalted for her; she didn't feel worthy of it. Thus, my need for support from her was not something to which she felt to give much, if any, attention. Gradually, indeed, she seemed to be treating me as others seemed to feel I deserved to be treated: as a young upstart, insufficiently experienced to make mature decisions, and, moreover, one (as they thought) who lacked Master's endorsement for building his work. (The fact that he never shared with any of them the instructions he'd given me left me with no standing in their eyes.) Thus, others of the directors, too, began singling out monks for various duties about which they never consulted me.

One evening a certain monk missed the group meditation. I made it a point to ask him where he'd been. "Ask Sister Shraddha," was his reply.

The next day I did ask her. She answered matter-of-factly that she had sent him on an errand. When I tried to explain that, in doing so without consulting me, she made it impossible for me to ask that monk ever again why he hadn't followed our rule, my explanation only aroused her indignation. Evidently she considered it presumptuous of me to imagine I had any right to interfere in her affairs. The upshot was that my hold on the monks gradually lessened, until it all but disappeared. The newer monks, especially, began reacting to anything I said with barely concealed condescension, as though they anticipated no problem, in the event they disagreed, in simply appealing over my head.

Worse still, there developed a tendency among

some of the directors to accept uncritically negative reports on any subject that were submitted to them.

My reaction to these difficulties was to ask inwardly, "What do *you* want of me, Master? I only want to do your will. I believe in cooperating with my superiors, and with Daya above all. But I find doors being shut one by one against me. All the enthusiasm I feel for building your work is being treated as if it demonstrated personal ambition. Why, then, did you encourage me in it? I want your will, but what am I to do when I find the instructions you gave me dismissed as though I were only motivated by self-interest? You *know* that isn't the case. Why don't they know it, who are far more in tune with you, and far more spiritually advanced, than I am?"

A Monks Ashram

At some point—I don't remember the year—the cottage in which most of the monks lived was getting far too crowded. Additional space was sorely needed. I approached Daya Mata and asked her if we couldn't construct an ashram for the monks.

She agreed with me as to the need. "But," she continued, "we haven't the money."

Well, I thought, if money is the only obstacle, then I must do what I can to earn it myself. My "solution" was seen by others as yet another of my "hare-brained" schemes. I have always found, however, that if I put my will to accomplish something I can bring it into manifestation. What looked like madness to them was a certainty to me.

I started an import business, importing items for

resale to our members, primarily: harmoniums, Indian gift items, even hammocks from Yucatán, Mexico. "How," some of our people with business experience inquired, "do you expect in that way to earn the money to build a whole ashram?" In fact, I was no businessman, and had never had the slightest wish to be one. I would earn $500 or $1000 in one month with my imports, then lose most of that amount in expenses the next month. My focus, however, was not on the money earned: It was on the positive energy I was directing toward making the ashram an eventual reality. That energy, I was convinced, would stir things up "in the ether" and bring success in the end. My thought was, why simply rest and hope the money would appear someday, out of thin air?

One day Daya Mata announced to me happily that Doris Duke, the tobacco heiress, had offered to give SRF $80,000. "We'll use it for the monks' ashram," she said. Her feeling was, quite naturally, that it was she herself, through her friendship with Miss Duke, who had attracted the money. I felt the money had come as a consequence of the positive energy I had been putting out. At least, I thought, my zeal for the project had put into Daya Mata's head the thought that the money should be used for the monks' ashram. (There were other needs in the work, after all, many of them pressing.) Both Daya and I were probably right. What did it matter? It was divine grace, ultimately, that had made the gift possible.

But the conviction that I'd had nothing to do with it had unfortunate consequences, for me. I had gone, as part of my affirmative campaign, to a devotee architect and persuaded him to draw up, without charge, a beautiful preliminary sketch for the ashram. I was thrilled by its simplicity and beauty. When the time came to consider the actual construction, however, that architect's sketch was not even considered. A motel construction company was approached and offered the job. The proposed design looked identical to countless two-storey motels in America: an L-shape with iron-work balustrades and two staircases leading up the outside to the second floor. Modifications on the design for rooms were kept minimal, though quite adequate, it was felt, to the monks' needs. An attempt at beautification was made in an attempt to appease the outrage I couldn't help expressing: The "L" angle would be truncated on the outside and adorned with a lotus design.

As part of my campaign to materialize my dream for an ashram, I had purchased a little, attractive painting and had had it framed. I couldn't afford much on my allowance of $20 a month, but my purchase had helped me in my efforts to bolster the visualization of the completed project that I was working to make a reality. My painting was now dismissed casually with the statement, "The directors will decide how to decorate the building."

My supportive willingness longed for outward sustenance. It was a flower wilting for lack of water. Surely, I thought, support ought to be a two-way proposition. Master himself had supported me in my efforts to work with the monks. To Vance Milligan, a newcomer, he had said, "You should mix more with Walter. You don't know what you have in him." In the new arrangement, however, I got the growing impression that no matter what I did, it would be viewed only as a presumption.

I and the other monks were brought in after the construction, to help decide on furnishings for the rooms. By this time I had little interest left in the project. It was only reluctantly, at last, that I moved into my new quarters.

Well, I consoled myself, I still had the church to develop as an arm of service to the work. There, if I concentrated on developing our lay disciple order, I might yet accomplish something, at least, for the spread of Master's work. There were obstacles here, too, of course. Sister Meera was in residence at the church. Though Daya assured me several times that Meera and I were in charge equally, Meera was my senior in both age and discipleship. She and her family had come to Master two years before me.

Nevertheless, Meera and I had a good working relationship. She was the only one who continued to come and have lunch with me—at the Hollywood restaurant, the Brown Derby—years after my ouster from SRF, whenever I visited Los Angeles.

Service Outlines

The good that I could accomplish through the lay disciple order was minimal, but it was at least something. Meanwhile, in the Center Dept., the rules still had not been approved, but the fact that change was in the air, and the uncertainty surrounding that change, won me hostility from certain of the center leaders. There wasn't much I could do about it except write friendly letters and try to assure them that we would all be able to do much more, working together, towards the spreading of Master's teachings than we could accomplish, each one working apart.

For myself, I was concerned also that our centers all work from Master's teachings. Some of the center leaders didn't seem to know the teachings all that well, and introduced variations they'd gleaned from miscellaneous reading. *Their* concern, on the other hand, sprang from a fear of too much regimentation. Heretofore they'd been given virtual freedom to do what they wanted. With the new outline of services I'd developed, few of them caught onto the fact that the outlines were optional. Fewer still understood that these outlines were only guidelines to help make their talks more instructive and interesting.

Since the time I left the Center Department, these service outlines have been cast into the form of service readings to be read exactly as printed. Such was not the case during my time. On the other hand, as far as I know, the Center Department has now established full control, and the centers don't seem to demur. I was concerned at first, when I heard of the shift toward required readings, that a committee of ministers meeting to prepare fifty-two service readings for a year would be likely to approach their task somewhat uncreatively. I could imagine them thinking in terms more of the numbers of weeks than of content: "Well, that's ten readings out of the way. Forty-two to go."

I remember a talk I was invited to give at an SRF meditation group in the late 'sixties, when I was no longer in SRF. The subject of that week's service reading was "Meditation in Daily Life." I thought to follow at least the outline of that reading. Before looking at the reading, I tried to "second guess" it. "There are two ways," I thought, "to approach this topic. One is to convince the listener that he should include meditation in his daily routine. The other is to give him helpful suggestions for *how* to include meditation in his busy life. The first approach would hardly be necessary for the members of an SRF meditation group, all of whom are presumably already meditating daily. Rather, the question in these people's minds must be 'how?' not 'whether?' But the question 'whether' is much easier to answer. A committee faced with fifty-two sermon readings to prepare would, I suspect, be inclined to take this easy way out." Sure enough, this was the approach taken in the reading.

Tours

I was satisfied that my work at the Hollywood church, and my sporadic tours of the centers, were accomplishing something, at least, of what Master wanted of me.

Three salutary experiences, well remembered, came from my tours.

The first happened prior to a lecture I was scheduled to give at the SRF center in Vancouver, Canada. I had written to Signa Schulz in Bremerton, Washington. Miss Schulz was the leader of our meditation group there. I'd said I'd be happy to meditate with her and the other members on my way to Vancouver.

Signa Schulz thought, "Well, if he's going to Vancouver to lecture, why not lecture also here?" She wrote me an enthusiastic letter announcing that she'd arranged for a hall for me to lecture in. I knew Signa had had no experience in arranging public activities of any kind. I could foresee an empty hall.

I telephoned her to share my dismay. "Miss Schulz, all I really wanted was to visit your little group. I know there are only three of you. Let us just meditate together quietly."

"Oh, no," she shouted back reassuringly (telephones were not as good then as they are now). "I have it all arranged. The hall is quite big enough to hold fifty people."

Ah well, I thought resignedly, it's all a cosmic dream anyway. I was certain the evening would prove a fiasco; nor were my expectations disappointed.

Miss Schultz met me at the ferry and drove me to the place I was staying. I inquired what she'd done to promote the lecture. Proudly she held out, for me to feast my eyes on, an ad that had appeared that day in the local newspaper. It was a tiny one-column-by-one-inch announcement: "Special meeting, SRF members," followed by the date, the time, and the location of the event. I already knew, of course, how many members we had: three. The announcement that this was to be a special meeting for SRF members automatically warned non-SRF-members not to come.

"Have you done anything more?"

"Oh, yes!" she replied cheerfully, as though to

reassure me that there had been more than one arrow in her quiver.

She proudly produced a sheet of paper that contained the same announcement. "I gave this to the local radio station," she assured me.

"Did you give it to any person in particular?"

"Well, no, the announcer wasn't available, so I left it at the desk with the receptionist."

I had no great hopes for the coming evening.

As the hour of the lecture approached, it began to rain heavily. I arrived at the hall with Brother Bimalananda, my companion on the trip. Signa Schulz had managed to coerce an impressive troupe of her own relatives into coming: cousins, brothers and sisters, about twelve children who squirmed restlessly in the two front rows. In addition to Signa Schultz and the other two SRF members, there was actually one "outsider": a lady who sometimes attended their meditations, and who, perhaps, hoped to find something of interest in my lecture.

I don't believe I have ever tried so hard to interest an audience. Perhaps in an effort to rise above the discouraging influence of heavy rain and the lightest possible attendance, I told stories that would ordinarily have had everyone laughing uproariously. I tried my best to make every point in my dissertation not only convincing, but interesting. I sought to touch on what I hoped were the audience's points of interest, and to build on those points.

The children squirmed, whispered to one another, and giggled. A lady seated by herself two rows further back (the seats around her were all empty) was surreptitiously turning the pages of a little book she tried to conceal in the palm of her hand. A man still further back kept looking at his watch, shaking it, then studying it again more closely. My best jokes fell on ears that had, to all appearances, lost their power of hearing; no one even pretended to think them funny. Meanwhile, throughout this fiasco, Signa Schulz kept smiling bravely and nodding brightly, as if to show me that she considered my every word a shining pearl of wisdom. Even she, however, failed to laugh at my jokes—meaning, I assumed, that she probably wasn't really listening at all: She was only exerting her will to make her relatives sit up and take notice. For my part, I was thoroughly enjoying the whole show.

"Never again," I told myself, "will I have a less responsive audience. As a speaker I can sink to no lower depths. What this means is that the future is full of promise of better things!"

As it turned out, however, I still had one notch lower to sink. After the lecture, Signa Schulz assured me with a bright smile, "Oh, I'm sure *many* more people would have come this evening if Gaylord Hauser [a popular health lecturer] had not happened to be speaking in town this evening." The lone "outsider," that woman who had come to my talk not in the capacity of relative, and not as an SRF member, but presumably out of some mild curiosity of her own, overheard Miss Schulz's remark.

"Oh, dear!" she cried. "You mean Gaylord Hauser was *tonight?*"

Bimalananda and I exulted later in the sheer comedy of it all.

Another salutary experience I had was during a lecture at our meditation group in Denver, Colorado. During my talk I made the statement, "I *promise* that you will find inner joy if you practice these teachings."

Dora Hirth, our meditation group leader there, said to me afterward, "When you said those words, 'I promise,' an electric thrill went through my entire body." Suddenly I thought, What right had I to make such a promise? A speaker, I reflected, must be very careful to speak from his own experience of the truth. But then I reasoned, yes, I *had* had that experience, and I did know what I was talking about. Yet her statement lingered in memory as a reminder never to make statements lightly. Indeed, I had not done so on that occasion.

Another useful experience came not from a tour to our centers, but from one arranged to set up lectures for a visitor from India, Swami Bharati Krishna Tirth, the Shankaracharya of Gowardhan Math, and the one person in India who might legitimately be regarded as holding a position of authority comparable to that of the pope in Rome. The swami had offered to lecture in the West, and had appealed to Self-Realization Fellowship to arrange lecture engagements for him, preferably at universities. Unfortunately, the notice he'd given was short. Universities are accustomed to prepare for such matters at least a year in advance.

I was told by my superiors to travel around the

country to visit various university campuses and do what I could do to book lectures for him. My first attempts were in Los Angeles. There the answer was uniformly negative. The notice was too short; SRF was local, and probably obliged to concentrate locally because it was unknown elsewhere.

San Francisco had another angle, also negative: What event of any serious value could come out of Los Angeles?

At last, a Los Angeles university reconsidered. Their acceptance of the swami sparked interest in a campus in northern California. These two acceptances gave one or two other universities the incentive they needed to invite the distinguished swami from India to address their students also. Very soon, campuses across the country were phoning and begging to be included in his itinerary.

Success, I mused, breeds success. An old adage, but never before had I seen it so dramatically demonstrated.

When Bharati Krishna Tirth arrived, SRF set up two public appearances for him. One of these was, I believe, at the University of Southern California, and another (again, if memory serves) was sponsored by SRF itself at an auditorium on Wilshire Blvd.

At the USC lecture, which many SRF monks and nuns attended, a young woman in the audience, unaware that she was surrounded by SRF disciples, exclaimed loudly to her companion, "I don't understand why this important person had the misfortune to select SRF as his sponsor. He can't have realized what a low-class outfit they are!" Her criticism continued at length.

I waited in ambush for her afterward. Other monks and nuns passed me on their way out, no doubt wondering why I was there waiting. When the young woman appeared, I asked her if she would please stop a moment.

"Have you had any direct experience of SRF?" I inquired.

"No," she replied, taken aback. "But I know what I've heard about them."

"Do you realize you were surrounded by SRF members, who were gracious enough (I didn't say 'timid') not to answer you as you deserved?" She was taken aback.

"I'm afraid I had no idea. But that doesn't make what I said less true."

"No, but since you've had no personal experience of SRF, that makes your words doubly offensive. I would like to invite you to visit one of the SRF churches and base your opinions on your own experience. As it happens, I myself have lived at the SRF headquarters for ten years. I personally knew and lived with SRF's founder, Paramhansa Yogananda, for three years and a half. I have never in my life known a greater man, nor have I been fortunate to encounter a finer group of people. I do not mean to convince you with mere words. All I ask is that you take the opportunity to come and see for yourself. Meanwhile, have the generosity and the honesty not to speak boldly on a subject about which you yourself admit virtual ignorance."

Definitely chastened, the woman apologized, then departed with lowered gaze.

For the other SRF-arranged event, I was selected to introduce the swami. Sister Tara, our chief editor and the person behind promoting this event, insisted that I write out my speech and present it to the Board for approval. I explained that I didn't know how to lecture in that way. Tara tried to insist. I replied, "When it comes to lecturing, let me do it my way." At last, since time was running out anyway, Tara capitulated.

A cannon shot had been fired, however, in what was eventually to become an outright war between us.

CHAPTER 5

Polarization

I have in my possession a Christmas card from Tara Mata in which her greeting contains these words: "To the first vice president of SRF from the second president." For years I thought those words, "from the second president," were a misprint, inasmuch as Tara was, nominally at least, the second *vice* president. It was not her way, however, to make errors of this sort, and in fact she always spoke as though she were the "power behind the throne." Once she remarked to me on the phone, "People say that Daya and I run the organization. Well, it's true. We do."

Tara Mata figures large in the story of my life; I can't really describe Ananda's origins properly without including an account of my relationship with her. Yet I must confess it is a difficult story for me to relate.

Tara was the most extraordinary person it has been both my fortune and misfortune ever to meet. There exists, I believe, a strong karmic link between us. She herself first stated this as a probability.

Tara was a great soul. Yet she possessed such an unusual personality that I find it impossible to describe her only from that point of view. She was a close disciple of Master, and was much loved by him. Master was also deeply grateful to her, for in her he found at last someone with the editorial skills he'd been seeking.

It was not his temperament to give his literary works the editorial polish they needed for the general reading public. Tara was the only one he'd ever met who combined editorial skills—hers were considerable—with spiritual depth and attunement with his consciousness. Other skilled editors there had been indeed, but these had lacked both spiritual insight and the necessary attunement; their skills were merely intellectual. Drawing on their readings of other teachings, they had intruded into his writings other, and sometimes incompatible, ideas. Master quite naturally preferred even unpolished writing to editing that distorted his teachings.

That Master needed an editor is more or less generally known. He himself made no secret of it. As he once put it, "Books in the astral world are written by infusing them with the writer's vibrations. On this material plane, things must be done with painstaking deliberation. Divine Mother disciplined me when I wrote my autobiography!"

The instrument of Divine Mother's discipline was Tara Mata. He was deeply grateful to her for her help.

To a person like myself, for whom writing has long been a major activity, it is obvious that conscientious writing requires careful working and reworking. Equally obvious to most writers, I imagine, is the fact that a great deal of this revision is merely mechanical.

Master's consciousness was too intuitive for him to be patient with these mundane details. What he wrote, though deeply wise and inspiring, was often what might be considered a first draft. Tara, in laboring to bring his manuscripts to polished perfection, would never intrude her own thoughts on his writings. More and more, as she worked on his books over the years, she found her attunement with Master deepening, until she no longer needed to check with him constantly, as she had in the beginning, to see whether she'd understood his full meaning. By means of this attunement, so he himself told me, she herself developed spiritually.

Tara was not, however, everyone's idea of a saint. Deeply spiritual, yes; deeply loyal to her guru, certainly; mighty of will, unquestionably so. She was also, however, eccentric to the point of demonstrating little capacity to relate in a normal way to others. She was opinionated to the point of refusing to admit the very possibility that different opinions from her own might have any merit. She was given to making sweeping generalizations, each of which sounded like a decree imperiously presented before a lower court, this material universe. She so lacked the quality of respect for others that her high-minded disrespect amounted virtually to contempt.

I remember once when the committee to which I belonged arrived at a consensus on some matter. A spokeswoman for the committee notified Tara by phone of our decision. "You're quite wrong," Tara announced in reply.

"But there are fifteen us of who feel this way!" protested the other.

"My dear," retorted Tara high-handedly, "that makes you just fifteen times as wrong!"

Tara practiced astrology—contrary, it should be said, to Master's wishes for her. Shortly after the opening of Disneyland, so I was informed, she had declared that that amusement park would never be successful: It had been opened on the dying moon. Some years later, after Disneyland was already one of the outstanding success stories in financial history, I said to her on the phone: "I understand you predicted Disneyland would fail."

"Oh, yes! What a *pity.* All that money they've poured into that place!"

Her opinions about people were quite as extreme. Intensely loyal to Master and to anyone who continued, in her opinion, to be a good disciple to Master (having Tara as judge made this forever an insecure position), she also had violent antipathies, particularly toward anyone who she felt failed to match her own definition of what a disciple ought to be—a definition that, as far as I could tell, included implicit agreement with her.

Mr. Cuaron, the SRF center leader in Mexico City, a close and deeply devoted disciple to whom Master once said, "I lost sight of you for a few lifetimes, but I will never lose sight of you again," got on the wrong side of Tara by disagreeing with her as to the way the work should be spread in South America. Tara, referring to him during one of our many telephone conversations, said, "Why, he's the greatest hypocrite that ever lived!"

Durga Mata was a devoted, even a heroic, disciple. Speaking of her to me, Master said, "When I met her, I said to her, 'You have come.'" Tara, however, told me, "Durga is totally lacking in refinement. [Durga had not had Tara's formal education.] The *only* reason Master took her in was that he so *desperately* needed help."

Dr. Lewis, Master's first Kriya Yoga disciple in America, and highly advanced in meditation, was dismissed loftily by Tara as too "insignificant" to merit serious attention.

When Debi Mukherjee, a disciple from India, suggested that the *Autobiography* be printed in paperback format to make it more easily available to people, Tara's comment to me was, "His suggestion is so ridiculous as to be irresponsible."

She even excoriated Daya Mata to me as "insincere" for not accepting certain of her own wishes for the work.

Yet Tara was able to say to me once with utter conviction, "I've never said an unkind word in my life."

Tara liked to cast people into types. She herself might be typed as having a sublimated artistic temperament: sublimated, because her artistic sensibilities were wholly devoted now to the divine search. Yet she was deeply sensitive to music and to visual beauty.

Master told her, after a visit he'd paid to the Louvre in Paris during his voyage in 1935 to India, "I saw some of your paintings there." All she would reveal to me was that he'd told her she had been a famous French artist during the Eighteenth Century. I was naturally intrigued, and read up a little on Eighteenth Century French artists. In my research I found a remarkable similarity to her in descriptions of the life and character of Watteau. I also was struck by one of Watteau's idealized scenes of a group of people relaxing amid the beauties of nature. The scene included a buxom young lady whose face held a remarkable similarity to a photograph of Tara herself when she was young. Had the artist's attraction to that form, I wondered, caused him in this life to be born into a similar body? Tara had, from all accounts, been extremely beautiful as a young woman. Beauty, however, meant nothing to her now. She had let her appearance go in her total dedication to serving Master's work.

Like many artists, she lacked social skills. It is not uncommon for artists to behave toward other people as though they weren't really human beings, but merely projections of their own artistic fancies.

Master told Daya Mata, with reference to Tara, "Keep her away from people." Unfortunately, that is just what Tara would never allow Daya to do. Tara was senior in discipleship to Daya Mata, having come to Master in 1924 (Daya came in 1931), and was sufficiently forceful to impose her will on the younger and forever-insecure-in-herself disciple, now the president.

I've long wondered how it is that people can be truly great in certain ways, and yet so very much the opposite of great in other ways—unless, indeed, greatness be defined also as being greatly flawed. Tara was flawed, certainly, but at the same time she *was* great. Personally, I much prefer greatness to mediocrity, even if that greatness include flaws that are outstanding.

A comparison comes to my mind of a stained-glass window. When the sun shines directly upon the window, the color in every pane is revealed in its full intensity. In dim light, however, as for example before dawn, the color is so poorly defined that, however great its variety, it may seem uniformly gray.

People, similarly, whose lives lack energy and driving force, may seem more virtuous than they really are simply because they haven't the energy to appear otherwise. Latent cruelty may appear in them as nothing but insensitivity. Deep-seated selfishness, too, may be excused by others in the same terms: insensitivity.

How often has a murderer been described later by his shocked neighbors in such words as: "He seemed like such a nice person!"

We don't know very well even those who are closest to us. Deep-seated traits may lie buried under the obfuscating mud of low energy and mediocrity. The spiritual power that will reveal our nature as it truly is will make it possible for us also to see clearly our own faults, and, recognizing them as obstacles, to discard them.

We are not responsible for one another. It is not our job to judge anyone. Supremely important for each of us is it to see that our own *direction* of development be toward a continuous expansion of sympathy, love, and understanding—above all by loving God ever more deeply. As Master told us, "God doesn't mind your faults: He minds your indifference." And as Sri Yukteswar said, "Human nature is ever unreliable until anchored in the divine." Even to be in deep communion with God doesn't signify, necessarily, that every root of our humanity has been dug up and exposed to the cauterizing rays of wisdom. Therefore, never grieve if you discover weaknesses in yourself. See to it only that your *direction* of development be ever toward God.

Tara had her faults, but I think she paid for them, too. Spiritual development does not excuse in us a single flaw, even as sincerity in fixing a roof doesn't excuse us from having the rain leak through the smallest opening.

Master's acceptance of each of us despite the infinity of our imperfections, while he worked with unceasing patience to bring out the flawless divine image within us, was the surest proof of his own soul-identity with the divine love that sustains the universe.

I will never forget one occasion when, speaking on behalf of certain others, I spoke critically of Dr. Lewis to Master, not because I had feelings against Doctor, but because I thought Master would want to know what those people were saying. Master thought I was speaking on my own behalf.

"When *you* have passed the tests through which Doctor has passed," he told me sternly, "*then* you may criticize!" To reaffirm his loyalty and love for Doctor, he immediately telephoned this long-time disciple. They spoke as old friends.

Tara had a tender nature, inwardly. Few people saw that side of her, however. She was like certain fruits: soft and sweet on the inside, rough on the outside. Most people saw only the outside of Tara, and were put off by her. As for me, I must say that I very much liked her. Her caustic speech I found stimulating; I saw in it an expression of the delight she took in using words colorfully. The Italians have a saying that covers this trait, *"Se non è vero, è ben trovato,"* for which a loose translation might be, "Even if it isn't true, it's well expressed." It wasn't that I agreed, necessarily, with her often drastic opinions, but often, too, I found them rooted in wisdom. I gained greatly from our association. My philosophy has always been that human beings are very much a mixed bag. Take what attracts you, and—in gratitude for that much good—overlook the rest.

Gradually, however, it became clear to me that Tara represented an attitude toward the work that was completely opposite to my own. This fact didn't greatly worry me at the time, for I couldn't imagine that her attitude would ever, by any possibility, prevail. Thus, I saw her in this respect as a harmless anachronism who would never play a responsible, to say nothing of devastating, role in shaping the future of Master's work.

Master himself had described this attitude of hers as it was revealed to him at the time of his first acquisition of Mt. Washington Estates. "As I stood in the third floor sitting room," he told us, "overlooking the city of Los Angeles, I thought, 'Now at last my mission begins!' Laurie (Tara), standing beside me, remarked at that moment, 'Now your troubles begin!'" Master laughed, "I've never forgotten those words." He'd remembered them, he said, because they were true. What he didn't add, because it wasn't his way to speak in self-justification, was that he hadn't come to this country to *avoid* troubles, but to do whatever was needed to bring his message of salvation to the West.

Tara didn't see his work in terms of bringing spiritual solace to the masses. As she herself told me many years later, "I thought he'd come to America to gather up a handful of disciples, then take us all back with him to India where we'd spend the rest of our lives meditating in the Himalayas." People, in her view, represented only trouble: a threat to the purity of Master's teachings.

I recall one of the monks, on her arrival at Mt. Washington one Christmas, greeting her fervently with the words, "I've been longing to meet you!"

"Well," she announced off-handedly, "you'll never be able to say *that* again!" Indeed, had that monk come to know her he'd probably have wished he'd never said it at all.

Tara was a hermit by nature, and didn't actually live at Mt. Washington when I knew her; her home at that time was a little house across the valley. For some of the time I knew her, she also lived near Master's retreat at Twenty-Nine Palms.

She approved of my enthusiasm for the work, but never realized that its direction was only incidentally toward strengthening the organization, but fundamentally toward reaching out to people with Master's message. To her, the needs of people were of very minor importance.

"What do they need with more books?" she once asked me, commenting on the six or seven books of Master's that he'd left in her care to edit and publish. "People have all the books they need." She seemed to think that only idle curiosity could motivate anyone to want his commentaries on the *Bhagavad Gita,* the New Testament, Revelation, Genesis, *The Rubaiyat of Omar Khayyam,** Patanjali's *Yoga Sutras,* and other priceless works that had come through him in a flood of divine inspiration.

It was, in fact, a statement of hers to me regarding the *Bhagavad Gita* that started the first ripple of trouble between us. Master had just been exulting to me that his *Gita* commentaries would be out by Christmas of that year, 1950. I was sent to Tara's house later that day with a few letters, and mentioned to her Master's enthusiastic statement.

"By Christmas!" she exclaimed. "It won't be *nearly* ready by then."

I quoted her reply to Master on my return.

"Always delays!" he exclaimed. "I will write her a note. You take it to her." My natural assumption was that he intended the note to be a scolding.

"I'm sorry," I said to Tara repentantly when delivering his note to her. "It's my fault."

As matters turned out, Master's note, whatever

*Years later, I edited and published his commentary under the title *The Rubaiyat of Omar Khayyam Explained.*

message it contained, was not a scolding. But from my words Tara could easily guess what had happened. My attempt to take the blame on my own shoulders erupted into a brief time of tension between Master and Tara.

Master took me to task, later, for giving insufficient thought to my words before uttering them. Others seized on his scolding to voice displeasure with me also. To them Master spoke in my defense. "Walter is *very* sincere," he said. But me he allowed no defense. "You must be practical in your idealism," he insisted.

Wise counsel, indeed! Still, I wonder what he would have said had she informed me that it would take another forty-six years, as it did, for his commentaries to come out in book form.

In my book, *The Path,* I omitted Tara's name. In the chapter "A Spiritual Test," I could bring myself only to refer to her as "the senior editor." In the last period of our relationship she hurt me so deeply that I simply couldn't write of her as kindly as I felt Master's disciples deserved. Certain things she had said to me went simply too deep: for example, her statement: "From now on, we want to forget that you ever lived!" Today only, twenty years after the completion of my book, can I view our relationship with detachment, and feel for her once again the friendly appreciation I once felt. It isn't that I now see she was right. Rather, I see that our two premises regarding the needs of the work were so fundamentally different that, given her nature, she couldn't have treated me other than the way she did.

I always knew intuitively that we would lock horns someday on our differences. I simply never believed she could possibly win. Her views were too utterly opposed to the basic needs of Master's missionary work; I was confident that he would never *allow* her contractive outlook to win out. I hadn't counted on being 12,000 miles away in India while she carried on a determined offensive against me.

For her part, I don't think it ever actually occurred to her that anyone could genuinely *want* to reach out to people and help them. Such a desire would only, to her way of thinking, be a cover-up for personal ambition. She was determined that her philosophy become the officially accepted one in SRF.

"Every work," she said to them repeatedly, "must have a guideline. Our own must be to ask ourselves in every situation, 'What is best for the work?'"

To me she said, after my appointment to the Board of Directors (it was she who had proposed the appointment), "In an organization, no one has a right even to *think* except the members of the board of directors."

CHAPTER 6

Six Blind Boys and an Elephant

Master enjoyed telling the fable, after so many years now well known in this country, of six blind brothers who received from their father the task of washing an elephant. Each boy was assigned to a different part of the beast: the tusks, the trunk, the ears, the sides, the legs, the tail. Each of them, unable to see the whole elephant, thought he could describe the animal from the part he was washing. Comparing their experience afterward, one of the boys said, "The elephant is like two long bones."

"How can you say that, brother?" protested the second. "The elephant is like a long rope hanging down from the sky."

"Ah, no!" expostulated the third. "The elephant is like a couple of large fans."

"I don't know how you can make such ridiculous statements," cried the fourth, "when the elephant so clearly resembles a large wall."

"Absurd!" shouted the fifth. "I know from experience that the elephant is four sturdy pillars."

"Brothers! Brothers!" complained the sixth, "I can tell you are all making fun of me. I know from *my own* experience that the animal you're making out to be such a marvel of complexity is like nothing but a piece of string dangling from heaven."

At this point their father entered the room. Hearing the altercation, he cried, "Boys! Boys! You are quarreling over nothing. All of you are right, and all of you at the same time are wrong."

"Respected father, how," they demanded, "can we be both?"

"I am able to see the whole elephant. Each of you has been washing only one part of it. You've been speaking from experience, I grant you, and to that extent all of you are right. But your experience is limited. It is only by pooling your knowledge, not by using what you know against one another, that you will arrive at an understanding of what the elephant really looks like."

Looking back over my years in SRF, I am forced to the conclusion that all of us were like those six boys. Each of us saw one, or perhaps even several, aspects of Master's work without comprehending its entire scope.

Tara's influence on Daya Mata, and through Daya on SRF, increased steadily—determinedly, on Tara's part. In the process, it gradually neutralized my own influence. She telephoned Daya almost daily and instructed her, speaking as a senior disciple, in the attitudes her junior must hold as president. If Daya demurred, Tara would accuse her of disloyalty.

"She can dish it out," Daya commented to me one day, "but she can't take it." Tara was resolved that her own view of the work be accepted as the proper view, to the exclusion of all other views. Tara even said to me once, "I've come to realize that those who are against me are against Master. And that means, they are against God."

Daya Mata had only me to influence her toward a people-oriented mission. In this position I see now that I stood virtually alone. True, Meera Mata did agree with me, but her agreement didn't amount to active participation. Practically speaking, she sat on the sidelines. The resistance to my philosophy was growing on the part of certain other disciples who had lived with Master more years than I. It was like a seesaw: Daya Mata at the fulcrum point; I at one end, never realizing that I was alone; the others grouped at varying distances on the other side of the fulcrum. Tara, the heavyweight in this analogy, sat firmly at the opposite end; she represented the polar south to my north.

Tara's influence stiffened a predilection already growing in the work. There had been a tendency anyway, seldom voiced of course, to consider public teaching and lecturing as a dance with delusion. The monks, whose responsibility it was to go out and teach, were generally looked upon by the nuns as second-class citizens, spiritually speaking. Daya Mata actually said once to Brother Anandamoy and me, "Let's face it, women are more spiritual than men." To remain behind the scenes, guiding and developing the organization through correspondence, and by sending out the lessons by mail, seemed to most of the renunciate disciples more in keeping with the deep-seated desire I suppose we all felt to devote ourselves to communing with God in meditation. If our role in this life was to serve Master's work, then the best way, surely, was to do it as much as possible from a position of obscurity.

Often, when a person feels duty-bound to do something that goes against his natural grain, he will hurl himself into it with even greater zeal than if such an action were natural to him. The one who pursues wealth out of personal desire will be less likely to deprive himself of other natural interests such as home, family, social position, and innocent pleasures. It is the one who doesn't want money, but feels in some way obligated to devote himself to its pursuit, who is the most likely in the process to become one-sided. This is all the more likely to happen if the assigned duty involves serving God.

Much as I wanted to cooperate with Daya Mata and to go along with the understanding Master's closest disciples had of his wishes for the work, I couldn't dismiss from my mind the things he had told me, personally. And I couldn't help becoming growingly aware that there was a discrepancy somewhere. My natural reaction was to question my own understanding of his wishes. Yet I *knew* what he had said. And I couldn't help wondering why he had encouraged me in a way so opposite to their priorities if there was a chance that I would fundamentally misunderstand his true wishes for me. I had never asked for that encouragement.

"Walter, you have a great work to do." On all but one of the occasions on which he said this to me, we were alone. On that single exception, the other person was a man who never really figured in the development of the work, and who later left it. When Rajarsi said to me, "Master has a great work to do through you, Walter, and he will give you the strength to do it," there were other monks present, but Rajarsi spoke so softly that even I had to strain to hear him. He uttered those words when I approached him for his blessing. (We were taking turns doing so.) It never dawned on me on any of these occasions that this information was being given to me privately for a reason. Yet the fact that it was so given has emboldened leaders in SRF to comment in recent times, "Kriyananda has a 'great work' to do, all right—on himself!"

"Your work is writing and lecturing." Considering the fact that Tara wasn't even getting out Master's books, what chance had I of getting any of my own works published through SRF? Everything that was intended for publication had necessarily to pass through her hands, and was editorially screened by her.

"Apart from Saint Lynn, every man has disappointed me. And *you mustn't* disappoint me!" I never quoted these words to others. Had I done so, it would have given the women disciples only one more reason to look down on the men disciples, though what Master was pleading with me was to understand and accept an aspect of the work that the women, even more than the men, had always ignored.

"No more moods, now. Otherwise, how will you be able to help people?" Were the others to try to reconstruct his advice for my benefit or for anyone else's, they would phrase it quite differently, probably something like this: "No more moods, now, or you'll get out of tune." Their advice would be directed inward, in other words, not outward. Master knew that I'd be motivated more easily by an appeal to my desire to help others.

Though he encouraged me to meditate, it was on serving others that he placed his main emphasis. "Your life," he told me, "is one of intense activity and meditation." The tone of his voice, as well as the secondary placement of meditation in the sentence, suggested that meditation was not his primary emphasis for me. Thus, perhaps I had misunderstood him when he announced, or Divine Mother announced through him, during the all-day Christmas meditation in 1949: "Walter, you must try *hard,* for God will bless you very much." After redoubling my meditative efforts for several months, I approached him and asked, "Sir, I keep trying, but I don't seem to be getting results." "You are trying too hard," he replied. "It becomes nervous. That is why, in the beginning, it is better to emphasize relaxation." His admonishment to "try hard," then, may have been intended to urge me toward the "intense activity" that he later predicted for me.

I am aware that this inference might be argued from more than one point of view. Yet it was evident that he wanted me to "try hard" also, even if not primarily, in the field of action. And it was in my efforts to obey him in this field that I ran afoul of others' demands of me. What they wanted of me was that I "slow down," not be so eager, wait to be told what to do and not keep coming to them with endless ideas for expansive ways of serving people. Novelty was not welcome to them. Every time I came up with a new proposal, their first reaction was, "Study other organizations and see how they've handled this problem."

Master also told me, "God won't come to you until the end of life. Death itself is the final sacrifice you will have to make." This must mean he saw my life primarily in terms of sacrifice. And what of "death itself" as a sacrifice? Did he mean martyrdom?

In answer to my question, "Will I find God in this life?" he replied, "Yes . . . but don't think about it." The unspoken, though guessed-at, inference from this statement was, "Meanwhile, you have a lot of work to do."

"Remember," he told me once, "you won't be safe until you achieve *nirbikalpa samadhi.*" These words were, I take it, a warning that I was destined to walk through minefields of temptation in my service to him. Thus, his reference to a life of sacrifice assumes special significance for me. How many times, since leaving SRF, have I had to "enter the camp of the enemy," keeping my mind sympathetically open to ways of thinking that were not my own in the hope of learning how to persuade other people to embrace higher ways.

My life of service to others has not given me much time to think of my own spiritual development. Again and again I have had to "shelve" that primary aspiration in order to obey a deep-seated impulse, as well as Master's directions to me, to bring others along with me. I find consolation at least in the fact that this apparent sacrifice has kept me from thinking very much about myself and my own needs. And it has brought me to the point of not knowing whether I even have any such needs. At any rate, I am aware of none.

To others, Master said, "Follow Faye." He never gave such counsel to me, though I worked more with her than with the others. To me, rather, his counsel one day regarding her was simply to maintain a certain distance.

"Sir," I had asked him previously, because my work brought me into frequent contact with her, "may I go to her for counseling when I can't come to you?"

He gave reluctant consent, then added, "But don't talk to her about sex."

"Oh, Sir," I remonstrated, shocked, "I wouldn't! And even if I did, she wouldn't."

"I wanted to say," he explained, "where the monks are concerned."

In retrospect, I realize that he saw my sphere of action as lying far from the activities of SRF. Once he tested me to make sure of my loyalty. A certain minister of SRF had left the work and was giving lectures and classes in the city of Long Beach, presenting Master's teachings as though they were his own. Master sent me to listen to his talks and report back. I think his wish was to see whether there lurked in my subconscious mind any ripple of attraction to what that minister was doing. There was none. I knew I could never be disloyal. Master indicated his satisfaction with me days before he left his body. Gazing into my eyes lovingly, he said, "You have pleased me very much. I want you to know that."

CHAPTER 7

Rights and Wrongs

In any confrontation of principle or of opinion, it is natural to ask, Who was right, and who, wrong? Who was the hero? who, the villain? Whom shall we applaud, and whom shall we hiss?

Human nature likes to be offered winners and losers. It also wants the winners to be on the side of right.

Life, however, is not always so simple. In my disagreements with SRF I think both sides were right—each of us for different reasons.

My predicament, however, as junior to those I was working with, was that I found myself repeatedly cast as being out of step with their wishes and their reality. As their subordinate, moreover, it wasn't my place to stand up boldly and declare, "This is what Master told me to do, and this at least, therefore, is what I must do." To have done so would have demonstrated a culpable arrogance on my part (in which case Master would never have given me such a charge) or such high spiritual advancement that I could stand before the whole world in my wisdom, like a modern-day Buddha, undaunted and undauntable in the work God had given me to do.

I was neither a male Ayn Rand nor a Self-realized saint. I *knew* what Master had told me, but—how could I help asking myself repeatedly?—was I perhaps mistaken as to his true meaning? My superiors must surely be wiser than I. As for me, I was forever unsure of myself. My lack of self-assurance, indeed, which sometimes amounted to gripping self-doubt, was a curse, but also a blessing—a strength as well as a weakness. It was a strength because it forced me to test my motives to make sure they were sincere. And it was a weakness not only for its paralyzing effect on my will, but also because it encouraged others in any doubts they entertained about me.

Daya Mata was the president. I believed and also taught others that we should follow her faithfully. "If by any chance she should happen to err on any issue," I told the monks, "God will help her to correct her mistake. Meanwhile, we will gain more, spiritually, if we obey her than we ever would by rebelling."

Thus, inevitably, I responded to any conflict between her wishes for me and what Master had said to me by turning my predicament inward upon myself. What, I asked myself, was wrong with *my* attitude? Why couldn't I simply do as she asked and leave it at that? My problem was threefold: first, she seemed to be asking less and less of me; second, I felt as though I were perched on an erupting volcano in my own enthusiasm to build the work; third, everything Master had said to me, in no matter how many ways I might have misunderstood it, held at least this much clear counsel: Do your best, and do it with enthusiasm. Unfortunately, I found my very enthusiasm to be coming ever increasingly under scrutiny.

And then, occasionally, my heart would rebel. "No, I can't possibly have misunderstood him. I *know* what he told me. I *know* what he wants of me. It is they who have misunderstood his wishes regarding me." Master, after all, was my guru. Whose counsel could be acceptable if it contradicted what he himself told me?

I wonder what I would have done had Master not told me so often, and so definitely, what he wanted of me. I wonder what any monastic *ought* to do in similar circumstances. For I had my own nature to contend with, and I found it difficult to adapt that nature to demands that sought to take it in a completely incompatible direction.

This question has no doubt been asked for centuries by renunciates who lived under a vow of obedience: What should a person do if that obedience entails suppression of his own nature? The yogic way is quite different: not through suppression, even of evil tendencies, but through striving to *redirect* every trait toward its highest, positive potential. Selfishness, for example, cannot be overcome by suppressing it. One of the best ways of overcoming it is by expanding one's sense of self to include the welfare of others in one's own.

Master worked with our natures as we were, and never *against* our natures. To work against the disciple's nature, he implied, would have a weakening effect on the will.

What should a monastic do, then, if he is told by a

superior to do something that conflicts with his own nature? What should he do when what is asked of him even defies common sense? Novices in monasteries have sometimes been told to plant flowers upside down in the ground in order to teach them "perfect" obedience. Can this be good for anyone? Can blind obedience really be termed "perfect"?

A certain amount of suppressive discipline may be good—as an inspiration, for instance, to renounce a rebellious ego. And if nothing else, it may help the novice to develop a detached sense of humor about things. Sister Shraddha, one of the SRF directors, occasionally made what I thought were unreasonable demands of me, and I found that the best response was to take them good-naturedly. As it turned out, by responding cheerfully I found we got along very well. In this regard I succeeded better, certainly, than others to whom she always appeared oppressively stern.

Too much of this sort of insensitivity on the part of the superior, however, and too much unquestioning obedience on the part of the subordinate, can only have a weakening effect on the subordinate's will power, and a corresponding hardening effect on the superior's ego.

To survive in an oppressive setting, the subordinate can only find spiritual peace by withdrawing within, mentally, while viewing the scene around him as a dream of God's. Thus, even suppression may prove a helpful goad to drive one deeper into prayer and meditation. It may thus actually be turned to good account.

For one whose energy and enthusiasm impel him outward, however, the problem becomes difficult. I'm not really sure what to suggest in such a predicament, though the obvious solution might be to ask for a transfer to some other field of service. In my case, such a transfer seemed out of the question.

For I looked on SRF as my pathway to God. I could not have imagined serving another work. If Master hadn't taken me out as forcibly as he did, I don't doubt for a moment that I would be there still—unless, indeed, I had died by this time, from ulcers.

Master praised me for my obedience. I tried always, however, to be *intelligently* obedient. Tara once, after my falling out with her, instructed me to do something—I think it had to do with the magazine in India. Feeling that she wasn't familiar with certain aspects of the matter, I asked her by letter to consider a further point. I assured her, however, that I would do what she wanted if she continued to be of the same mind. Her reply came by cablegram: "Your nature is disobedient beyond human comprehension. Do as I said immediately."

Those were confusing years for me.

Was Daya—was Tara—were any of them wrong? I've decided it simply isn't my business to judge. I present the problem as it appeared to me. To me, it appeared insoluble.

CHAPTER 8

I Go to India

For three years in a row—1950, 1951, and 1952—Master planned to go to India. Each time his plans were canceled, the last time by his physical death. The plan every year was for me to go with him. He wanted me, as I understood it, to travel around the country ahead of him, lecturing and preparing people for his arrival.

Daya Mata went to India in 1958 to fulfill his primary reasons for going. Ananda Mata and Sister Revati accompanied her. I met them in Indonesia, and completed the journey in their company.

Before their departure from the States, I flew to Hawaii, Fiji, New Zealand, and Australia. The plan was for me to give lectures in Auckland and Sydney. This was my first voyage westward from America.

Hawaii was a one-day stopover, only. I got to see the island of Oahu, thanks to a cousin of one of the monks. The cousin took the day off from work to show me around. In Fiji I planned a two-week rest, much needed after months of intense activity in Los Angeles prior to my extended stay in India. (I had long been under the impression Master wanted me to develop his work in India, though he never actually said as much.)

Shortly after my arrival in Fiji, however, my vacation plans met a snag. Some 380,000 Indians lived on the main island, Viti Levu. Swamis seldom if ever came there. In Nadi (pronounced Nandi) I found myself in great demand. Before I knew it I found myself addressing 700 people in a large auditorium. Soon, seeking my hoped-for break from activity, I went to the little town of Navua. There also, however, the news of my arrival in Fiji had somehow preceded me. Again I was sought out. In Suva, the main city of the island, a lecture program was set up for me. It was difficult to plead my need for rest, with so many people hungry for spiritual teachings. For me this proved also a golden opportunity to get a taste of Indian culture before actually landing in India.

From Fiji I flew to Auckland, New Zealand, where an SRF center thrived under the leadership of Reginald Howan. Here, and again later in Sydney, I was introduced to an aspect of my future work with the public that I hadn't anticipated, and that I didn't know how I'd explain to Mt. Washington.

I was the first person from the Mother Center ever to travel "down under." Mr. Howan, delighted that I was coming, was yet in a quandary as to how much to publicize my visit. On the one hand, he naturally wanted as many people as possible to hear me. On the other hand, a doubt arose in his mind: Was I a good enough speaker to address general audiences? I was a monk, accustomed to a fairly sheltered life. What if I showed no aptitude for lecturing to worldly people unfamiliar with the very word yoga? If I proved inept as a public speaker, to invite a large crowd might even be disastrous for the work he was trying so conscientiously to build there.

He compromised. A large reception was held, at which I got to smile, be garlanded with flowers, say a few words of appreciation, and participate in a delicious banquet. Subsequent gatherings were all planned for center members and friends. I was to be in New Zealand two weeks. Mr. Howan had rounded out my program with a tour of the island, a Kriya Yoga initiation for those ready for it, and informal chats with him, his wife, and other members.

After my first lecture, however, everyone regretted they hadn't planned anything public after the reception. A great flurry of activity ensued: advertising, the hiring of a large hall, press and radio interviews. Six hundred people attended the lecture, which proved a great success.

For the first time I discovered that, in order to attract large audiences, I needed to become known as a personality, or at least as a good speaker. It was insufficient to be known as the representative of a large organization. How, I wondered, to convince the people at Mt. Washington of this need for self-promotion, when they all did their best to remain behind the scenes? Master, after all, had not told them his plans for me. Could it be that he, too, didn't expect them to understand? To them, such publicity was anathema. Nor was I myself interested in it for any reason other than my desire to reach out to as many people as possible with Master's teachings.

The situation arose again in Sydney, Australia, the next stop on my journey. Constantin Tenukest, our center leader there, was even more fearful of harmful publicity than Mr. Howan had been. Convinced, however, after hearing me, he too went to the effort of hiring a hall and promoting a public lecture for me. Six hundred and fifty people came.

It also helps, I discovered, to present the evening *as* an event. The fact that I had come all the way from America was undoubtedly an attraction: My presence was news!

Thus, I learned that the most effective way of drawing an audience was not only to highlight the speaker's name, but to present him as interestingly as possible. What would my fellow disciples at Mt. Washington do with this information, once it was presented to them? Should I even tell them? In a wish to be as effective in my public speaking as possible, and not wanting them to curb my effectiveness because of their own lack of experience, I decided to say nothing, but to let things work themselves out in their own time. Even to raise the issue, I feared, would condemn me in their eyes as *wanting* publicity.

I met the others in Djakarta, whence we flew to the island of Bali for two weeks of rest—at last! In Bali I had many adventures that I'd enjoy relating, but, having selected a single thread out of the complex tapestry of my life, I must pursue its course faithfully. Those adventures were diverting, but would be a diversion from this account.

From Bali we traveled to Bangkok, whence I also took a side trip alone to Angkor Wat. Our next stop was Rangoon, Burma. And then, at last, Calcutta, where we arrived late in a September evening in the midst of a heavy monsoon rain.

A large group were waiting to greet us at Dum Dum airport. I had told Master in 1950 at his desert retreat, "I think it would be easy for me to learn Bengali."

"*Very* easy!" he'd replied, then pointed to his eyes: "Chokh," he said; to his nose: "Nat"; his mouth: "Mukh"; his ear: "Kan": his hand: "Hath." I never forgot this little lesson, though I found no time for further study until shortly before my departure for India, when I acquired a simple Bengali primer. Now I addressed myself proudly to Swami Brahmananda: "Ami mangso khai na" (I don't eat meat). Appreciation for this brave effort got me off on the right foot.

I soon found, however, that, mainly because most of the people we met spoke fluent English, I had little opportunity to practice Bengali, or, later on, Hindi. Years later, in Italy, I became relatively fluent in Italian in a matter of a few weeks. During four years in India, however, my knowledge of Bengali and Hindi remained comparable to the status of a relative newcomer to America, who can make his wishes somewhat known, but who wouldn't dream of giving a lecture in English.

Our home, during that first year in India (Daya Mata and the others returned to America after one year), was an ashram in Baranagar, a little town outside Calcutta. The grounds were large—perhaps three to five acres—and separated from surrounding factories and a tannery by a high wall. The ambient noise didn't intrude too much, therefore, and the vibrations in the ashram were peaceful and inspiring.

CHAPTER 9

My First Year in India

That first year I devoted much of my time to helping Daya Mata in her mission in India. She had gone there to familiarize herself with the work in that country, to regularize it if necessary, and to help the Yogoda Satsanga Society members (YSS is the Indian affiliate of SRF) to know their new president. I accompanied her in most of her public appearances, where I was often asked to sing an Indian *bhajan* (devotional song) or two at the start, to set a spiritual atmosphere. Daya Mata herself was not accustomed to giving lectures, but she easily won people's hearts and made Master real for them by her simple presence.

I ran numerous errands for her in Calcutta, sat in on many meetings, and did whatever I could to make her stay in India easier for her. For gradually, as time went on, things grew increasingly difficult. The problem was with the workers themselves. None of SRF's Indian representatives appeared to have any idea that Master's birth had brought an earth-revitalizing message. To them, SRF/YSS was another ashram, merely, in a nation rife with thousands of ashrams. His teachings, in their opinion, were true, but perhaps a little over-Americanized for Indian tastes. They considered us, certainly, too American to understand or even fully to appreciate the ancient ways of India. To bring us "up to snuff," they treated us to many traditional worship ceremonies—*puja*s, *yagya*s (*yajna*s), impossibly dull dissertations on the *Bhagavad Gita,* and Sanskrit readings, followed by clumsy English translations of other *shastra*s (scriptures)—and then, of course, explanations of numerous local customs and the deep reasons for each.

At first we entered wholeheartedly into everything. We felt humble devotion as we prostrated ourselves, then meditated, in various temples and places of pilgrimage. We visited Tarakeshwar and listened entranced to stories of miraculous healings that had taken place there. (Daya Mata herself experienced a healing the day of our visit.) We visited the beautiful Jain temple in Calcutta. Daya and the others visited Benares (I was not with them this time), and the home of Lahiri Mahasaya. Together we visited the home of Ram Proshad, the famous Kali devotee of the Eighteenth Century, composer of still-popular devotional songs to the Divine Mother. We visited the Kali temple in Dakshineswar, where the great master Sri Ramakrishna had lived, worshiped, and found God. We visited Belur Math, founded by Ramakrishna's disciples. We visited Sri Yukteswar's ashram site in Serampore, and his seaside ashram in Puri. We visited Master's school at Ranchi, of course. The list of places we saw and of saints we visited is endless. To all of us, the time spent in these ways was deeply inspiring.

Gradually, however, we also began to observe that, in the midst of all the *puja*s, *yagya*s, and dissertations on the *Gita,* Master and his teachings were being given a back seat. Where was the emphasis, among his own devotees, on Kriya Yoga? Where, the attempt to show his mission as special? Every effort, rather, seemed directed toward presenting it as being firmly rooted in a tradition too ancient ever to be challenged. As for his organization, our leaders there considered it a matter for gratitude, certainly, that SRF was able to support its Indian branch financially. Thus, the Indian representatives weren't obliged to devote excessive worry to raising the money themselves to support the work. What SRF's assistance also accomplished for them, however, was lull them to sleep as far as any zeal for the work was concerned.

The Indian mentality is not much inspired, in any case, by organizations. The Ramakrishna Mission, established about a century ago by Swami Vivekananda, has convinced people by its work of founding schools that organizations can, in fact, do good work, but as far as inspiration went, this had to be sought from saints individually, or within oneself in meditation. Daya Mata won people's hearts not nearly so much in her capacity as president as by the fact that they saw in her a person with deep devotion to God. Her monastic title, when we first went to India, was Sister. Indians, however, found it more inspiring to think of her as mother. Accordingly, after her return to America in 1959, she persuaded the

Board of Directors to approve a change in her title from Sister to *Mata* (Mother).

The longer we stayed in India, the more clearly we realized that we didn't really have an organized work there. Oh, true, our Indian office sent out printed lessons to students in various parts of the country—but not to very many students. Indeed, the student enrollment was negligible. As for any outreach on Daya's part, it slowly became apparent to us that she was being carefully hemmed in as though to prevent her from having any major impact on matters there. With loving smiles, nods of appreciation for her saintly example, and numerous functions given in her honor, her efforts to change and re-energize the work were nevertheless given the soft-pillow treatment: the vigorous punch that lands only to be gently absorbed, its impact neutralized by a feather stuffing of silent opposition.

As our mounting displeasure began to be apparent to others, attempts were made to fix the blame for whatever wasn't right on other people—never on anyone present at the time, of course. We—Daya Mata especially—were subjected to endless hours of gossip and accusations. Unfortunately, many of those accusations appeared to be not without merit.

The time actually came when certain officials in the work conspired to get us sent out of the country. The police arrived one day at the Baranagar ashram with a notice to the effect that if we didn't leave India within ten days we would be deported. We had by this time, fortunately, made a few influential friends, who were able to get the order rescinded.

Our first year in India, begun with so much joy and inspiration, became increasingly sad for all of us.

"What will happen to the work here?" Daya wondered aloud in anguish one day not long before her departure.

Sister Revati, who was with us, raised her chin in an expression of staunch faith. "*Master's* here," she declared. "*Master* will protect it!"

"Master," I couldn't help retorting, "has been here for the past forty years, and what has he done?" I knew there was no point in expecting him to act except through the agency of willing disciples. God Himself accomplishes His will in this world through human channels; He even sends His awakened sons on earth to redeem sleeping souls.

The story of our first year in India is primarily Daya Mata's to relate, or ours to relate about her. The thread I have selected for the present account, however, is that of my own role in serving Master's work. My frequent trips to Calcutta on Daya Mata's behalf, my support role during her many visits and pilgrimages, were, I hope, useful to her, but they add only minor twists to the thread I've selected for these pages.

Singing Bengali Songs

One aspect of my presence at Daya's public appearances did, I found, win me a measure of public attention also: namely, the devotional songs I was asked to sing. Much to my surprise, my notoriety began preceding me wherever we went. The first thing our hosts did, when we arrived, was bring out a harmonium and request me to sing. I was happy in this way to bring people a greater appreciation for what Master had accomplished in America. It offended me, however, if anybody gave me credit that was withheld from Master.

This happened during a visit to the south of India. It was after a short stay in Madras, where we had a small center. I then proceeded on to a well-known ashram to the south.

This was the first time an SRF representative had gone there, and I had announced my arrival well in advance, writing in my official capacity as director of the SRF Center Department.

The advance notice made no impact.

"Have you heard of Paramhansa Yogananda?" I inquired as I was being led to the office to be registered as a guest.

"Oh, yes," was the indifferent reply. "But . . . there are so many nowadays."

I was given a space in their most primitive guest house. My sleeping section was divided off from other sleepers by a simple sheet of canvas, open at the top and at the bottom. For myself I didn't mind, but I couldn't help thinking this was no way to show appreciation to Paramhansa Yogananda for the great work he did on India's behalf in the West.

I asked if I might receive a tour of their extensive property. No car was available, I was told. And that was that.

The following day a Calcutta devotee arrived who had been working on a project for them. A car was immediately placed at his disposal for a tour of the property. This devotee happened to be a friend of mine. He asked me to join him. Of course, they had to consent.

After the tour, which was provided *gratis* for him, they asked me for ten rupees to cover my part of the tour.

My Calcutta friend afterward exclaimed, "Why, haven't you heard of Swami Kriyananda? He's a wonderful singer. You *must* take this opportunity to hear him sing Bengali *bhajans*."

A gathering was convened. I sang a few songs. Later, at a scheduled *satsanga,* a few people observed me seated in deep meditation, and were well impressed. Quite unexpectedly I found myself greeted on all sides with great warmth and affection. The receptionist (the man whose reception had been so casual the day before) invited me to meet their general secretary. This gentleman, I had been informed previously, was too busy to see me. He received me now, standing—as a hint to me, I felt, to keep my visit as brief as possible.

This sudden recognition given to me personally, when no one had paid me any heed as a disciple of one of the great gurus of our times, was, to me, doubly offensive. Wordlessly the next day I paid my bill, and left by the first bus for Madras.

Resistance to Lectures in Bengal

Knowing that Master had planned for me to lecture in India, Daya Mata urged me to set up lectures during the little time I had available. By the local Indians, however, I was generally discouraged, either overtly or by their patent lack of enthusiasm. I remember one of our Indian directors devoting an hour one late afternoon to trying to assure me that I was quite untrained to speak before the spiritually sophisticated audiences of Bengal.

Finally a Bengali friend did arrange a lecture for me at the Maha Bodhi Hall in Calcutta. The lecture was well attended, and well received. No further doors opened for me as a speaker, however. Kriyananda wasn't, after all, what was happening that year. It was Daya Mata's time, quite properly. Moreover, my own appearance was against me. I looked younger than my thirty-two years, and even thirty-two was too young to impress most of my listeners, who were far older than I. Age, to a degree not appreciated by most Americans (citizens as we are of a young culture), receives primary respect in the most ancient of all lands: India.

Redoing the Lessons

The main work I was able to accomplish that first year had to do with the Lessons. These were in lamentable shape—so poorly printed, for one thing, that many of them were barely legible. They also cried out to be presented in such a way that the Indian public, unaccustomed to receiving lessons of any description by mail, could be convinced that it was worth their trouble to study them.

While I was on the central committee in America, I had argued repeatedly that the lessons lacked universal appeal. I had made a study of this matter, and had found that a majority of our students dropped out by the end of the first year. In another such study I learned that, out of those who remained faithful longer than a year, those who had read *Autobiography of a Yogi* were several times more likely to continue their studies than those who had come to us through magazine advertisements. I therefore recommended that we concentrate our advertising on promotion of the *Autobiography.* In time, this policy—my recommendation was approved—notably improved the statistics on student-perseverance.

Nevertheless, I kept pleading with the committee that it was the lessons themselves that needed revising. "We'll never get this show on the road," I kept insisting, "until the lessons are redone."

Master had informed me that he hadn't organized the lessons himself. Nor was it the actual teachings that needed revising: It was their presentation. They had been arranged in their present format by a devoted disciple of Master's who, though a wonderful soul, had had no experience with the public or, for that matter, with teaching others. Louise Royston couldn't realize what presentation would be the most effective in terms of reaching people's actual understanding, satisfying their immediate needs, holding their interest, and answering their latent doubts before those doubts even arose.

Lacking experience, her approach was based on another theory altogether. It was designed to keep the student associated with SRF for as many years as possible. Her reasoning, sound enough in itself, was that in this way the student would gain the most, spiritually—not from the lessons, only, but from the added benefits of pilgrimage to Master's colonies, advice by correspondence, and, above all, by inner attunement with the line of gurus. Her reasoning was, as I say, sound. The problem was only that by the end of the second year we had almost no students left.

By now I'd had nine years of experience working with the public. I asked myself, What is the student really interested in when he subscribes to the lessons? His chief interest, obviously, lies in receiving a course on yoga. Presumably he is *eager* to learn this new science. And he wants to feel that this particular course is giving him more than he could ever receive through reading a book.

What the present course did, instead, was start the student off on side issues. It eased him into the water gently by stressing such matters as loyalty to the work—with which, so far, he was hardly acquainted. Miss Royston had decided that the beginner would then be inspired by a beautiful lesson Master had written on the subject of friendship.

Next, pursuing her policy of dragging the lessons out, she had stretched to several weeks lessons on techniques that Master had been accustomed to teaching in a single evening. Each lesson was short, padded with repetitions, and contained as little information as she felt she could get away with presenting at a time, all with the thought of giving the student time to digest what he was receiving.

Again, deciding that it would be a good idea to include an inspiring and instructive story with each lesson, but finding that the available stories were fewer in number than the lessons, Miss Royston stretched the stories, too, over as many lessons as it took to make the number of both equal.

Looking at the matter from the new student's standpoint, eager as he probably was for information, I couldn't help feeling that he'd rather receive his instruction "hot and heavy," at first particularly. As for the stories, he'd rather complete them in a single lesson—particularly one of the simpler stories such as "Big Frog, Little Frog." (To keep the student wondering for a week or longer whether those frogs make it out of that bucket of milk struck me as trying his patience unnecessarily.) Even if condensing a story into a single lesson meant that the student wouldn't receive a story with each lesson, I felt he'd greatly prefer to know what the story was all about, and not be held in unbearable suspense for weeks in a row.

My reasoning also was, as I said, that the beginning yoga student wanted his information "hot and heavy." Fill the early lessons with teaching, I thought, including as much material as possible about any one technique in a single lesson. After a year of such intensive study, the student would no doubt be relieved to relax a little, having so much material already to absorb. A year, I considered, would be enough time for tightly packed teaching. After that would be the time to stretch things out a little.

My outline wouldn't necessitate reducing the number of lessons. The whole course could remain the same in length. Nothing need be disturbed, therefore, in any existing office procedure.

I knew that Master had given to Sister Mrinalini the job of rewriting the Lessons. Until the completion of her job, however, it seemed to me that a revised presentation would keep more students faithful to the path. Perhaps, I thought, if I did this revision in India, Mt. Washington might like it well enough also to incorporate it in the lessons they sent out—at any rate, until Sister Mrinalini's course made its debut. Thus, I thought enthusiastically, our lessons could begin to hold students at last, and our student membership to grow in number instead of remaining more or less constant over the years.

Armed with my ideas for this project, I presented them to Daya Mata for her opinion. She liked them, and told me to proceed with the plan.

Having no office to work in, I did all the work in my bedroom. For one year the floor of my room was covered with piles of paper as I arranged and re-arranged the lessons to correspond to my ideas. At the end of that year, I was well satisfied.

There followed another task: typing everything out. For this work I hired inexpensive outside help, limiting my own part to careful proofreading and correction. It thrilled me to think that here we finally had a product that Indian students would appreciate for its clarity, its conciseness, and its practicality.

Unfortunately, a year and a half later, when I fell out of favor with SRF, it was decided that my work on the Lessons should be scrapped. The Indian lessons, it was felt, should be brought into line with the lessons being put out by Mt. Washington—"in case," Daya Mata explained, "students should ever move to India and want to continue their lessons without change or interruption."

My concern at all times was the spiritual needs of the devotees. I accepted the official decision without demur, but it was painful to me to see those needs being subordinated to bureaucratic considerations.

Dubey

During our first year in India a man began attending our meetings whom Daya Mata came gradually to look upon as the fulfillment of Master's prediction to her concerning the work there. "The people in India," he had told her, "will organize the work themselves." We had met no one among our Indian representatives at that time who could be counted on to fulfill that prediction. This man, however, appeared to have the necessary ability, if only he could be interested in serving Master's work.

Binay N. Dubey was his name. He was the founder/president of a large hospital in Bengal called Niramoy. He was a *"pukka"* (perfect) organization man, being uninterested in reaching people through lectures and other direct outreach, but competent to organize a smoothly running office and keep it functioning efficiently. Daya Mata considered organizational efficiency the paramount need of our present work in India. For that purpose, among the Indians we'd met, Binay-da, as we called him (the *da* means "older brother"), stood alone.

Binay Dubey began to follow us about from place to place. Often he admitted to me quite frankly that he had no personal commitment to our work, but that he found inspiration in Daya Mata's company. In time, as her influence on him grew, he came to feel drawn toward a broader commitment.

Binay-da spent much time in visiting other saints. Being independently affluent, he had few personal responsibilities, though he may still have been running Niramoy from a distance; this I don't know. Thus, he could devote himself to seeking *satsanga* (good company). More and more, the *satsanga* he sought was the company of Daya Mata.

Binay-da and I were friends, too. We spent many hours together. His devotion I found attractive. "Binay" means "humble"; in many ways, the name fitted him admirably. In other ways, however, he was very proud. He wasn't an easy man to understand.

Often he said to me, "You all from America are mere children compared to these people. You don't even imagine the tricks they can use to take advantage of you. They may praise you lavishly, convincing you of their sincerity, yet all the while the people around them will know they are simply poking fun at you." He made this remark, and similar statements, so frequently that I began to think, "If simplicity, devotion, and kindness are not enough to touch people's hearts, I would rather be laughed at and have done with it! God is the only one I'm trying to please. What do the opinions and the superficiality of human beings matter?"

Kamal-da, a man prominent in the movement started by devotees of Ananda Moyi Ma, remarked to me years later, "I was well impressed by Binay-da at first. But I came in time to realize that he is too much of a politician. Since then, I have kept my distance from him."

Other Indians whom I respect have reported to me other traits in Binay-da that, if true, are not worthy of applause. These friends insist that he justified himself with the explanation that such behavior is normal for his own land-owner class, the *zemindar*s. It isn't normal for a yogi, however. In Binay's defense, I would add that these people may have had personal motives in speaking against him. In *their* defense, on the other hand, I must say also that he'd given them good reason, as we shall see, for their antipathy.

So again, as I've already stated, Binay-da was not an easy person to understand. And I must repeat that, speaking personally, I liked him, though in time I found in him also a tendency to be so condemning of others that at last I avoided his company as much as possible. Still, I did like him! And he, for his part, claimed to see something in me that inspired him second only to Daya Mata.

His influence on Daya reinforced her own conviction that the heart of Master's mission in India, no differently from in the West, was the institution itself. I will not say this was an error on her part, though it went quite against the priorities I myself saw for the work and the directions Master had given me, personally. Still, Daya Mata was the president; it was her job to be right in such matters.

Master, meanwhile, was pulling me forcefully in another direction—the one at which he had hinted in his discussions with me from almost the beginning of my association with him.

Ranchi

Somehow, I had always been under the impression—mistaken, it would now seem—that Master wanted me to remain in India and build his work there. He spoke to me several times of his wishes for the Indian work—by no means so much, I'm sure, as he did to Daya Mata. Perhaps, in his talks with me, he was thinking of the work I myself would be doing much later in America.

About his school in Ranchi, for example, he told me:

"Most of the boys, after graduating from our school, went on to live in the world. As far as spreading this message was concerned, they were a loss to us. What we have now in America is much better. People come to us when they are grown up and know what they want to do with their lives. Someday it will again be possible for us to concentrate on developing schools, but that time is not now."

After the start of my troubles with SRF, Tara Mata wrote to the directors, "My common sense tells me that we should do what Master himself wanted: develop his Ranchi school." Binay-da followed up on this suggestion by announcing to me, "The Indian government has a program for helping schools. They will match whatever funds we put up. In this way, we will be able to grow twice as quickly."

I was in enough hot water by this time already, and therefore refrained from arguing the point. Inwardly, however, I thought, "If the government gives us even a single rupee, its accountability to the public will oblige it to control the entire enterprise."

So it happened, in fact. Spiritual teaching received less and less emphasis in our Ranchi school until it was virtually eliminated.

Nearly twenty years later, one of the SRF/YSS monks in India confessed to me that the only spiritual education the children were receiving at that time was outside the classroom. The instruction was given to those few youngsters who expressed personal interest. "But," my informant then hastened to assure me, "we hope someday to get back to Master's ideal of an all-rounded education, including instruction in his yoga techniques and meditation."

Well, if nothing else, Master was pointing my own mind toward adult education. I have developed schools since then at Ananda. These came into being, however, within the larger context of an already-thriving adult community.

Office Management versus Outreach

Part of my problem in India stemmed from my belief, which as I've said may have been mistaken, that Master wanted me to develop his work in that country. Binay-da's plan for me was that I devote myself to the position of office manager. I'd had the necessary experience, it was true, but my own inner direction was growing stronger and stronger to do what Master wanted of me. I knew he didn't want me doing office work anymore.

"Binay-da," I protested, "were I to take on that job, it would be another twenty years before I saw the light of day again!"

"Quite right," he replied matter-of-factly.

India herself had been drawing my heart in another direction altogether. Master had told me to lecture, not to be an office worker. Daya Mata herself agreed with me on this point, and encouraged me to travel around the country, giving lectures and classes. I suspect she also felt that my absence would give Binay-da more freedom to develop the work at its center. (My recognized enthusiasm for new projects may well have suggested to her that it would be easier for him to work quietly in his own way, without "interference" from me.) But certainly she also saw merit in having someone out "in the field," bringing in new members. Binay himself saw no real need for me to travel. He wanted me on hand in the office, while he directed my activities from his home in Calcutta. This was part of his ongoing resistance to getting too much involved in the work, personally.

I did not take easily to being directed by him. Though older than I, he was not only new in the work but not yet even committed to it. Even while traveling with us, he had applied for acceptance by other ashrams, and at one time expressed interest also in following Ananda Moyi Ma, to whom Master in his autobiography devotes an inspiring chapter.

Ananda Moyi Ma

I myself spent many inspiring days in the company of this great woman saint. I experienced no diminution of loyalty in being with her. I did, however, find my natural predilection, which was a disinclination for the institutional outlook, receiving support from her own disinterest in organizations. Referring to the work her own disciples had built in her name, she often remarked to them, "It is *your* organization." When they tried to read to her from their society's magazine, she often laughed gaily and said, "It's your magazine. Why bother me with it?"

I referred once in conversation with her to "my kriya yoga"—my intention being to differentiate between Lahiri Mahasaya's technique and the many other types of kriya yoga that are practiced in India. Her correction was instantaneous: "No, *my* kriya yoga!" I smiled appreciatively at her emphasis on the universality of the ancient teachings.

Ma once visited the Aurobindo Ashram in Pondicherry. Later, in the magazine published by that ashram, it was reported that *their* Mother Meera had gazed at Ananda Moyi Ma with so much spiritual power that Ananda Moyi Ma had been forced to look away. Ma's devotees were naturally outraged at this slight. But Ma herself only laughed. "Isn't it true," she asked, "that if *their* mother had been the first to look away, you'd all be saying it was because *she* was not able to endure the power of my gaze?" She then went on to explain that the reason she'd looked away was simply that she had noticed that one of her devotees hadn't been given a place to sit. She was concerned on his behalf.

I loved her spirit of universality. It was something to which my own nature aspired, particularly in contrast to our own increasingly rigid definition of Master's work as an institution. Universality, I felt, was the right way to reach people: not to talk organization to them, but to appeal to the truth of *their own being.*

Ananda Moyi Ma showed a special affection for me. Among her devotees I came to be known as her *"chhoto chele"* (little child). Once she told me, "Many come before this body,"—she rarely used the personal pronoun in reference to herself—"but none attract me as you do." Once she said to me also, "You can ask anyone here: People have been with this body twenty and more years, but no one has received the depth of explanations you have."

She was reported once to have stated, out of my presence, "Kriyananda is like a honey bee. Here is a lotus resting on a large leaf. Many frogs are in the pond, croaking loudly. Kriyananda swooped down, took a sip of the nectar, and away he flew."

I was able to have with Ananda Moyi Ma the outer relationship I would have loved to have with my Guru. At the time I came to him, however, I was too young and new on the path not to feel always a profound awe before him. With Ma I could be completely natural, like a child. I used to address her as *"tumi,"* the familiar form of "you." Most, I imagine (though I don't know), addressed her as *"apni,"* the form of respect properly used when addressing an elder, especially one who is deeply revered. To me, Ananda Moyi Ma was like my own spiritual mother. I felt no conflict between my love for her and my one-pointed devotion to Master. Master was completely my own. Nothing and no one could have diluted my loyalty and love for him.

In fact, one day—sensing, perhaps, the test I would soon undergo with SRF—Ma said to me, "What would you say if I asked you to stay here?"

Immediately I replied, "Well my answer would of course be, No." To her, however, organizations meant nothing at all.

When news reached her, some time later, of my dismissal by SRF, I am told she strode back and forth as if greatly angered. Years, and much suffering, later she told me, her expression warm with compassion, "If you had asked to be allowed to come and stay here, you would have been made welcome." God and my guru, however, so arranged matters that for ten years I was denied a visa to return to India. By the end of ten years, I had already founded Ananda and was committed to carrying on this work I had begun in Master's name.

Master couldn't have got me out of his organization except violently. I was completely loyal to it, and so committed in my heart to helping it to grow in any way I could, that I would never under any circumstances have left it of my own volition.

It is clear now, however, that his wish for me was that I serve him independently of his organization.

CHAPTER 10

My First Lecture Tour

Daya Mata and her party left India in about September 1959. Shortly thereafter I traveled to the Himalayas, where I made a quiet retreat near the village of Lohaghat, in the Almora district. Fern Hill Estate was a large property owned and managed by an English family. I had been invited to stay in a large house, unlived-in and somewhat abandoned in appearance, but perfect for the seclusion I was seeking. Complete silence, spiritual reading, and long hours of meditation prepared me for a lecture tour I was to begin in October.

The tour began in the town of Simla. My seclusion had proved deeply inspiring—indeed, life changing. The thought came to me one day in meditation to see Master as residing in my listeners. Thus, my service to both him and them could be given a single focus. What I would address, I decided, was not people's personalities, but the soul within them that longed for release from the limitations of delusion. I would appeal to my Guru to enter their consciousness and transform it.

Speaking thus to people's souls, I found I was reaching them on a deep level.

Simla

My visit to Simla gave me an opportunity to learn several important lessons. One of them concerned the need for promoting public lectures.

Though Master himself had used publicity to promote his "campaign" tours, I felt some hesitancy on this point. It was after my week in Simla that I became convinced of the need for publicity. Several people came to me on my last day there, literally in tears. "If only we'd known of your visit sooner!" they lamented. "Now it is too late."

Another important discovery was the corroboration I found for my conviction that people didn't need to be converted—except, as I put it, to their own higher Self. Binay-da especially, and also many of my fellow disciples, would, I knew, look askance at my representing a teaching without trying to convert people to it. They would have considered my approach, from the organization's standpoint, "irresponsible." Yet even in terms of their priorities, my approach was effective. Many more people were drawn to this path than would have been had my approach been sectarian. Because I clearly believed in this path as exemplifying universal truths, they also believed in it.

In my emphasis on universalizing truth, I also sought to show the relation between specifics and universals. Thus, I tried always, when telling a story, to show its broad, and then its immediate and practical, implications. I also tried to generalize my answers to people's questions and comments, so as to help everyone in the room with my answer rather than satisfy only that particular person. In stories about Master, also, I tried to show what his example could signify for my listeners in their own lives.

It was important, I also realized, to show the link between the specific and the universal. I discovered that it helped never to tell a story that didn't have some general import.

I was invited one afternoon to speak at a women's college. The principal, during her introductory remarks, said, "When I was a young girl, I was taught whenever I saw a swami to fold my hands reverently and bow to him. Let us all welcome Swamiji in that spirit."

In my reply I said, "If you bow to me as a human being, your respect is offered to someone as fallible as you are. But if you show it to the ideals I represent, then I must state that I, too, bow to those ideals. In return, I bow to all of you as images of the Divine Mother, whom I worship in my heart."

I learned another priceless lesson, this one a technique for winning restive audiences.

It was another afternoon. My audience was to comprise the students at an all-men's college. I misjudged the walking distance, and arrived a full twenty minutes late. The student body president, who had invited me, met me on the street, his entire demeanor expressing agitation. His voice shaking, he tried to dissuade me from proceeding with the program.

"Can you hear them up there?" he asked. Indeed, on the hilltop above us there was a rising swell of hundreds of voices raised in angry protest. Feet were pounding loudly on the floor. The occasion seemed to me definitely inauspicious.

"It isn't only that you're late, Swamiji, and that this is the final function of the day before they leave for their villages. The boys have also just finished signing a petition *in blood* in protest against China's recent incursions onto Indian soil."

Indignation at China's totally unexpected aggression was readily understandable. Simla was near the Tibetan border, whence the incursions had come.

"Swamiji," pleaded my host, "let me cancel your lecture."

"But I've given my promise. I must honor it, if only with a brief appearance."

"My fear, sir, is that they may not honor you!"

Nevertheless, I climbed the hill and climbed up onto the platform, smiling. The college principal nervously introduced me, then sat down. I think I recall him mopping his brow. The boys looked up at me with expressions that implied, "This is the last straw!"

Obviously, unusual tactics were called for. I reasoned that if I started right in with a dissertation on yoga, I would soon find myself facing hundreds of highly vocal critics. Instead, I launched into a denunciation of China's incursions: the topic concerning which their interest was already fully aroused.

My opening was unexpected, and most welcome. I soon found them nodding their heads in agreement as I presented arguments that, I hoped, hadn't even occurred to them. Soon their sympathies were wholly on my side.

I slid gradually into my announced topic: yoga. I emphasized that the lack of peace in the world is due largely to the peacelessness human beings experience in themselves. Yoga, I said, is a panacea for world unrest. What, I asked, had China shown that it could give the world? An oppressive political system, and a readiness to dominate others through warfare. India must of course defend herself; the *Bhagavad Gita* sanctions defensive war. But what unique gift had India to give the world? It might rightly be summed up in a single word: yoga, and the inner peace that develops with yoga practice. I emphasized the power of inner peace to effect beneficial outward changes in the world.

When I finished, the pandemonium began again—but this time it was a pandemonium of applause. The students wouldn't let me go. They plied me with question after question. After half an hour the principal stood up and pleaded with them to stop asking so many questions. "The buses are ready to leave for your villages," he cried repeatedly. "If this goes on any longer, you will miss them." Eventually, concerned over those waiting buses, I myself declared, "I'm sorry, but I'll answer no more questions."

Patiala and Chandigarh

From Simla I traveled to Patiala, a city in the Punjab. Here I stayed in the large compound that belonged to the home of Dewan Balkishen Khosla, the former chief minister to the Maharaja of Patiala. My lectures were held in the public library, which filled to overflowing every evening, thereby breaking all records for attendance. No doubt it was the unusual fact of being an "American yogi" that drew people initially. What kept them coming, however, was Master's emphasis on the up-to-date practicality of the yoga teachings, and their compatibility with the findings of modern science. People were used to hearing lectures on spiritual topics supported by lengthy scriptural quotations.

A representative from nearby Mahendra College asked me if I would consent to speak to their student body, and I accepted. Many of the faculty members, and many more students influenced by their teachers, were dedicated communists and scorned anything that smacked of religion—that "opiate of the people." They despised anyone who believed in God. This, I was warned, was not a tame audience. Guest speakers had been known to be shouted off the platform. Conservative elements in the college, not wanting to see this foreign visitor disgraced, urged me to cancel my appearance. I insisted on honoring my commitment, however.

To play it safe, the principal decided to invite only the faculty and the graduate students. The hostile professors, pledged at first to treat me with courtesy as a foreigner, soon began hurling questions that were designed to embarrass and confuse me. I answered them calmly, with a smile. Several of their questions I was able to turn back against them, much to their discomfiture when everyone else laughed.

"How can you stand there and talk so confidently about God's love," one of them asked scoffingly, "when science hasn't even proved that there *is* a God?"

"I certainly can't offer proof of God's existence," I replied. "But I do know this: What I seek in life, and what I think we all seek, is happiness. I have found that when I experience love, I am happy; when I don't experience it, I am unhappy. Loving expands my sympathies; lack of it contracts them. If in the continued expansion of love I choose to see a demonstration of God's existence, where is the harm? You can have your definitions. I prefer to concentrate on what I've found by experience. Frankly, I think what we all want in life is not theories, but love." The audience laughed appreciatively. That professor, whether silenced or won over (I've no idea which), asked no more questions.

The graduate students were delighted. But the undergraduates launched a protest at having been, as they felt, discriminated against. A day or two later, a much larger gathering was convened for me out of doors. This one, the whole student body attended.

The principal later asked me how they might include Master's yoga teachings in their curriculum. Alas, I couldn't suggest a way. Here I saw demonstrated, indeed, the need for an efficient organization behind what I was presenting. We had the organization. We were still far from having the requisite efficiency.

I was invited also to address a college in Chandigarh. This city, designed by the French architect Le Corbusier, struck me as wholly inappropriate to the Indian landscape. Its straight lines and sharp angles are far too Western for the soft roundness of India's ancient civilization. Indian consciousness is not rough-hewn, like a rock newly fallen into a river bed. It is a stone rounded after centuries of erosion by the waters of time. A Parsi architect, Mr. Ghista, the acting architect of Patiala (he was designated "acting" only because he hadn't yet obtained the necessary university degree) impressed me as the kind of architect India needs. His buildings were modern, yet simple, and graceful, with long, sweeping curves that hinted at an inherent ability to adjust to life's vicissitudes.

In Chandigarh, it seemed to me that even the students had assumed into their consciousness some of the unfeeling efficiency that Indian officialdom was trying to assume in its efforts to become Westernized.

New Delhi

I returned first to Patiala, then proceeded to New Delhi.

SRF/YSS had a small center in New Delhi at that time. The members there showed a hesitation over my coming similar to that which I'd encountered in Auckland and Sydney: the fear that whatever I said would fail to have universal appeal.

"Let us plan for a large audience," I said to them on my arrival.

"Yes, Swamiji," they replied. "We can get a school room for about thirty people."

"Thirty people? I was thinking in somewhat larger terms. We'll need a large tent."

"A tent? A large—tent?" They looked shocked, as

though made suddenly aware that the difference between the Americans and the British was that the Americans were mad. Very reluctantly, under my prodding, they rented a tent large enough for eighteen hundred people, and set it up in an empty field in Main Vinaynagar, a community in an outlying district of the city. Printed posters were put up. My hope was that a sufficient number of people would be intrigued at the prospect of hearing a talk by an "American yogi" to fill the tent. Indeed, I had felt the inner guidance to get a tent this size.

The afternoon of the lecture arrived—dreaded by our members. Our little flock gloomily anticipated the worst. I meditated beforehand in a house adjoining the field, where one of the members lived. Four o'clock arrived, the hour of my scheduled appearance. The center leader knocked timidly on my door.

"We have a good crowd, Swamiji," he announced miserably. "About one hundred people." One hundred, in a tent large enough to hold eighteen hundred! This could not in any way be called a "good crowd." It was disastrous. I asked him to wait. Seven minutes passed; the crowd had increased to two hundred. Later I learned that another member had been walking back and forth outside the tent moaning, "Our reputation will be ruined!"

"Let us wait a little longer," I repeated.

At the fifteen minute mark the crowd had swelled to six hundred. Rising from my seat, I agreed to begin.

Indians are not known for their punctuality. By the time I reached my dais in the tent the crowd had swollen to two thousand. The tent was full to overflowing.

And I learned something more during this lecture: It is easier to unite two thousand people in a single vibration than it is only six people. The enthusiasm was so great that most of those present attended the follow-up series of classes, also.

Word of this "American yogi's" lectures spread rapidly through northern India, along with the news that he was making the ancient teachings attractive to the modern mind. Invitations began to pour in from all over. I spoke in East Patelnagar, at Birla Temple, and in other parts of the city. Thousands came. In addition to classes I gave Kriya Yoga initiations. Soon it was obvious that the indifference I'd been shown in Bengal was by no means the reaction of India as a whole. Clearly, a definite place existed in India's heart for Master's teachings.

CHAPTER 11

Fresh Water for Dirty Drains

This period lives in my memory as one of the spiritual highlights of my life. The joy and inner freedom I'd experienced during my seclusion in the Himalayas lingered with me still. Nothing, I realized, was important except loving God. If I could bring people onto the path, that was gratifying; it was what I myself wanted outwardly more than anything else. But this dream of life would last only a few years. What counted most was that I felt convinced, in my heart, that God alone mattered.

I had built a bonfire, mentally. Constantly I offered into that fire every lingering attachment, every latent desire.

Ananda Moyi Ma said to me at this time, *"Tomar bhab khub sundor"* (your spiritual attitude is most beautiful). God gives us such periods from time to time, to encourage and reassure us. Much work yet remained for me, however, before I could claim this sense of soul-freedom for my constant companion.

Some time later I said something to Ananda Moyi Ma about the love I was feeling in my heart. She cautioned me quietly, "Intense feeling in the heart can flow downward in the spine as well as upward." She was telling me, I felt, to make a conscious effort to direct my heart's energies up toward the spiritual eye. I didn't find this such an easy practice at that time, however. I was basking too blissfully in the heart's inner freedom.

Back in Calcutta, I was faced more painfully than ever with the dilemma of institutionalism versus my concern for people's hunger for truth. While on tour I had understood that the way really to spread Master's work was to inspire people with his teachings and example. If I'd had a harmonious team of co-workers, as I have today at Ananda, I am certain that we'd have been able to serve the needs of countless thousands, and that Master's name would by now be loved and revered throughout India. Instead, he remains little known. (One thing that pains me is that, in anthologies of Twentieth-Century Indian saints, I have yet to see Yogananda's name even mentioned.)

I had no such team to work with. Binay-da was friendly, but not much interested in my approach to spreading Master's work. In this respect, he was more American than Indian. What mattered to him was a strong organization.

I didn't, and still do not, want to argue against that idea. He himself kept saying, "Instead of presenting ourselves with black-and-white alternatives, of either . . . or, why don't we think in terms of both . . . and?" I agreed. Yet apart from Binay, and realizing also that what he really wanted was to lure me away from my ideas, not to embrace them himself, I felt a psychic morass surrounding our work as it existed then. To me it seemed that, if we proceeded in his direction, a quarter of a century would pass before the work even began to accomplish anything noteworthy. There was too much deadwood, too much sleepy energy, too much commitment to doing things as they had always been done, too much resistance to new ideas.

On my tour, many young people had expressed to me a desire to join our ashram. The energy I knew they'd encounter in Dakshineswar and in Ranchi, however, would be spiritually deadening to them. I couldn't in good conscience urge them to come there.

Kashipati, a young man in Main Vinaynagar, said to me with tears in his eyes, "I read *Autobiography of a Yogi* a few years ago. I was so inspired that I went straight to Yogoda Math in Dakshineswar and joined the ashram as a monk. But gradually I became so disillusioned with the absence of spiritual inspiration there that for a while I even thought seriously about committing suicide. This was the one path I had found that I felt I could have faith in. And then this, too, proved a complete disappointment. It is only your coming that has reawakened my faith in spirituality, and in Master's path."

I told Binay-da this story, and said to him, "You see? We just *can't* ask people to come here until we're in a position to give them the help they need."

"Doesn't matter, Brother," he replied dismissingly. "Let them come. When they leave, others will come."

His was a businessman's approach to the situation. But surely it could never be that of a devotee.

What occurred to me as the best possible solution was one to which I have resorted successfully again and again in my life: Don't waste time transforming old energy, but concentrate on developing a positive vortex of new energy. Once the positive vortex grows strong enough, it will either absorb the old, transforming it automatically, or cause it to dissipate for lack of cohesion. This was how I had succeeded in organizing the monks. It was how I succeeded, later, in building Ananda despite much internal dissension during our early years. It is how Master taught us to work on ourselves: Do what you can do; don't worry about the obstacles that are beyond your strength. I was convinced this method would work well for us in India.

I had been well received in northern India. In Bengal, however, especially in our own organization, the old ways were so entrenched that I wondered what, apart from dynamite, could ever dislodge them. I pleaded with Binay, Why not build an ashram in New Delhi? We could welcome applicants to a new way of life that we'd be able to develop from scratch, following Master's ideals. New Delhi, I reminded him, was presently the heart of India. Everything flowed from that heart. The country looked to New Delhi for guidance in everything. A spiritual work established there would become known throughout India almost over-night. A good ashram there would become a model for ashrams everywhere.

"Just think," I enthused, "of all the young people who graduate from college and want new ways of doing things, new ways of looking at life. That's exactly what Master's teachings can offer them.

"I don't mean to starve our work here in Calcutta

and in Ranchi," I continued. "It can be left to continue as it is. You and I could visit here regularly, and give them whatever encouragement they would accept. But *you* could live at the Delhi ashram, too. Together we could establish a strong work there. I would travel around India, drawing people to our work. I am sure the work itself will then flourish.

"And then," I concluded triumphantly, "perhaps in five years, when we have a strong, well-trained group of devotees in New Delhi, we could bring twenty or twenty-five of them back here. It would take that many to turn this local energy around effectively. Their fresh energy would act like buckets of fresh, clean water to wash out the clogged drains and enable them to function again."

Dubey didn't want to quash my enthusiasm, but I don't think he shared my vision. I'm still convinced it would have worked. His mind, however, was on more immediate problems.

First, there was his own uncertainty about this path. Did he really want to participate in our work? Often he voiced his doubts to me on that score.

Second, he was on familiar ground where he lived.

A true Taurean, moreover, he was more comfortable working with the known, however difficult, than launching into the unknown. There was no certainty that we would even be able to get land in New Delhi. He himself had not experienced my success there.

As for money, he conceded that we could raise a fair amount. He had already suggested that we sell the Baranagar property, from which we might realize some five or more hundred thousand rupees. Indira

Devi, moreover, the Maharajmata of Cooch Behar, had told me she wanted to contribute 400,000 rupees to our work. She had become friendly to us while Daya Mata was still in India, and continued to invite me to her home occasionally for lunch. So—there was the money we'd need for the project. Binay didn't close the door. For him, nevertheless, Delhi was only one of several irons in the fire, all of them waiting to be sorted out by the patient alchemist, time.

Master, meanwhile, had plans for me that I could not have imagined at the time. In retrospect, it looks as though he planned to use on me the same tactics I myself had found helpful: Don't try to change the old energy; instead, create a new energy vortex.

CHAPTER 12

I Return to America

I returned to America in April 1960, for a visit. Stopping off in Japan on the way, I visited some of its famous gardens and had *"darshan,"* as they put it in India, of the huge statue of Buddha at Kamakura.

My return to Mt. Washington lingers fondly in my memory: the love of my brother monks, the enthusiasm and affection of the members in our Hollywood church, Daya Mata welcoming me joyfully, eager for news of developments in the work she had left with such a heavy heart only eight months before. I was happy to be the bearer of good tidings. Things were looking up there, I told her. She was delighted to hear my description of the tour in northern India.

When I told her of my proposal for building an ashram in New Delhi, she pondered the matter, then said, "It is an idea worth pursuing." She added:

"Stay in touch with Binay. Work with him." I assured her that this I intended to do.

While I was in Japan I received a cablegram from Mt. Washington informing me of Dr. Lewis's passing. I was sorry for the loss not only of a friend, but of one more man among the old-time disciples. Dr. Lewis had been an example to us all of sincere loyalty to the guru and of depth of realization. I'll never forget the longing in his eyes, once, as he spoke to me of being with Master again.

Shortly after my return to Mt. Washington I was voted into his place on the Board of Directors and as the first vice president. It was Tara Mata who proposed the appointment, based on her reading of my horoscope. (Later, again based on her reading of the same horoscope, she demanded my dismissal from SRF.) Well, I suppose I was the natural choice anyway. I was the head monk, the director of center activities, and had been described a year earlier by Daya Mata as the senior minister of SRF. A man was needed for the Board, which otherwise would have consisted of only women.

Much of my time in America was spent in discussions with Daya Mata about our work in India. I also spent time with the monks, and spoke at several of our churches. Memories come crowding in now, most of them filled with joy.

Most of them . . . but not all. At this time a cloud entered my life, and posed a serious threat to my spiritual development. It represented the commonest of all obstacles on the path.

Romance was not a part of our way of life. We were renunciates, dedicated to the single life in our service of God. But we were human beings also, and not immune to normal human feelings. The important thing was that we sublimate those feelings in our love for God—our Divine Mother, rather than any human beloved. For many, this was not an easy task. Our American upbringing militated against outer renunciation. Our culture, in the form of countless influences, militated against it. These were difficult influences to combat.

I myself had had two crosses to bear in my self: spiritual doubt, which by this time I had for the most part overcome, and the desire for sex and romance, over which I felt by this time that I'd achieved at least noteworthy victory. The tendency toward spiritual doubt lingered still in my subconscious, however; it emerged occasionally in the form of bouts of self-doubt. And the desire for human love, though no longer mixed, to my conscious awareness, with physical desire, yet found expression in the thought that human love was an attractive manifestation of love itself, the "divine passion."

Master had occasionally discussed this aspect of cosmic delusion with me. Certain of my readers may be displeased to see it described as a delusion, but indeed, anything that can divert the mind from one-pointed focus on God, the Sole Reality, deserves no other description. Master assured me, however, that I would win out over this universal foe.

Self-doubt impelled me once to ask him to whom I might go for counseling on this issue, when he was no longer with us.

"Speak of it to no one," he replied.

"Not even to Dr. Lewis? to St. Lynn?"

"No," he replied firmly. "No one. You have a great work to do, and no one must know."

Though it is my nature to be frank and open—to a fault, Master sometimes said—I have always honored these words of his, and have said nothing about this matter. I mention it here only because of a determined campaign that has recently been launched by my enemies to destroy me through lies and innuendoes.

Master himself reassured me, "You will be all right," whenever I spoke to him on the subject. "This tendency isn't deep in you. Be strong in yourself."

I valued renunciation not only in the abstract, but as a personal ideal. When I took my vows in 1955 as a swami, however, it was not a declaration, "I am free!" Rather, it was an affirmation, "I will do my utmost to become completely free in this life." Sometimes I would fantasize that on my deathbed I would joyfully realize that I was free at last from this greatest of all delusions.

For who doesn't have it, in one form or another? Master was praising one of the monks to a small group in Encinitas, saying, "Look at him. He feels no attraction to the opposite sex."

One of the young men in the group, new to the monastery, said, "Yeah, Sir, but look at him. It's because he ain't got no energy."

"That's the truth!" Master admitted with chuckle.

People who expect perfection from those who have embraced the path of renunciation do not themselves realize how difficult such perfection is to achieve. A young woman at the Hollywood church used to mock me for maintaining a certain distance between us. "There's a young man in my office," she chided me, "who never shows any interest in us girls, yet he's perfectly natural with us. What's wrong with you? Are you weaker than he is? He isn't even on the spiritual path!"

Refusing to be drawn into an argument, I remained silent. But I thought, "And what do you know about this man's life outside the office? He probably has a girlfriend to whom he is completely loyal."

One of the young women in the church told Meera Mata one day, "That Kriyananda! He's the cutest thing on two legs."

Meera told me about it later. "*Miss* Baldwin," she'd replied indignantly, "Our ministers don't . . ."

"*have* legs!" I finished for her. We had a good laugh about it. But certainly the rule about our maintaining a certain distance from women was less for our reputations than for our own spiritual safety.

Most women, fortunately, respected my impersonality, and made no attempt to draw me out of it.

"The important thing," Master told us, "is never to admit defeat. If ever you say, 'I am lost,' it will be so, at least for this incarnation. But if you keep on making the effort to be good, God will never let you down. No matter how many times you fail, get up and try again. Always remember this: A saint is a sinner who never gave up."

Virtue is not static. Usually it should be defined by the *direction* toward which one is growing. To criticize others is to draw to oneself, by the inexorability of karmic law, the very fault one has presumed to criticize in others.

"Intense love in the heart," Ananda Moyi Ma had warned me, "can flow down the spine as well as up it." Was it foresight that had caused her to utter these words?

There was a nun at Mt. Washington who had once harshly criticized another nun for leaving the ashram and marrying. The karma for that criticism now became her nemesis. She fell in love with me. The anguish on her countenance and in her eyes was too much for me. This was a weakness of mine: I couldn't bear to see another person suffer. Before I knew it, I found myself drawn into an emotion that I had hoped to have left behind me forever. I struggled against it, but to no avail.

It is not difficult to fall into a ditch. The difficulty lies in climbing out of it. What with the intense feeling of abandonment I experienced, years later, in my dismissal from SRF, the loneliness of that period of my life, the absence of any external support for my longing to live for God alone, it was many years before I achieved true freedom again in my heart—a freedom greater, with God's grace, than any I'd ever known previously.

Just see the heart-rending twists of fate: This very nun became, years later (perhaps in attempted expiation of her own sin), utterly dedicated to my undoing.

How to account for the bitter ironies of life? A few evenings ago I was watching the movie "Casablanca" on video. How sweet seemed human love in that story,—how sweet, that is, for a time. And how inevitable, perhaps just because of its sweetness, was the story's ending in tragic unfulfillment! Such always, whether late or soon, is life's drama. When I first met Master, I said to him, "I don't see marriage for myself. For others it may be fine." He answered me promptly by pointing out how disappointing human love is for everyone, eventually. This world is set up in such a way that only God's love, finally, can satisfy the heart, for only God's love is real. Only God, truly, is forever our own.

Meanwhile, to learn that lesson to our very core, how many heartaches must we endure! How many almost unbearable hurts! How many betrayals!

Lest any reader of these pages think my relationship with this nun was the cause of my later dismissal from SRF, I hasten to add that it was never known to others. The reasons for my separation from the organization will be explained later, in another chapter. Define them how one will (it may be stated here), they were essentially political.

That relationship may, however, have had an indirect influence on what happened, for it threw me into a state of inner confusion and despair. I knew I wanted only God. I had no intention of leaving my quest for Him for any lesser attraction. But how could I manage to realign my heart's feelings so that all its energies flowed once again upward, toward Him alone?

I had said once to Master, "I would commit suicide rather than fall into temptation!"

"Why do you speak of suicide?" he asked me, scoldingly. "Keep on trying your best. You *will* come out of it in the end."

Suicide, then, wasn't an option for me, though there were times when it appeared attractive. I would simply have to learn to live with myself and do what I could with the tools I had (my outer traits, that is to say, whether good or bad). I *would not* allow this flaw to become an obsession. If the battle proved too difficult to win for now, there were others I could fight that, in the process of fighting, would develop my strength to face the greater battles.

I, too, like Tara, had an artistic temperament, with the weakness that often accompanies it of finding inspiration in romantic moods. The essential thing was to direct those moods toward love for God alone.

Fortunately, I have also been blessed with an ability to separate myself from my heart's feelings. Even during times when outer tests have brought me the greatest pain and suffering, for example, my ability to compose happy music or to write or teach with a consciousness of inner joy has remained unaffected.

Thus, though I went through much soul-searching and anguish, my months in America were on the whole positive and joyful. Daya Mata and I discussed, as I said, the situation in India. She endorsed my proposal for starting an ashram in New Delhi. Though we discussed other matters, especially her wish that I support Binay-da, paramount in her eyes seemed to be that I continue my efforts to reach out to people through lecturing.

This left a need for another monk to be sent to India to help with the work at our national headquarters. The monk I would have liked to work with was Stanley Guy (now Brother Achalananda), with whom I had a friendly relationship. Tara, however, reading horoscopes again, told me, "Allen Marsh is the one to be with you. Your horoscopes are compatible." My heart sank. Allen (Brother Sarvananda) was the main one of all the monks who had been the most prompt to go over my head on the slightest difference of opinion. Still, Allen it was to be. "It's all a cosmic dream," I reminded myself. I wasn't going to place my personal wishes over what others thought best for the work.

As things turned out, my fears proved fully justified. Allen, once he realized which way the wind was blowing for me, did his utmost to undermine my position and to place a negative twist on everything I said and did in his reports to Mt. Washington. These reports were later quoted to me in "proof" of my wrongdoing.

I returned to India in the fall of 1960 by way of Europe, where I visited our centers in England, France, Switzerland, and Italy. From Europe I went to Israel, where I toured Galilee and visited a kibbutz. So many stories I could tell! The apparent miracle, for example, over the Mount of Transfiguration in Israel; my impressions of the Israeli kibbutz; the tragic consequences to our work in Europe of Tara's dismissal of our main leader there; my first exposure to Italy, Italians, and the Italian language; my visit to Sri Lanka and the time I spent there with my parents, who were then on an around-the-world tour—even my brief impressions of Iran, where I stopped for an afternoon on my way to Sri Lanka (or Ceylon, as it was called then). But I must stick to my theme no matter how tempting it is to follow these detours.

From Sri Lanka I flew to Madras. I had two hopes in mind: one, a few days of seclusion prior to resuming my work for YSS; and, two, a visit to Sri Rama Yogi, known as Yogi Ramiah to readers of Paul

Brunton's book, *A Search in Secret India.* Master had met Yogi Ramiah at Ramana Maharshi's ashram during his 1935 return to India. Speaking to me of that meeting, Master told me, "We walked about the ashram hand in hand. If I'd had another half hour in his company, I could never have brought myself to leave India again. He was a great and fully liberated soul." This was more than Master had said about Ramana Maharshi himself.

"Paul Brunton," Master added, "later told me that Yogi Ramiah had materialized before him and requested a photograph of me."

I traveled to Nellore, then out to the little village of Buchireddypalayam, where Sri Rama Yogi (as he was now known) resided. Again, I would love to describe this four-day visit in detail. Some day, perhaps. For the purposes of these pages, however, it is best that I limit myself to one snippet from our conversations.

Sri Rama Yogi had received several letters from Daya Mata. "What are her responsibilities?" he asked me.

I explained her worldwide duties as president of SRF/YSS.

"What a burden!" he exclaimed, dismayed for her.

"But, Sir," I protested, "to speak of her duties only as a burden would imply it was bad karma that raised her to that position. It might even imply that the main requirement for the position of president in a spiritual organization be that one have sufficiently bad karma for the job!"

Rama Yogi smiled. "Of course I didn't mean it that way. Rather, she has the *good* karma to have been placed in a position where she can work out certain outward tendencies more quickly. But that doesn't mean that being the president is in itself a good karma. For others, such a position wouldn't be fortunate at all; if it didn't coincide with their own karmic needs, it would be *only* a burden. For Daya Mata, it is a burden also, but one that can also help and strengthen her."

Back in Madras, a fervent prayer to Babaji opened up for me a house in Kodaikanal in the Nilgiri mountains, where I spent ten days in seclusion. And then it was on to Calcutta.

CHAPTER 13

The Delhi Project

Binay-da was reluctant to see me leave Calcutta for New Delhi. I postponed that trip, accordingly, and remained near him for several months. Our discussions centered on the work and how to develop it. The alternative to starting afresh, as I wanted to do, was to concentrate on clearing out (as I put it) the clogged drains.

Even while cleaning out dirty drains, however, the focus of one's attention can be on cleanliness; it needn't be on dirt. We can try to be solution-oriented, not problem-oriented. Binay's mind was problem-oriented.

He talked for hours of how "useless" this person was, what a "parasite" that person was, what an "enemy" that third person was. He took delight in declaring over and over, moving his thumb back and forth in a gesture of determination, how he would "smash" this one, "force" that one to obey his will, get rid of that other one. "These are all useless people, Brother," he repeated again and again. He spoke mockingly of people who, in my view, deserved sincere respect. There was no one in the work, in his opinion, worthy of anything but our contempt. They were all slackers, time servers, self-seekers, petty schemers, bereft of the slightest hint of spirituality.

I was there to help him. When he expressed doubts about this path, I was there to encourage him to fuller understanding. Whenever I felt myself tempted to plead that he stop loading me to the gunwale with negativity, I found myself having, instead, to bolster his faith, in the process expressing sympathy and understanding for his problem with doubts.

After weeks of these harangues, and no glimmer of a suggestion as to how we might improve matters except by "driving the rascals out," I felt there was nothing more I could do. Certainly I didn't enjoy these endless denunciations of everything and everybody. I was becoming more and more depressed. New Delhi appeared to me our only hope.

Delhi it was then, and Binay agreed to let me go there and try my luck.

More than luck was needed, as it turned out. When I arrived in New Delhi, I sought out friends and told them of my plans. They put me in touch with a man they knew, a Mr. Ratti, who was on the council (or whatever it was called) for Delhi State. Mr. Ratti laughed scornfully when I told him of my plan.

"Delhi is a government town, completely," he informed me. "Nothing can be done here without the government's permission. And the government's priorities are strictly set. Schools and factories are needed. Hospitals are needed. Businesses are needed. Residential communities are needed. Who needs ashrams? The country is crowded already with too many ashrams. India is a secular state. You will find no one anywhere in New Delhi to support you in your ideas."

"What about land outside the city?" I inquired. Friends had taken me to see land in the direction of Gurgaon. It seemed far enough outside the city limits.

"All land surrounding the city has been designated as a 'green belt' area. No construction of any kind is permitted there."

My "inspiration," if it may be called that, was to do anything rather than return to the downward spiral of negativity in Calcutta. Did I feel inner guidance to work here, against such a host of contrary indications? No, I had to admit to myself, I did not. But in the absence of inner guidance, what was I supposed to do? Should I simply give up? To give up was, to me, unthinkable. Thus, I came to a decision which was to have a lasting influence on my life.

I committed myself to a massive undertaking without prior inner guidance. What I have learned from that experience is instead to take one step at a time, listening inwardly all the while until something inside me "clicks" and I really know what to do. Otherwise, to try arduously but blindly for too long becomes tantamount to presumption.

It isn't that what I was trying to do was wrong. Certainly I was doing it with good intentions. But I think Master didn't want to give me inner encouragement on a course that, he knew, was destined to end in personal disaster for me.

Facing nothing but rejection no matter where I turned, I reaffirmed a conviction I have always had, supported by repeated experience in my life, that seemingly impossible events can often be brought to pass by the sheer power of will.

"By my will," I declared with concentrated determination, "I will make this dream a reality!"

The Campaign

I had been invited to live in the home of Dr. and Mrs. T. N. Bhan, at Kashmiri Gate in Old Delhi. They had a small cabin in their garden. I was invited to live here. Rani Bhan and her son Indu helped me in my campaign to interest the government in my project.

I was informed that 2,000 other societies had tried unsuccessfully to get land in the green belt area. My reaction to this disheartening news was a stronger-than-ever resolution to succeed.

Land on the outskirts of town was unavailable, since it was in the green belt area. Well, I didn't want land on the outskirts anyway. For a population mostly dependent for locomotion on buses, walking, and bicycles, the outskirts were too far away for any viable public activity.

A certain wealthy man, Shree Gupta, visited the home of the Bhans one day. "Swamiji," he began, "I have the perfect place for you. It is a yoga ashram on Mandir Lane, just next to the Birla Temple, and very close to the center of the city. It is also in the green belt area, which curves into the city at that point in a sort of loop."

To be in the green belt and at the same time within the city was very attractive.

"How do you propose I get this property," I inquired. "Isn't it already functioning as an ashram?"

"It is," he agreed. "Nevertheless, I have studied their by-laws, and I've learned that it would be a simple matter to take it over. Their decisions are made by a majority vote of its members. No restrictions are placed on who may become a member.

"What I propose to do," he concluded, "is buy up enough memberships to vote the existing leaders out of office, then give the ashram over to you."

I was appalled at this want of scruples. I knew such things happened in the business world, but I would be no party to any such plan. I declined his offer, not even with thanks.

Shree Gupta, however, as it turned out, could not imagine I would seriously refuse his offer. Proceeding with his scheme, he bought up the necessary number of memberships, voted out the existing leaders, then came to me one day with the proud announcement: "Swamiji, the ashram is yours!"

Again, and all the more forcefully because of my disappointment in having had no other promises of success, I rejected his offer. I've no idea what has become of that ashram since then. I don't believe I ever saw Shree Gupta again, though I have one other recollection of him, an amusing one.

He and his wife came one day to tea. Referring to her, who fortunately understood no English, he announced, "She was a cow in her last life." I glanced over at her. She was sitting relaxed, her features fixed in a vapid smile while her jaw worked gently in a manner not unreminiscent of a cow chewing its cud.

One thing did impress me favorably about Shree Gupta's proposition, however: the *area* in which the yoga ashram was located. It was amazingly tranquil considering its proximity to the heart of the large city. Across Mandir Lane from the ashram there was a large, beautiful tract of land, useful for nothing at all in its present condition. If no land in the green belt area was available, I thought, why could I not at least try to get this ideal piece and forget about the outskirts? I resolved to do my very best.

My Campaign

I gave serious thought, not to my own needs, but to those of the government of India and, even more specifically, the city and state of New Delhi. New Delhi, I reasoned, was not only the economic and political hub of the country, but also the heart of a new country that aspired toward international recognition and respect, especially from wealthy countries in a position to help her with gifts and loans. Prestige was important to the government leaders, particularly to Pundit Jawaharlal Nehru, the Prime Minister. If I concentrated on the international aspects of this project, might it not exercise an appeal for them beyond any I could excite on behalf of an ordinary ashram? If so, could I not devise some means whereby *both* needs would be satisfied—ours, and the government's?

How could it be made a reflection of something Master wanted? Well, I reflected, he had written in the first edition of *Autobiography of a Yogi* that he hoped someday to have a "yoga university," flying the flags of all nations as symbols of international co-operation and good will. His very last speech, the evening of his *mahasamadhi* (conscious earthly passing), had been a plea for international cooperation—for taking the best of each nation and uniting that good for the greater welfare of all mankind. This was a bit grand, perhaps, as an initial concept for our ashram, but a work devoted to this ideal, as Master's surely had always been, would not be expected to spring out immediately in full-blown perfection.

It came as second nature to me to think of ever new, more expansive ways of manifesting Master's teachings, as long as those ways were in tune with things he himself had done or at least aspired to do. It would take vision to build his work in India. My concern was only to keep that vision true to the essential mission of spreading Kriya Yoga.

International? Why, we *were* international. It would only be emphasizing our strengths to draw attention to that which was already a fact.

Would Kriya Yoga fit into this scene? Yoga was India's greatest contribution to the world. In any discussion of international unity, Kriya Yoga could be offered proudly as central to this ideal.

Might subjects other than Kriya Yoga, introduced by people more outwardly attuned to international harmony, dilute our own special emphasis? No, why should they? Ours could be a place that made a focus on yoga its special contribution to a larger good. It would be absurd to use our ashram as a center for teaching anything and everything. From our own central focus in Kriya Yoga we could relate meaningfully to other groups possessing different interests.

Master had said repeatedly, "We are not a sect." What better ground than this fact to help draw India out of its ancient inter-sectarian rivalries?

As I contemplated these ideas, I grew increasingly enthusiastic thinking of the good that could spread outward from this Delhi project.

Contemplating the importance to the Indian government of international approval, I visited the ambassadors from various countries and solicited their expressions of support. A few of them answered positively. Each positive reply became another arrow in my quiver.

I then went to the chief ministers of various ministries in the central government. Their approval, I felt, could be vital in persuading the Delhi government at least to listen to my proposal. A number of these men expressed sympathy with my idea, thereby adding more arrows to my arsenal.

To awaken further interest, I described the international nature of my own background: born in Rumania, educated in Rumania, Switzerland, England, and the United States; fluent in several languages; conversant in others.

Finally, realizing that Delhi State, albeit under the general supervision of the central government, was focused more locally, I considered the rationale behind the green belt area itself. The green belt was intended as lungs for the city. Lungs, however, suggest trees, not barren open spaces. There were few trees in the green belt, and most of them little more than spindly sticks, surrounded by a few listless shrubs.

There was one park in the green belt, however: Buddha Jayanti Park, clear evidence in itself that the government was not absolutely opposed to any development that might further its idea of providing lungs for the city. Only in Buddha Jayanti Park was there any greenery worthy of mention: flourishing trees, broad lawns, flower beds—acres of natural beauty.

I wrote a letter to Bhagwan Sahaya, the chief commissioner of Delhi State. In my letter I addressed the city's, not my own, needs. I pointed out that the green belt was, for the most part, anything but green. "As far as I can tell," I continued, "it serves the city mainly as a public latrine." I went on to discuss Buddha Jayanti Park, and how that park, at least, succeeded in providing Delhi with lungs. "Even a state as wealthy as Delhi State, however," I went on, "could not expect to finance the development of parkland throughout its thousands of acres. The obvious solution, then, is to allow individual institutions to undertake the development of certain approved areas of the green belt.

"I am aware," I continued, "of the government's ban on the construction of buildings in the green belt. However, even Buddha Jayanti Park could not exist had it not been permitted to erect certain minimal construction: a restaurant, for example, to feed the visitors who come there. These buildings are really no more of a threat to the city than the rocks they replace. What they make possible, however, is the natural greenery that exists for acres all around them.

"If, therefore," I concluded, "you consider allowing certain approved institutions to develop certain parts of the green area into places of public inspiration or enjoyment, it would be necessary to allow them also to construct certain minimal facilities, subject to your approval, in order to carry on their own activities."

I mentioned in my letter, of course, the numbers of ambassadors and chief ministers who had already found my proposal attractive.

Bhagwan Sahaya telephoned me a few days later and asked if he might see me. We fixed an appointment, and I went to his home in a hopeful mood.

"I like your proposal," he told me. "India, however, is plagued with too much sectarianism. How could I be sure that this place you're asking for, assuming we grant you permission to develop it, would not degenerate into yet another bickering sect?"

"Well, our founder declared many times publicly that we are not a sect."

"Words are cheap. Can you give me anything more substantial than that?"

"Well," I replied, "we welcome people from all religions to our talks and *satsang*s. Paramhansa Yogananda in fact called his work in America a 'church of all religions.'"

"I don't know of an ashram anywhere that isn't happy to welcome people from other religions to its functions," he replied with a sardonic smile. I realized I'd have to think quickly. I hadn't anticipated this question. Then I said:

"We would allow groups from other ashrams to

hold meetings at our facilities." This seemed a safe offer, even a desirable one. It would be wonderful if other ashrams could be inspired to join hands with us in a kindred spirit of universal good will. As for the "bickering sects," I didn't think they would come, given their fiercely territorial spirit. I saw no danger to our own integrity, therefore, in this open-handed proposal. We would gain, I thought, from such a wholesome interchange, provided we ourselves remained centered in our own practices.

Bhagwan Sahaya considered the matter a few moments longer. Finally he said, "Very good. I can sway the Delhi commissioners to your idea. Only one obstacle remains. Because this idea of a green belt comes down all the way from the highest levels of our government, Pundit Nehru himself will have to be convinced before we can proceed any further."

"Fine," I said. "Then would you speak to him on the matter?"

"Oh, no," he replied. "That is something *you* will have to do."

"I! But I can't even imagine how to meet him."

"I'm sorry, but I can't help you there." He implied that to do so would be sticking his neck out farther than he dared. What he seemed to be saying was, I'll give you what you want provided you go first to the moon. I was reminded of those impossible tasks fairy tale princes were given if they wanted to marry the princess. Considering that, in those stories, the penalty for failure was invariably the loss of their heads, the comparison seemed to me not entirely unapt. The penalty for failure to see and convince

Nehru would still be the final and complete rejection of my proposal.

I See Nehru

The Bhans were, like Nehru himself, Kashmiri brahmins. In India, communities like this are more close-knit than comparable groups in America. Rani Bhan knew an elderly cousin of Nehru's. She suggested we pay her a visit.

The cousin received Rani affably. After some discussion on a variety of homely topics, the subject was raised of an introduction to Nehru's daughter, Indira Gandhi.

"I'll be happy to put in a word for you," said the cousin. And so it was arranged that I meet Indira Gandhi.

An appointment was made, and Indira Gandhi received me, though with obvious reluctance. To her mind, she was only seeing me as a favor to her elderly relative.

"Please state your business quickly," she said, quite haughtily. "I am busy packing for a trip to Paris tomorrow. I'm supposed to address a conference there."

"Do you speak French?" I asked, demonstrating interest in her plans.

"Yes," she replied coolly.

"Where did you learn it?" continuing our discussion in French.

"Somewhere you wouldn't have heard of, at a small school in Switzerland called Beau Soleil. It is in the mountain village of Villars."

"Beau Soleil!" I exclaimed, amazed. "Why, I went to school almost next door to it, in the village of Chesières. We used to walk by your school every day on our 'promenades.' It was there that I, too, learned French."

She thawed completely. We chatted awhile longer, in French. She then said she'd be happy to recommend to her father that he spare me some time. Our talk ended by her taking me out into the garden and "introducing" me to two cute tiger cubs that had been presented to her father and her as a gift.

Things had begun to look brighter.

Realizing how important a recommendation from a secretary could be in the life of a busy executive, I made an appointment to see Nehru's secretary. The secretary was favorably impressed with my proposal, and promised to put in a good word for me with his boss.

Another happy coincidence occurred. As an example of pure serendipity, Jayprakash Narayan, the former number two man in the government, happened to visit New Delhi at that time. I knew him, having met him a year earlier, again fortuitously: We had traveled together in the same train compartment from Calcutta to Benares. I hadn't known who he was at the time, but we'd got into a discussion on cooperative communities—a subject that interested me deeply—and he'd appreciated my ideas. I paid him a visit now. Expressing pleasure at seeing me again, he concluded:

"I shall speak to Punditji on your behalf. If he is as

well impressed with you as I am, I don't think you will encounter any problem."

There was one thing more I did, hoping it would assist me in convincing Nehru. Realizing that, busy as he was, a picture would speak more instantly about my project than any abstract discussion, I painted a large design of how I hoped the property would look when it was developed.

In the painting I waxed fanciful, imagining an almost Disneyland-like series of hills made to look like miniature Himalaya mountains (the land already had the necessary hills), concrete-insulated caves for residents to minimize the visual impact of residences on the land, a temple (which I depicted also for the cover of a promotional brochure), and trees and grass everywhere.

Rani, her son Indu, and I, armed with my large painting, went to meet Nehru as he came out on his daily way to the office. He paused briefly, looked at the painting, said a few words, then remarked that he would arrange to see me.

A meeting with Nehru was less promising than it sounds. He was known to be extremely quixotic. One never knew whether he would be in a gracious mood, or shout at one never to plague him again with such utter nonsense. A further problem was that he was known to be antagonistic to religion in general.

The day of our meeting proved inauspicious for him, but auspicious for us. News had reached him of the death of a dear friend. Instead of his frequently irascible mood, he was quietly thoughtful. He heard me out, then asked a few pertinent questions. He smiled when I spoke of my deep convictions against sectarianism, which I saw as a cancer in the body of the world's religions. Altogether Nehru gave me forty minutes of his time, which, I was told later, considerably exceeded the time he normally gave to ambassadors. At the end of our discussion he said, "Your idea attracts me. I shall make it a point to walk the property. If it meets my approval, you shall have my consent."

And so, with almost miraculous suddenness, what had so long seemed an impossibility had become an actual probability. People who had been shaking their heads, grinning their skepticism, began really to sit up and take notice.

Nehru did in fact walk the land a few days later. Shortly thereafter, he gave the project his formal blessing.

****

And there you have the entire story behind what ended up being the greatest test of my life.

For decades, SRF representatives have replied to inquiries with the stock answer: "If you *only knew* what he did!" There is nothing more anyone could tell you than what I have told here. I myself know the whole story much better than anyone else. If my actions seem as outrageous to you as they did to my fellow disciples, then I have no further explanation to offer you. I must accept your condemnation as at least *your* judgment on the matter.

SRF members have sometimes written me anonymously to say, "No corporation would put up with what you did." Since they all write the same thing, it seems safe to assume they've been coached. Well, to them, whoever and wherever they are, I have this to say: I am the president of a fairly large and successful corporation, international in scope: a place called Ananda. If anyone representing us abroad showed so much loyalty, dedication, and creative zeal, I would wine him (non-alcoholically, of course), dine him, and thank him with tears in my eyes. It is with spirit like this that Ananda has grown and, with Master's grace, flourished over the nearly thirty years of its existence.

A photograph had been taken of me meeting the Dalai Lama. It seemed perfect for promoting the new project. I told my Indian friends to look for it to appear soon on the cover of "Self-Realization Magazine."

CHAPTER 14

The Reaction

Daya Mata used sometimes to tease me for being what she called "naive." In one respect she was right. I trusted in friendship, and believed that ours superseded any mere organizational consideration. I often expressed myself to her without giving my words careful thought, as friends will. I couldn't help the frustration I felt at her not giving me a chance to do certain things in which I believed, and I couldn't help feeling let down when, faced with others' criticism, she often failed to back me in a project to which she'd given her prior consent. But we were friends, and she knew I'd stand by her always.

I wrote her on May 14, 1961, about my success with the Delhi project. That date is indelibly etched on my mind. I was completely confident that there would be joyful celebrations at Mt. Washington upon the arrival of that letter. I had, after all, just completed a major campaign for Master, and had emerged victorious. From now on, Master's work in India, which had been for us such a heartfelt disappointment, would flourish. It would attract devotees and ashram members from all over by the hundreds. It would become one of the great spiritual lights in modern India. From today on, SRF-YSS would be known and revered as one ashram where principles were placed ahead of sectarian differences. Master's teachings would be practiced everywhere.

I hadn't been able to write much, previously, I explained, because there really was nothing to report except the disheartening news of a long list of adamant refusals. As a commentary on years of opposition to my ideas, I couldn't resist adding, in effect, "See, I *can* get things done if I am given the opportunity."

Daya Mata told me later, "After reading your letter, I passed it on without comment to the other directors." Was she telling me that she'd never told anyone about the project, nor that I'd been working on it with her consent?

I mentioned in my letter that I'd be going to Darjeeling for a needed vacation, as my time in Delhi had been exhausting to me. I'd be at the vacation house of the Maharani (actually the Maharajmata, the mother of the present Maharaja) of Cooch Behar. I hoped soon, however, to get word that Pundit Nehru had given his approval to the Delhi project.

Word of his approval came while I was resting and meditating in Darjeeling. That same day, I believe it was, a telephone call came from America. It was from Tara Mata:

"We . . . do . . . not . . . want . . . that . . . property!"

We had a bad connection; I didn't understand her at first. "Yes!" I shouted. "With God's grace we have Nehru's permission at last."

"We . . . do . . . not . . . want . . . that . . . property!"

came the statement again, each word this time enunciated distinctly and at maximum volume.

What was I to say? This completely unexpected refusal would mean a colossal humiliation for me, but what did that matter, after all? I hadn't done all that work for myself. If after everything the idea was rejected, then that was that. There would be other ways of serving the work. Without pausing even to think my thoughts through, I replied, "All right. If that is your decision, I'll abide by it willingly."

"We . . . do . . . not . . . want . . . that . . . property!" she shouted a third time. "You'll be getting our letter shortly."

And that was that. I hung up, then commenced adjusting my mind to these new and very different circumstances. There was no sadness in my heart, though I was probably feeling slightly numb. Whatever God and guru willed for me was my will also.

The disastrous shock came the following day in the form of a letter, some twenty or thirty pages long, written and signed by Tara Mata but intended to be read as though coming from the entire Board.

I was accused of deceitfulness and "crafty guile" in deliberately concealing from them the work I'd been doing. "You wanted to get us so compromised with the Indian government that we'd have no choice but to go along with you. Your scheme was to split the work and set yourself up as the new guru in India. You lied to us. You connived for personal power. Your attitude reeks of personal ambition. You're a megalomaniac, hypocritical, treacherous to the last degree. You refused to work with Binay, who is doing everything he can in Calcutta to serve Master's work. Nothing you can ever say or do in future will permit me ever to trust you again."

I am paraphrasing her words. The letter, as I say, went on, single-spaced, for at least twenty pages, all of it vitriolic, accusatory, and utterly damning.

I couldn't believe my eyes. I took a long walk, and, in Tara's jeering words later on, "wept buckets."

"You can do what you like with the Delhi proposal," I wrote back. "I am not attached to it. But please," I pleaded, "*please* don't misjudge my motives."

"Shame on you," came the angry reply, "for trying to justify your actions, first, and now your motives. Master *never* let us try to justify ourselves. Your motives are impure, and worse than impure. They are completely self-motivated. You are a traitor to your guru. You are his Judas. You are so disobedient, so insulting, so unbelievably presumptuous that Master drew you to him only near the end of his life to spare you getting the bad karma you'd certainly have received when you left him, hurling insults as you went. You've lied, you've cheated so often that you can no longer even faintly tell the difference between right and wrong. Your delusions of grandeur have inflated your ego to the point where your head is likely to burst. There isn't anyone living in any of our colonies who isn't more spiritual than you. And unless you do something to improve that atrocious personality of yours, you will make nothing but enemies wherever you go.

"You told Nehru we aren't a sect. I admit Master said we aren't one. Well, we *are* a sect.

"And now you say you're tired. No true disciple would ever admit he's tired. Sometimes Master worked us to the limit of our strength, but he *never* let us say, 'I'm tired.'"

Again, this is only a paraphrase. Tara's answer was much longer, and much more vitriolic.

I will not detail the events of the following year. They were many, and very painful, marking as they did my slow, inexorable descent into total disgrace. I tried valiantly to keep on serving Master to the best of my ability. Nothing else mattered to me. But no matter what I did, I was told I should not have done it. And no matter what I didn't do, I was told I should have done it. I was so utterly bewildered that I wondered if I understood *anything* any more. Whatever I did or didn't do was denounced categorically. Still, I kept the flag of my divine resolution high. I was determined to go down trying my best, if go down I must after all.

And so it appeared: that I must. For months I could feel Tara's thoughts hurled at me in anger from America as she demanded that I be ousted from the work. Later I learned that she'd kept on insisting, "Unless we get rid of him, fifteen years from now he'll be strong enough to divide the work."

In July 1962 I received a cablegram summoning me to New York. Why New York? I wondered. Our centers were in California. Why a safe 3,000 miles from Los Angeles? Deep down, I knew the answer.

Yet I was determined to play my part as a disciple, let come what would.

I landed in New York on Saturday, July 28th, 1962. Tara and Daya were at the airport to meet me. During the taxi ride to the Pennsylvania (now the Penta) Hotel, where we had reservations, not much was said. Tara looked up into the sky and said something about Jupiter's and some other planet's positions in the heavens. Clearly, she saw this as the astrologically appropriate time for whatever bomb she intended to explode. But I blocked the thought out of my mind. I couldn't, I *wouldn't* believe what I knew I must soon face.

The following morning a large manila envelope was shoved under my door. I opened it and found it to contain a document some thirty pages in length by Tara, and a number of letters by other people. The gist of it all was that I was through forever in SRF, and a very good riddance to me.

Later, when I asked to see them, they agreed. I spent two hours on my knees in front of them, my hands crossed on my breast in an expression of unbearable anguish, incapable of assimilating the enormity of this tragedy. I pleaded with them to reconsider their decision, in which I'd had no say at all.

"I'll do anything. Write it down and I'll sign it that I'll never do anything anymore in the work but wash dishes. I didn't come here for position. I didn't come here to be vice president. I came here only to serve my Guru and find God. Why can't I just render him some small service? What I do doesn't matter to me."

"Never!" was Tara's reply. "The least toehold and you'd only worm your way to the top again."

"The only 'top' for me," I protested, "is serving my guru and God."

"Never!" she repeated. "From now on we want to forget that you ever lived."

She paused, then tilted her head back and gazed at me deeply as if reading my entire life. "Can you tell me," she demanded, "why everything you've ever done has ended in *disaster?*"

The question surprised me. I thought I'd been successful at quite a number of things, and couldn't think of any failures, what to speak of disasters.

After a puzzled pause, I inquired, "Would you give me an example?"

For a moment she was nonplussed. Then she quickly dismissed the matter with a wave of her hand. "That's your technique, see? Asking questions to get the other person confused. But don't you know it takes spiritual power to attract the money you wanted for building things?" She continued: "You can never succeed.

"We don't want you ever to lecture again in public. We don't want people to know Master ever had such a despicable disciple.

"You are never again to set foot on any SRF property.

"You are never again to contact any SRF member.

"You are never to tell anyone you are Master's disciple.

"Never again," she added with a loud sigh of relief,

"will we have to listen to the projects concocted in that fertile brain of yours.

"You think your motives are pure. Well, I assure you, they are *most impure.* You tried by careful scheming to get yourself made the new SRF president. Well, it didn't work . . . did it?

"You'd stop at nothing short of murder to get what you want!" she then repeated herself with careful deliberation, emphasizing each word: "nothing . . . short . . . of murder!

"But I will see to it before I die that others see you the way I do. You shall *never* get back into the work. I have the power to know you better than you know yourself."

Daya said little during this interview, though at one point she interjected a few words in support of Tara's position.

Tara returned to the fray: "Your things will be sent to you from Mt. Washington."

"But," I protested, "I don't want *anything!* All I own I've given to Master."

"Oh!" she cried, sneeringly. "How dramatic! Well, I'll tell you what you do. If there's anything you don't want, just drop it in the trash can in the corridor of this hotel."

She asked me how much money I had.

"I have about a thousand dollars left from my travel expenses."

"You may keep that."

She then produced a letter she'd written for me to sign, resigning my membership on the Board of Directors and my vice presidency. I signed it readily;

those positions had meant nothing to me. Smugly she took the letter from my hand and gazed at it, then at me, with an expression of relief as if to say, "Well, that's over with. We've got what we came for."

After the meeting, pleased with how it had gone, they decided between them to give me another $500. Tara flew back to Los Angeles that same afternoon.

The following morning, bright and early, the phone rang in my room. It was Tara. "Were y'able to get the check cashed?" she inquired brightly. I hadn't yet learned there was to be a check. Perhaps she thought I'd dashed to the nearest bank to cash it before they could stop payment.

Coincidentally, my parents had just landed in New York from a vacation in Europe. They were staying in Scarsdale, north of the city, and I'd been able to get in touch with them.

"Just think!" Tara exclaimed. "Isn't it wonderful how Master has worked this whole thing out?"

I was too amazed at this example of insensitivity to reply. Tara, on finding that I didn't share her enthusiasm, demanded, "Don't you think it's wonderful? Why are you silent?"

"I'd rather say nothing."

"That's your trouble, see? You're secretive. You're a schemer." She started in on another long diatribe delineating my innumerable imperfections.

I saw Daya again briefly that day. She regretted that I'd already paid my hotel bill, but I wouldn't let her reimburse me.

My father took the train in to New York to fetch me. We had lunch together. "Well, well," was all he could think to say when I told him my tale of woe. Mother was more vocal in her outrage, when I saw her later in Scarsdale.

"Why," she cried, "since the time you were a baby, you never *once* told a lie!"

What could I say? I knew she was right. To give voice to my agreement, however, would have been tantamount to taking sides, when it seemed to me that what was needed was for me to remain open to any possibility of truth in the disastrous accusations that had been made.

From Scarsdale, a few days later, Dad, Mother, and I drove across the country to their home in Atherton, California.

It was excruciating agony to find myself living a non-ashram life again, in an ordinary family albeit the family of my birth, serving my parents instead of serving my guru.

It seemed to me that I was being asked to bear the karmic weight of all those who had ever betrayed Master, whom he himself had forgiven, while his disciples raged at those people's treachery.

(above) With Daya Mata and Ananda Mata in India

(above) A photo of me taken in 1959

(left) I am feted by Indian devotees on the day of my departure from Patiala, India, where I gave a week of classes in November 1959. Behind me to the left is Dewan Balkishen Khosla, my host. The class series was described as "the greatest success in our history."

(left) In Allahabad, India in 1960 at the Ardha Kumbha Mela. The Kumbha Mela is a spiritual gathering held every twelve years. The ardha, or half Kumbha is held midway between Kumbhas. Two million pilgrims attended.

The Delhi Project

(above) Prime Minister Jawaharlal Nehru and Rani Bhan. (I took the photo.) Nehru is examining my painting of the projected ashram, prior to his visit to the site and giving his approval. The picture shows the large park entrance and approach to the temple. Caves for men and for women are depicted to either side of the entrance. Behind the temple: a large pond with garden. The total size of the property was twenty-five acres.

(above right) A painting I did, an artistic fancy, depicting the Delhi project; intended for a cover to promote the project

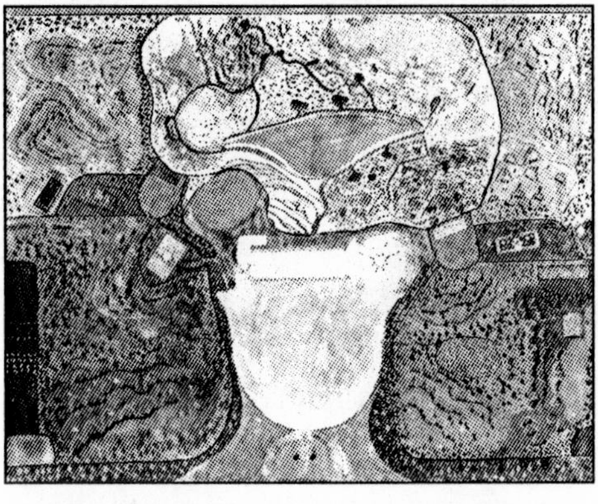

(above) A watercolor I painted to help people conceptualize the Delhi project

CHAPTER 15

Retrospect

Looking back now, thirty-four years (to the day, as it happens) after that meeting in New York, it is clear to me that everything that happened was for a divine purpose.

From SRF's point of view, they weren't ready to develop the work into a world mission of the magnitude Master had visualized. Tara was opposed to the whole idea. Daya saw her own role as putting into smooth working order whatever Master had already started, but not as developing his work to a further stage.

When I asked her once, in the 1950s, when we would begin to develop Master's idea of world brotherhood colonies, her reply was, "Frankly, I'm not interested."

In all these forty-four years since his physical death, SRF has spread very little beyond what Master started: a church in Fullerton to replace the former chapel in Long Beach; a church in Encinitas; a church in Pasadena; one in Richmond that the members had wanted already during Master's time. And that's about it. YSS has undergone even fewer changes.

So fixed was I in the consciousness of spreading

the work, as Master had encouraged *me,* at least, to do, that I simply couldn't imagine that this was not Daya's goal also. I see now, however, that it never was her goal. It is pointless for me to ask, Why not? It was not to her that Master gave that responsibility. He did give it to me.

I suppose it would have been possible for her to accept that he had given me this job, and to let me simply go ahead with it. But had she done so, she would have felt the need to control what I did—and from a basic outlook altogether different from my own. Without Tara's influence she might have been able to embrace both ideas. But it would have been like trying to mix oil and water. Tara was the catalyst for something that needed to happen. The full extent of the injustice done to me must be balanced against the full extent of what I have been able to accomplish since then, in Master's name. I could never have accomplished any of it, had I remained in SRF.

Nor do I suppose for a minute that the suffering was mine alone. That Daya suffered deeply I don't doubt for a moment. Tara, six years after our New York meeting—in 1968, the year I started Ananda—suffered a massive stroke. Indirectly I learned that she had told someone later, "I know this happened to me to teach me compassion." She died two years after that. That the others suffered also can be inferred from an event that took place in a restaurant in Westwood or Beverly Hills (I forget which).

I had been staying with a second cousin of mine in Westwood. Daya Mata, who had offered to see me when she could, agreed to meet me for dinner. She arrived accompanied by Mrinalini Mata and Ananda Mata. This meeting, like the others, was cordial but strained. Daya said she would soon be traveling to San Francisco for reasons she didn't explain.

"Good," I said. "My parents' home is in Atherton, south of San Francisco. Perhaps you can visit us."

"If they'd allow me in the door," she replied, doubtfully.

I fell suddenly silent. How could I reassure her? I was certain my parents would not make her welcome at all. There ensued a long, embarrassed pause.

Shortly thereafter they left. All three of them were weeping. I, too, was weeping. What could any of us say?

Trying earnestly to see matters from their point of view, I realize that I was the one out of step with their priorities. This doesn't mean I was wrong. And it doesn't condemn them in their priorities. Even Tara's harshness to me, though in itself appalling, was necessary to get me off onto another track in my life. I was too loyal for less drastic treatment to have worked: I would always have been turning to them for guidance, direction, and advice.

Tara's deliberate intention was to destroy my faith—in myself, primarily; in Master's path, also, as my own path to God; and in thinking there was anything at all that I might do to serve him further. I was not a friend of hers any longer. I was an enemy—an arch enemy, for I was a threat to her guru's mission as she herself understood it. Even today, SRF ministers have been heard to refer to me as the "anti-Christ." She had a powerful will. I think most people, treated by her as she treated me, would have been pulverized.

There was one weakness, however, to Tara's attempt at a knock-out with a single, massive blow. If it didn't succeed, there would be nothing left for her to follow up with. She tried repeatedly to undermine me in other ways after my dismissal, but these attempts were feeble compared to what she had tried already. They never worked.

Unfortunately for her, my way of fighting is very different. For one thing, I never fight against; I fight *for* what I believe in. For another, my way of fighting is not the sudden knock-out blow, but an application of steady pressure, and an unrelenting search for new angles from which to apply that pressure until victory is achieved. Our natures are different. She gambled on beating me by brute force. As often happens, however, what wins is not fire, though it destroy the forest, but earth, which, if its power is centered beneath the surface, calmly produces a new forest. Tara, in her involvement with astrology, might have done well to consider this difference between us: She was a fire sign; my sun, astrologically, is in an earth sign. She saw strength in my chart, which is why she said, "If we don't get rid of him now, in another fifteen years he'll be strong enough to divide the work." She thought to win against me by striking while I was, as she believed, weak. What she didn't understand was that I hadn't the remotest wish to divide the work. I was, and am, loyal to it to my core. But she foresaw correctly that the track on which my own destiny would take me was a separate track from theirs. She could not imagine any separate track running parallel to their own. None of them have imagined such a possibility.

Fifteen years later, it is interesting to note, was the year my book, *The Path,* was published. This book, as you probably know, is an account of Master's life from the point of view of a disciple. It describes at the end of it the founding of Ananda Village.

Sant Keshavdas, a spiritual teacher from India, exclaimed to me while visiting Ananda many years ago, "What a lot of *tapasya* [spiritual penance] you had to do to create this place!" How right he was! Good never comes easily, especially when it goes against established trends. Master demonstrated that truth in the difficulties he himself faced throughout his life.

What Tara didn't know was that her very attack on me, and the untruths she told about me, were an essential element in giving me the spiritual power to succeed in this work. For the truth has to come out eventually. If it cannot come out in one way, it will find another way. The greater the lies told against a person, the stronger he *has to* grow in the truth. If in this life those lies succeed in destroying him, that power of truth will manifest in him in another life. Truth *has to* come out. That is the karmic law.

Tara didn't succeed in destroying me. Instead, her attempt to do so was an underlying factor in Ananda's eventual success.

Every time Ananda has been unjustly attacked, indeed, the very attacks have only increased our power to succeed. In the present attempts against us, we keep marveling to see how very much stronger we've become, simply by standing up for the truth as we know it and doing our best to continue with our work.

In the beginning, as I have said, Daya Mata was willing to see me outside Mt. Washington, as a friend. One day, Tara Mata, hearing that I'd been invited to give classes at the Academy of Asian Studies in San Francisco, called Dr. Landrum, the head of the Academy, to persuade him to cancel my classes. Failing in this attempt, she telephoned me and launched into her usual diatribe against me. The talk lasted a long time, as her phone calls did. As usual, moreover, the conversation was one-sided. I particularly remember her telling me, "You ought to be grateful to me for talking to you like this. I don't give many people the benefit of my wisdom." She continued:

"You haven't the character to be a teacher. You're vengeful. You're vindictive." It went on and on.

Finally, unable to endure these denunciations any longer, I exclaimed in exasperation, "It isn't everyone who thinks the way you do."

"Who?" she demanded. "Who thinks otherwise?"

"Don't ask me."

"Who? I demand to know."

"I'm sorry, you have no right to ask."

"Is it Sahaja?" Sahaja was her "right-hand man" in the Editorial Department.

"Sahaja supports you in everything."

"Can you tell me why such a high, spiritual soul as Sahaja has such utter, implicit faith in me?"

A line like this, I reflected, belonged in a Broadway comedy.

"Tell me," she again insisted. "Who?"

I wouldn't tell her. She surmised, however, that her "betrayer," according to her somewhat unusual definition, was Daya Mata. In consequence, she demanded that Daya give up seeing me. Daya, to keep peace, decided she had no other choice.

Today, Daya characterizes my action as "foolish," but I wonder how many people could have remained silent under such provocation. Perhaps my "foolishness" consisted in not simply hanging up on Tara—a rudeness of which my nature (unfortunately, in this case) was incapable.

Daya Mata told me after my dismissal, "Tara worked on me for months, ordering me every day to get rid of you. It reached the point where I saw she was quite capable of destroying the organization rather than not get her will. Even my presidency was being threatened." (I could just imagine Tara as the new president!) "At last, losing my composure, I shouted at her, *'All right!'* I wonder that everyone at Mt. Washington didn't hear me."

I had a meeting with Daya Mata in Pasadena in 1970, after Tara's death. "Even on her death bed," Daya told me, "she was bitter against me for what she considered my 'betrayal.' Shortly before she died, she actually cursed me."

I've often wondered what the nature of that "curse" might have been. Certainly Tara couldn't have done anything so ridiculous as swear at her. Nor do I imagine she said anything like, "Because of what you did to me, you'll come back for three incarnations as a Tithiri bird." (I offer this as a gem I discovered in a south Indian temple. It was the threatened penalty for spitting in the temple precincts.)

What Tara said must have been something more like, "Because you didn't cooperate with me in my endeavor to destroy Kriyananda, you will see that he will succeed in his endeavors." I imagine she carried this thought further, since Daya said it had been a curse, but I prefer not to speculate further. Only this, or some very similar, statement could account for Daya's determination in SRF's present attacks to complete my destruction. Daya Mata views Ananda, and me especially, as a threat to Master's very mission.

At that same meeting in 1970, however, Daya told me, "I've never accepted the things Tara said against you."

Did Tara fall from the realization she'd attained? It is difficult to imagine that she retained that state. At the same time, I believe she cannot have fallen very far. Her lack of charity—of compassion, as she is reported to have put it—would be a flaw, spiritually, one for which she would have to seek atonement. I doubt that her words to me, "I've never said an unkind word in my life," could have been uttered by her at the end of her life. Therefore, I feel, she must have fallen somewhat. But, knowing her as I do, I cannot believe that that flaw wasn't balanced out to a large extent by her devotion and faith, and by her life of deeply sincere sacrifice in service to God.

Daya Mata told me in 1970, "Master told her not

to practice astrology, but she kept up her practice. *That's why she fell.*" (The italics are mine.) In other words, Daya, too, believes she fell.

There were other reasons, besides, for thinking so. For one thing, Master had told Daya, "Keep her away from people." It wasn't only Daya's fault that Tara wouldn't let her obey this advice. I cannot but think that Tara's involvement with people proved at least as harmful to her as it did to those people.

I had noticed, moreover, a growing pride in Tara. It seemed clearly evident in her statement to me that whoever was against her was against God. My own thought in this matter is that her work of editing, in which it was her business to correct Master's words, awakened in her the delusion that it was her business also to correct his ideas. It began, I imagine, with a deprecation of his command over English. I remember her saying to me once with a throaty chuckle, "Even as William he never mastered the English language." This thought grew to the point where she could simply declare, in defiance of his statement that SRF is not a sect, "Well, we *are* a sect."

Whatever it was, an aberration like this would be more like a superficial wave in her consciousness than a profound flaw. Was it a spiritual fall? I am certain it deserves to be called only a slip. Her wrath, after all, was motivated by a desire to protect her guru's work, however mistaken her perception of the need. It was not motivated by a desire to harm me except incidentally toward that end.

****

A strange episode occurred several years ago that may or may not shed some light on this whole situation.

A man flew to Ananda all the way from New York City with the sole purpose of seeing me. After our visit, he flew straight back to New York.

He'd had a vision, he told me, and had been instructed to share it with me.

"I saw you with Master in a monastery two or more thousand years ago. He had put you in charge over the monks. Tara was your younger brother in that life. You were very magnetic, and commanded a following. Unfortunately, your prominence went to your head. You turned against Master, and, drawing many students away from Master, created your own following. Tara remained loyal to Master, and was adamantly opposed to what you had done.

"In this life, she was still influenced by her anger against you at that time. But in this lifetime, so I was shown, your motives are completely pure; there is none of that old rivalry against Master left in your heart. Tara was living out a dead scene.

"When she died, she realized what a great mistake she had made, and longed to ask for your forgiveness. She wants to beg you for it through me." At this point, the man stood up and asked if he could embrace me on her behalf, and if, with the embrace, I would give her my forgiveness. I did so readily, marveling all the while at the strangeness of this encounter.

Could there be any truth to his story? Certainly, one passes through many lives, and many errors, before finding the Eternal Truth. Master himself told me, about my past lives, "You were eaten up with doubts." Doubt was my greatest flaw.

I can only thank God that that flaw lies in the past. Perhaps it is because of my desire to expiate that mistake that I have such a deep longing, in this lifetime, to help others to pass through the white waters of spiritual doubt and to sail out onto the calm ocean of divine faith.

CHAPTER 16

Afterthoughts

The Sufi woman saint, Rabbi'a, lay on her deathbed, her body ill and in pain. Three disciples of hers came to console her.

"He is no true lover of God, after all," said one, "who is not willing to suffer for God's sake."

"This smacks of egoism to me," replied the saint. Another of the disciples attempted a correction:

"He is no true lover of God who is not *happy* to suffer for God's sake."

"More than this is needed," she replied.

"Then *you* tell us, Mother," said the third. "What should be the right attitude for a lover of God?"

"He is no true lover of God," she said, "who does not forget his suffering in the contemplation of the Supreme Beloved."

How well have I met this last condition? How well have I met even the first? God alone can judge. I know, for instance, that I was willing to accept whatever God gave me. But I wasn't willing to accept that God didn't want me. And in that thought, I suffered. I felt happiness when I thought that perhaps He had done it to help me, not to punish me. But I must say, it *looked* like punishment. I reached the point, after some time, where I could forget the pain at least during my prayers and meditations. Contemplation of His loving presence reduced any other consideration to non-existence. But I also had very serious questions to face in my life. Mine was not a serious physical illness, like Rabbi'a's, about which I would have been able to do nothing. It was spiritual suffering, and a need for inner *direction.* This was not a suffering to be forgotten, like Rabbi'a's, but one to be contemplated and understood.

People often counseled me, "Forget it!" Daya Mata herself said to me, "Cut the cord! You just have to create a new reality for yourself." It was asking the impossible of me. I had embraced Master's work as my reality. For me, there could be no other.

I even said to Master once, "It was this, or nothing."

"That's the right spirit," he replied solemnly.

I *had to* understand what he wanted of me. "Even if you yourself have forsaken me," I cried, "I will not—I cannot—forsake you. You may spurn me, but you cannot ever get rid of me." I knew in my heart, of course, that he would never spurn me. Hadn't he told me at our first meeting, "I give you my unconditional love"? But it looked like spurning, at first, and Tara did her best to convince me that that was what it was.

Out of my anguished soul-searching came the insights that made Ananda, and the books I have written, and the music, and all the things Master has inspired me to do since. It was not easy, but good things don't ever come easily. They must be earned.

What happened, as I shall relate in Part Two of this book, was that the effort I put forth to build the work during my years in SRF molded my understanding, and gave me the necessary insight to build Ananda, and to do the other things that have been accomplished since then.

Those early years were necessary, for they gave me the experience I would need for everything I did in future. I bless the experience, now, more than I can say.

Many of the principles I learned during my early years were what made Ananda possible. For example, my reaction to the dictum, "In any situation, be guided by the simple consideration, 'What is best for the work?'" gave birth to the two fundamental guidelines of Ananda. The first is, "Where there is adherence to truth and right action, there is victory." And the second, "People are more important than things." Armed with these twin principles, Ananda has steered its way through countless tests and difficulties, even when it seemed that by following them we'd be courting disaster.

That is the story that remains to be told in Part Two.

I do not regret anything that happened in the past. During my recent seclusion, when I examined my heart's memories I found only a great sense of sweetness and gratitude. Thank you, Tara. Thank you Daya. You have done more for me than I can ever repay.

Part Two

CHAPTER 17

Getting My "Sea Legs"

The goal of this book is to take the reader down the road to a place that has become known in the world as Ananda: a community (now there are several of them) and a religious mission dedicated to spreading the message of unity in religion, and of Self-realization, as taught by Paramhansa Yogananda. Ananda, a Sanskrit word, means divine joy. The Ananda communities are spiritual havens for thousands of people, some hundreds of whom live there, while others are associated with them and with the work Yogananda has given me to create. Many people visit these communities from all over the world, or are helped through the internet and through our outreach programs, as well as through my books and recordings: three million-or-so copies sold of over seventy books and over 300 pieces of music; nearly 200 editions published or under contract in eighty-two countries (at the present writing), and in twenty-some languages.

"Living Wisdom" schools thrive under Ananda's sponsorship—though not under its control. The schools are based on principles that I outlined in a book, *Education for Life,* which has been received favorably by educators in America and abroad. Thousands visit Ananda's retreat facilities annually at The Expanding Light near Nevada City, California, and at Ananda Assisi near Assisi, Italy. Some sixty-five meditation groups in America and abroad serve as channels of teaching and inspiration for spiritual seekers in their own areas. The creative and enthusiastic activity of Ananda members keeps this movement vital and growing. A continuous stream of letters, telephone calls, and testimonials attest to people's deep gratitude for Ananda's role in their lives.

In short, Ananda's is a success story—a success achieved in the face of what at first seemed overwhelming odds, and of trials that sometimes shook it to its foundations, but that were conquered by faith, devotion, and hard work.

I've said all this not to boast, but because the reader may like to know in advance where, generally, this book is headed: whether toward tragedy, or toward a happy ending. It is an adventure story, reminiscent in some ways of the communitarian efforts of the early Pilgrim Fathers in America; and of the move westward, later, to open up new territory and seek a better way of living. The *finis* of this story, like that of America, is victory.

I ended Part One with what looked personally like devastation. It resembled, in a way, the bombing of Pearl Harbor: unexpected, and meant to force sudden and complete defeat. That raid, however, was only the beginning of World War II in the Pacific. Much followed, ending in America's victory and—dare I hope for a similar ending to my story?—the conversion of the attackers to friendship and to peaceful, world-embracing ways.

To change the metaphor, you who read this may want to know early what kind of carpet I'm weaving. Will it be in dark colors, or in bright? Will it be sad, or triumphant? In fact, as you will find, it contains many colors, all of which I hope will not only please you, but will deepen your faith. To me it has been a wonderful and rewarding experience. As I look at Ananda today, I am deeply grateful for everything that happened. For Ananda has developed into a wonderful way of life. It has drawn to me thousands of devotees and true friends. And it has given all of us the chance to share with millions of others the truths I received from my Guru. The story of Ananda has been many times over worth the struggle and sacrifice that brought it into being. I look back on the years of uncertainty and doubt, and think what a privilege and joy they have been for me.

Many threads went into the making of this carpet. All of them were important to the overall design.

My departure from SRF seemed to me an unalloyed defeat. I had been thrown out, excluded from everything I believed in and loved in life. I had been warned under pain of dire retribution to sever every bond with the past. "Never again set foot on any SRF property. Never contact any SRF member. Never let anyone even know you are Yogananda's disciple. Never ever again expect in any way to serve his work or his teachings. Never again lecture in public. Never . . ."—what, I asked myself: breathe? As Tara put it to me, "From now on we want to forget you ever lived." When I asked her, "But what shall I do? My whole life is dedicated to serving my Guru!" she replied casually, "Just take any job that comes along."

Master had predicted to me, "Your life is one of intense activity—and meditation." Tara wanted me to refrain from spiritual activity altogether, except meditation. Master had been thinking of my spiritual development. Tara had been trying only to get me "out of their hair." Was it possible that she'd seen me in a truer light than he? Had I, perhaps—to lend credence to such a possibility—gone downhill spiritually in the ten years since his death, to the point where my service to his work was a menace to it, not an asset? I had developed the organization in many of its aspects: the monks' way of life, the head office, the centers, the public services, the lay disciple order. In India I had, provisionally at least, re-organized all of the lessons. It had been my ardent desire to make Master's name, life, and teachings known in India, and I had labored incessantly toward that end. Even if, as Tara proclaimed, my motives were "most impure" (I was convinced they were not), did not all that work count at least a little bit in my favor?

Evidently not. When Tara "ousted me," as she put it, she heaved a dramatic sigh of relief saying, "Never again will we have to listen to the projects concocted in that fertile brain of yours."

I have always been divided inwardly as to how to direct my energies. One inclination has been a deep desire for the hermit's life. The other inclination, equally deep, has been a longing to help others who suffered from spiritual doubt and lack of high purpose in their lives. Master had encouraged me in this second direction. I remember him saying to me once, "No more moods now, Walter. Otherwise, how will you be able to help others?"

In the matter of work, I had often felt as though I were sitting on a volcano, unable to repress the creative pressure within me. To Tara and to some of the others, this creative urge was merely a proof of my strong ego. "Why must he keep coming up with new ideas?" they'd ask each other. "Can't he just humbly wait for us to *tell* him what to do?" Enthusiasm, however, was basic to my nature. To suppress it would take more egoic effort, it seemed to me, than simply to let it flow. I didn't see the things I'd done as *self*-expression, but only as expressing the energy, enthusiasm, and inspiration I had received from God.

This dilemma wasn't resolved by their dismissal of me. In time, I concluded that, since Master's words, "Your life is one of intense activity," had been meant as a direction for the whole of my life, I must always heed them. "Intense activity" had seemed a command, not a prediction. The question before me now was, "*What* activity?" Even to ponder this question, I needed to get back to my own center. This, to me, meant going first into seclusion.

On the other hand, if I'd really disappointed Master, then perhaps his plans for me had changed. In his commentaries on the New Testament of the Bible, he'd written, of Judas after the Crucifixion, that instead of hanging himself for having betrayed Jesus he should have devoted the rest of his life to seclusion, meditating on God. Tara had called me a Judas. If my actions really were a betrayal of my Guru, or even a disappointment to him, perhaps he'd want me to do likewise. Tara, certainly, would be relieved if I did. Was a hermit's calling what Master wanted for me, now? I admit I hoped so. I was too deeply hurt to want to face anyone. If this was what he wanted, however, no doors opened to welcome me into that garden. I tried my best to find a place for seclusion: Every door to it was locked even as I turned the handle. The only doors that opened, with many a push from behind to pass through them, were toward lecturing, writing, and "city streets": that "intense activity," in other words, which Master had told me was to be my way of life.

Meanwhile, I had to adjust to the dramatically changed circumstances in my life. I also needed to redefine my relationship to those I had considered dear friends, and not only my seniors in discipleship. The worst of it for me was that I still loved and respected them. Could I *really* deserve the amazing things they had said to me? No one had ever accused me of anything remotely similar. Master himself had told me what he wanted me to do. It had been in a tone of command, not of compliment, that he'd said, "Walter, you have a great work to do." He had expressed confidence in my ability to serve his cause. In fact, everything he'd told me contradicted the things Tara was saying. Whom was I to believe? Yogananda was my guru; I hadn't ceased to be his disciple.

It is normal to try to justify oneself. This I simply

refused to do. I felt it was important to be completely truthful—with myself as much as with others. Continued wandering in delusion held all the attraction, for me, of a nightmare. Indeed, the very subtlety of delusion's power terrified me. To my thinking, it would be ridiculous to turn away huffily with injured pride, as if to say, "Well, I'll show *them!*" However common such a reaction, I felt no inclination toward it. And I determined that, no matter what I did, it would not be in reaction to anything external to myself. I would be guided by what I felt inwardly to be *right and true.*

In every crisis in life, one faces at least two alternatives. The first is, by means of that crisis, to grow spiritually. The second is to accept defeat. Master had said, "God will never let you down so long as you make the effort. If ever you tell yourself, however, 'I've failed!' it will be so for this lifetime, anyway."

There is, of course, a third alternative: revenge. But this was an absurd choice, and not even tempting for me. It would only drive more nails into the coffin of delusion. Master said also, "Circumstances are always neutral. It is how you *react* to them that makes them seem either happy or sad." I was blessed by this supreme crisis in my life to learn many lessons from it. I think what I learned may also help others in their own trials. For I don't in any way consider my case unique in the intensity of pain it caused me. Every human being faces suffering, loss, disdain, and self-doubt in his life. What I was able to learn will help, moreover, to explain certain aspects of the story of Ananda, and will give an important clue to its eventual success. For what made Ananda possible was not money or influence or scientific gadgetry (such as solar energy): Primarily, it was *attitude.* Ananda means joy. What made Ananda possible was, above all, the determination to make inner joy a priority.

SRF's rejection of me had no impact, fortunately, on my dedication to Master's teachings or to him as my Guru. My superiors claimed that I'd failed. Much more important to me was the question: had I failed my Guru? I could not honestly accept that my work in India had been a mistake—except in its personal consequences for me. What I'd accomplished seemed to me still a wonderful thing. The SRF directors' judgment of the Delhi project, and of me in consequence, seemed to be coming from a different set of priorities altogether—priorities that I couldn't for the life of me even comprehend.

My faith in what I'd done, however, left me in the "Wonderful Land of What Might Have Been," as my father put it. How should I proceed now, in "real life"?

My first step had to be to find my own center again, and not react to these events like a weather vane, turning with the shift of wind. The way others treated me was their business. The way I behaved toward them, and my reaction to their treatment, was my own.

Should I stop loving them, merely because they rejected me? The best reason for loving others, I reflected, is not because they love us, but because love is a gift we all have to give, freely and spontaneously.

Love is not something bought in a shop, or bargained for like a merchant: "Love me, and I'll love you as much in return." I was simply happier, giving love, than I could possibly be in withdrawing it. Were I to stop loving now, merely because I'd been rejected, I would only lose twice!

Master, I reflected, was always wholeheartedly charitable to all. He demonstrated perfect respect for everyone's individuality. I'd never seen him subordinate a person's spiritual needs to the needs of the organization. Moreover, he had told Daya Mata, "When I am gone, only love can take my place." Love and respect, then, must be my own guidelines.

Tara had spoken of my "atrocious personality." Well, apart from the fact I'd attracted many friends in my life, if by "atrocious" she meant something different from being liked by people, the least I could do was what Master always did, and in my case do it more than ever: put other people's needs ahead of anything I might want of them. Thus, later on when creating Ananda, one of the basic principles I insisted on was: *"People are more important than things."*

Above all, now, contemplating the choices before me, my firm resolution was to continue my quest for God. This would be the foundation upon which I'd raise any structure I was called on to construct in my life. My Guru had given me specific guidelines. To obey these also, then, was a priority.

On the other hand, wisdom dictated that I adjust my activities to any reasonable advice I received from others, particularly from SRF's directors. Was Tara's advice reasonable? The fact that she'd not allowed me to reason with her in return, but had instantly denounced the attempt ("I don't want your opinions!"), made it clear that it wasn't even her *intention* to be reasonable. Was she, then, being intuitive from such a deep level of insight that there was no need for reason at all? So she claimed, but it certainly didn't seem so to me. Intuition ought to meet common sense half way; it is never *un*reasonable. Everything Tara had said seemed beyond reason, certainly, but not *above* it. Moreover, what she had said flew in the face of the guidance Master himself had given me. I resolved, however, all the same to give her every benefit of the doubt, and to do anything she advised that seemed within reason. I wouldn't let myself believe Tara really wanted my destruction.

An essential key to right living is to be guided by that which increases one's sense of inner freedom. In this freedom, moreover, there should be a sense of expansive happiness. Does this teaching seem self-centered? I'm not speaking of *selfishness.* Selfishness is the complete opposite of centeredness in the divine Self. Yogananda praised "divine selfishness" as a key to right, spiritual action. Always, he said, we should ask, "What can I gain, spiritually, from this situation?" For without inner development, what have we to give anyone? We are responsible above all for ourselves. This means among other things being responsible for our own reactions to life. If those reactions give us no inner happiness, it is a sure sign that they are misguided, and will be of no use to us.

Anger, for example, would only have buried in the soil of my subconscious the hurt I felt. Too much was at stake, I felt, for me to shove it out of sight and pretend the problem didn't exist.

People sometimes asked me why I was living with my parents now, instead of in the monastery. Many others in my position would have tried to justify themselves. I refused to do so. I didn't say I'd left for any of the various reasons that I could easily have invented. Instead, I replied frankly, "I was kicked out." I knew that there were some who would say—if not to me, then to one another—"He must have done something terrible for them to throw him out." I preferred calumny against me to telling a lie. The calumny was, I knew, in any case inevitable.

For a time, I actually had to remind myself that the Bhagavad Gita says, "The soul cannot be destroyed. It is a part of God, who is immortal." No fault, then, however damnable, can forever cloud our true Self. If I really was as bad as Tara insisted, then the only thing for me to do was continue doing my best to be better.

One thing she would never be able to take away from me: my longing for God. She had denounced me as insincere. Well, apart from the fact that I had heard Master say to a monk who had criticized me, "Walter is *very* sincere!" I had to accept that it was God, through my Guru, whom I needed to satisfy.

I had given my life to serving my Guru. To me, this had once meant serving his organization. SRF, for me, however, had always stood for something far deeper than an institution. Above all, it stood for the message Paramhansa Yogananda had brought to the world. When I first came to him in 1948, for some reason it hadn't occurred to me, while reading his autobiography, that he even *had* an organization. I wonder, now, whether I'd even have gone to him, had I heard first of the organization. It was his spirit and the magnificent sweep of his teachings that always attracted me. I accepted the organization, once I'd met him, but only because I so wholeheartedly accepted *him.*

CHAPTER 18

"Your Work Is Writing and Lecturing"

By an interesting coincidence, one month before Tara summoned me to New York I had already been thinking that a book was needed, one I might even write myself. This would be the first of the books Master had himself told me to write.

The idea was inspired by an article I'd just finished reading in *Span,* the *USIS* (United States Information Service) magazine in India, written by the head of the philosophy department at MIT (Massachusetts Institute of Technology). The author reported on what was, he said, a major trend in modern thinking. Many people, having been exposed to Darwinian evolution, nihilistic materialism, and the construction often placed on Einstein's Theory of Relativity, had come to the conclusion that life is meaningless.

As I studied their reasoning as presented in the article, I saw that what I'd learned from Paramhansa Yogananda and from the ancient teachings of India utterly refuted it. What a service it would be, to combat those delusions thoughtfully—not by calling them ridiculous (which they were), but by following their own line of reasoning carefully and demonstrating *in its own terms* that it simply didn't work.

This inspiration, I realize in retrospect, was God's way of showing me where He wanted me to direct my energies. My Guru had said to me, "Your work is writing and lecturing." I had remonstrated with him at the time, "Sir, haven't you yourself done everything already to present the teachings?" His reply had shown a degree of shock at my obtuseness. "Don't say that! *Much* more is needed."

My dismissal from SRF didn't set me working on that book immediately. I was too flattened out by all that had happened to me. Gradually, however, I realized that dismissal had released me to do what Master had told me to do. Indeed, if I'd remained with SRF I would never have had the freedom to do it. Even if I'd been given such freedom, the organization would never have published my writings. It had quite enough to do in getting out our Guru's writings.

Thus—as I say, gradually—I rediscovered my true priorities. They had always been to promote the teachings: not to build the organization (which many of my fellow disciples felt I'd done well), but to go deeply into Master's thoughts, and to inspire others with them. What I'd wanted from the beginning was to share joyfully with as many people as possible his words and ideas, for it inspired me to think how much people everywhere needed them.

Even the organizing work I'd done had been toward this end: Never had I had another one. It was, as I now believe, Tara's reason for branding me as "insincere." In fact, I *was* "insincere" to her way of thinking, for I'd considered it only a regrettable necessity to have to organize the work. Even my way of organizing had always been motivated by the need for "inspired simplicity." Tara felt, quite rightly, that my real interest was not in the pipeline, so to speak, but in the water that flowed refreshingly through it. Indeed, I'd always imagined that all of us saw the organization as a means to that true end: spreading the teachings. Tara, however, had never shared that aim. Even in 1925, when Master acquired Mt. Washington Estates as the headquarters for his mission, Tara's only comment (which Master often quoted wryly) had been, "Now your troubles begin!" To Tara, people were a threat to the purity of his teachings, not the very purpose for his teachings.

"What do they need new books for?" she once said to me on the phone, referring to someone who had urged her to finish editing Master's books. "They have all the reading material they need, to find God."

Divorce is, or should be, a two-way thing. SRF had tried to divorce me, but their action never had—*has* never had—either my endorsement or my support. I supported the organization because I thought Master wanted me to do so, and I shall never withdraw the love I feel for it since it is the work he himself founded. I am not *anti*-SRF, merely because SRF is anti-Kriyananda. I am simply an ardent champion of the teachings of Paramhansa Yogananda. I support SRF in anything they do to promote his ideals and his message. The point where I withdraw from the field is that, to my mind, SRF is not *itself* that mission. Its purpose is to promulgate Paramhansa Yogananda's mission as a way of serving the needs of people.

After my separation from SRF, I cast about for ways to serve Master that would not place me in competition with them. Best of all, it seemed to me, would be to find something SRF didn't even want to do.

The book I contemplated could, I reflected, be one such service. SRF would never undertake such a labor. The book might be, for all that, a means of drawing people to God, and indirectly to Master's teachings. It would be for those who wanted to believe but couldn't, owing to the insidious influence of modern education. Nihilism exerts a strong influence in today's world, and has brought widespread spiritual confusion.

The book I contemplated writing would be also for those to whom religion seems a barrier to understanding, not the guide it can and should be to *higher* understanding.

CHAPTER 19

Seclusion vs. Outward Activity

Living at my parents' home necessitated my fitting in with their lifestyle. This wasn't always easy. My father, especially, had no understanding of the life of a devotee. I remember him entering my room one evening without knocking. I was meditating, and had lit a stick of incense to provide a spiritual atmosphere. Without apology he remarked, "It smells like a lady's toilet in here!" Of course, I stopped inflicting incense on them from then on, which was probably all he'd wanted.

I tried to fit in. Certainly, however, our priorities differed. I served them as well as I could, and told myself that in doing so I was serving God. Much of the time, however, I simply lay on my bed, staring at the ceiling.

One evening Dad and Mother announced they'd been invited by friends of theirs, the Watson Deftys, to their home for cocktails. They asked me if I'd like to join them. The Deftys lived a short distance up the road. "Why not?" I thought. Anything, surely, was better than lying here, doing nothing!

The cocktail parties my parents gave, and occasionally attended elsewhere, were of the usual sort:

people standing around talking, drinking, and laughing. At these events I'd hold a glass of water in my hand and let people believe, if they liked, that I was "nursing" a glass of gin.

Among the guests this evening were a couple from Bengal, India, named Dr. Haridas and Mrs. Bina Chaudhuri. I knew nothing about them, but was delighted to have a chance to speak Bengali again as a sweet reminder of the years I had lived there. The Chaudhuris responded with friendliness and charm. After a while they expressed amazement that I could actually carry on a conversation in their language, and not merely offer the usual contribution to international amity by saying, "*Kamon achhen* (How are you)?" They asked me my name. When I told them they cried, "Kriyananda! Why, we have the records you made of Yogananda's chants! Oh, please, you have to come and sing for our reunion honoring Mahatma Gandhi's birthday in October." They had, they informed me, an ashram in San Francisco, and were devotees of the Indian saint, Sri Aurobindo.

I'd been warned by Tara to do no public speaking. ("The least effort in that direction and we'll expose your constant treacheries!") I still felt honor-bound to obey her, though of course no actual obligation was involved since I was no longer under their authority. I therefore declined the Chaudhuris' invitation, in spite of their pleading.

Dr. Chaudhuri, however, would not take No for an answer. He telephoned me repeatedly at my parents' home. Later, he explained that he'd felt strongly guided by my Guru to draw me into public speaking again. As often as he called, I refused. At last, however, the thought came to me, "I'm getting no other guidance. Maybe Master can't reach me through these clouds of unhappiness. Could their invitation be his way of sending me guidance? Suppose it is: Shouldn't I give at least this one invitation a try?"

Finally, though with trepidation, I accepted.

Curiously, as I sang that day at the Chaudhuris' ashram, the Cultural Integration Fellowship, I felt Master's presence in my heart for the first time in over two months. By no means was it my *desire* to be in the public eye. Indeed, a part of me had always resisted speaking in public. Once I'd pleaded with Master not to make me a lecturer, but he'd only replied, "You'd better learn to like it! That's what you have to do." How very much less did I want that role now!

After my song, two people came to me separately and asked me to sing for their groups as well. One was a representative of the Indian association at U.C. Davis. The other was the secretary of the Dutton Club, at the Unitarian Church in San Francisco. I refused their invitations. Inwardly, I found myself trembling. Once more, however, the telephone calls came, repeatedly. They showed the same determination Dr. Chaudhuri had done not to take No for an answer. At last, and for the same reasons as before, I accepted.

Dr. Chaudhuri then invited me to speak to his congregation. And Dr. Landrum of the American Academy of Asian studies invited me to teach a course there. My heart shrank within me. Yet I asked Master in meditation: "Is this your guidance?" Certainly, the response I'd been getting was astonishing, both for the unexpectedness of the invitations and for the insistence with which they were extended. I was astonished again when several people came up after these events and said they'd felt great joy coming from me. *Joy?* I was conscious only of intense inner suffering! Yet, as I thought further about it, I realized that I'd been experiencing joy in my heart all this time on a deeper-than-conscious level. Joy was actually helping me now, in some manner I could not explain. Somehow, it fueled the intensity of my pain. How this was I cannot say even now, but joy was masquerading as sorrow, and deepened the feeling I was experiencing at that time.

Tara, at about this time, telephoned Drs. Chaudhuri and Landrum and virtually ordered them not to permit me to speak in their institutions. She then telephoned me and accused me of disobeying her. "You remember what I told you by cablegram in India? I wrote, 'Your nature is disobedient beyond human comprehension.'"

I replied, "But I didn't offer myself! I did my very best to refuse."

"Oh yes, I know," she replied with heavy sarcasm. "You just sat around at public gatherings, making yourself noticeable and hoping they'd invite you!" There was no point, I realized, in even trying to reassure her.

Dr. Landrum approached Dr. Chaudhuri and asked him, "What should we do?" Dr. Chaudhuri replied, "It seems to me we should go by what we see." And so, their invitations stood. SRF reacted by refusing to fill any more orders from them for Yogananda's books. (Grim revenge!)

Thus it was, gradually, that I found myself thrust back once again into the arena of public speaking, despite my earnest efforts to shun this role. Indeed, what I really wanted still was to find some way of becoming a hermit.

I approached Swami Ashokananda of the Vedanta Temple in San Francisco, and asked if I might pitch a tent on a corner of their wooded 700-acre property near Olema, California. I hoped to be able to live on consecrated ground. In India, such an arrangement would have been perfectly normal. Ashokananda consulted his directors, however, and announced that the place was reserved for their own members.

I then went to Big Sur on the California coast, hoping to find a place on government land where I might seclude. I was told I could stay in the National Forest for two weeks, but no longer.

Someone then suggested a group of hippies in Big Sur. After a visit to their encampment, however, I realized that their lifestyle was not suitable to what I was seeking.

Next, a friend told me about New Camaldoli, a Roman Catholic hermitage in Santa Lucia south of Big Sur. The prior there, Dom Roggi, gave me permission to stay—"for now." The guest master, Dom Pedro Rebello, hoped I would convert to Roman Catholicism and join their order. But how could I do that? Deeply grateful as I was for their hospitality, my life-commitment had been made long ago. No circumstance could possibly change it.

As it was, I had committed myself, short-term, to giving weekly classes at the American Academy of Asian Studies in San Francisco. Thus, what with regular trips to the city, I couldn't remain full-time at the hermitage, though I did live there for the better part of every week. I was deeply grateful to the hermits for their welcome, and for the kindness they showed me.

During my last month in India my parents had purchased a car in Europe, to tour the continent. They'd offered to give me the car on their return to America. Binay Dubey, the YSS secretary, had urged me to get it shipped to India, where the organization would put it to good use. My parents hadn't yet done so, however—fortunately, as things had turned out. They now offered to give it to me in California. First, I told them I'd like to think about it. In truth, possession of any kind in my own name, especially of something expensive, was abhorrent to me. I was a renunciate. Now that I would be traveling back and forth weekly between New Camaldoli and San Francisco, however, I realized that I'd need a car.

New Camaldoli provided a greatly needed respite. The hermits enjoyed discussions with me on the more mystical teachings of Christianity, including those of the Eastern Orthodox Church and the Hesychasts. They were also eager to draw me out on India's spiritual traditions, particularly on the higher teachings of yoga. In the literature they shared with me I was able to study ancient Christian writings, and grew increasingly enthusiastic about the book I'd been contemplating.

In my parents' home I also had a chance to meet and discuss with university professors and scientists, who occasionally visited there, and to go over with them points that had challenged me in that *Span* article. I had already intended to write an introductory chapter, before addressing the spiritual aspects of the subject, on the prevailing science-inspired point of view. The more I discussed these matters with these guests, the clearer it became to me that this would be a very long chapter indeed! In fact, it ended up becoming a whole book, named *Crises in Modern Thought.* It took me sixteen years to write it and get it published, then another ten to revise it and publish an improved second edition. Now, finally, in the year 2001—thirty-nine years since its inception—it will appear in its third and (I really believe) final edition with a new name: *Out of the Labyrinth.* Thirty-nine years is a long time to bring one book to completion! This particular one has always been important to me, however, though it hasn't been the most widely read of my books. *Crises in Modern Thought* (or, in its final form, *Out of the Labyrinth*) forms the basis for much that I've taught and written during these intervening years.

New Camaldoli could never have been my permanent home. I worked for them willingly as they'd asked me to do, but inwardly I suffered, thinking, "The service I'm rendering, though certainly in a good cause, isn't serving my Guru!" I knew, and also deeply believed, that all true religions are one. As a disciple, however, my dedication was to my Guru. My convictions of universality couldn't alter the fact that my human heart had been dedicated in service to him—to him specifically, not just in a broad and universal sense. I had therefore to leave New Camaldoli at last, after a restful and inspiring stay of six months. Several of the hermits maintained ties with me—notably Father Thomas Mathus, who now lives in the parent house of the Camaldolese order in Italy.

Much happened during the following years. There is little point in detailing all of them, interesting though they were. My purpose in writing this book is to explain what led to the founding of Ananda. Thus, much that might in itself interest the reader—like those stories I hinted at in Part One concerning my visit to Bali—must be passed over.

For some time, I couldn't give much thought to creating a community. To have done so then would have been unrealistic. I hadn't the money. My father believed that I, as a grown man, needed to make my own way in the world. Occasionally I received small honorariums for lectures and concerts, but nothing like what would be needed to purchase land and start a community. Moreover, I met no one who was even interested in the idea.

Always since childhood, however, I'd cherished this dream. Several times over the years I'd asked Daya Mata when we might begin the community Master had spoken of so often, and with such fervor. The last time I'd broached this subject, she'd dismissed it. "Frankly," she'd replied, "I'm not interested."

The fact that Master *was* deeply interested, however, started me thinking that if indeed I did start a community, it would at least create no conflict with SRF. Thus, it seemed a safe avenue to explore, if matters changed in a practical way.

For the present, however, I still sought seclusion determinedly. If SRF's directors had bought me a cabin in the woods and ordered me to "stay there!" I'd have obeyed them implicitly. That might have been a reasonable solution, but it hadn't turned out that way. Indeed, at every turn my dreams of becoming a hermit received a complete lack of support from the Universal Beneficence. Instead, I was thrust repeatedly toward public speaking.

Undeterred from my eremitical plans, however, I studied brochures on little islands in the Caribbean. The prior at New Camaldoli had suggested I try a place in Lebanon called *Charbel Macluff,* where, he said, many hermits had lived. I thought also of India, and was actually invited by the great woman saint there, Ananda Moyi Ma, to come and live in one of her ashrams. The Indian government, however, had received a report that I was a CIA agent, and also a Christian missionary in disguise. (An Indian friend of mine, a lawyer in New Delhi, told me years later that he had seen my file at the Home Ministry, and had personally noted that SRF was behind efforts to get me banned from India.) Thus, for ten years I was unable to get a visa for India. By the time I was permitted to return there, I had already become committed to the development of Ananda.

Meanwhile, Mexico seemed an inviting possibility.

That country, being geographically near to me, seemed the best place to begin my "project" of becoming a hermit. I never reached there, however. Dr. Chaudhuri, in his loving efforts to guide me toward what he felt my guru wanted, arranged that I stop on the way and visit friends of theirs, Nick and Lois Duncan, who had a ranch in Sedona, Arizona. The Duncans—no doubt coaxed by Dr. Chaudhuri—invited me to seclude in a cabin on their property, for which the utilities would be free. In return, they asked if I'd speak regularly at the weekly Aurobindo gatherings in their home. It wasn't much to ask of me, and I gladly agreed.

I made a three-months adventure out of living on ten dollars a month for food. This "adventure in eating" (does it sound like the title for a gourmet cookbook?) was rather fun. I trained my palate to enjoy, or at least to accept, powdered instead of regular milk. I made chapatis (the Indian version of Mexican tortillas) instead of buying bread. I convinced myself that a tablespoon of dessert was quite as good-tasting as a bowlful, and thus made one dish last a week. I cooked daal (split pea soup), which was cheap and nourishing. I made corn tamales (again, cheap and nourishing). And I shopped the local markets for "specials." I did lose some weight, but on the whole I did marvelously well.

And I made good friends, many of whom kept in touch with me for years after I left.

After three months, the Duncans followed an earlier schedule of leaving for India to visit the Sri Aurobindo ashram in Pondicherry. It would be inconvenient for me to stay there any longer. Should I now proceed, I asked myself, to Mexico? Christmas was approaching; I decided to spend it with my parents. After that, I would resume my quest for seclusion in Mexico.

CHAPTER 20

A Choice Is Thrust upon Me

God had other plans for me in this life than becoming a hermit. He now gave me a dramatic demonstration of His intentions.

After Christmas, the Chaudhuris invited me to a Saturday evening dinner party at the home of one of their students, Ethel Appleby. I was scheduled to leave two days later for Mexico. We parted on the street outside, and they wished me a safe journey. Somehow, for some days I hadn't felt that I'd really be leaving. Even now, the journey seemed unreal. Still, with friendly waves we bade one another goodbye.

The next day my plans were altered drastically. Dr. Chaudhuri, during his Sunday sermon, collapsed with a heart attack. When the news reached me, I knew I couldn't possibly leave. There was no one to take his place at the ashram. That afternoon I telephoned Bina and asked if she'd like me to substitute for him until he recovered.

"Oh, thank God!" she exclaimed. "I was afraid to ask you, knowing you were so keen on leaving. But—do you really think you *could* do it?"

I moved into the ashram, and lived there for one year. It was January 1964, when my life entered a new phase, altogether different from the hermit's life but surely what God wanted of me now. The least I could do for the Chaudhuris, after all they'd done for me, was help them in their time of need.

I gave the Sunday services and mid-week classes, and received in return meals and lodging at the ashram as well as an honorarium from donations for my talks. The rest of every week I had free. I took the opportunity to do research at the public library for the book I was contemplating. I read scientific journals, and took out books on various subjects, scientific and philosophical, relating to the subject of meaninglessness. It was fascinating to familiarize myself with ways of thinking that were so diametrically opposed to my entire belief structure.

I was tempted to dismiss what I read as utter nonsense. No good would result from doing so, however, for I was hoping to help people who were infected by this kind of reasoning, and who, consequently, had lost faith in life. I wasn't interested in convincing those with an actual preference for believing in nothing. Many of them, I knew, found a certain comfort in meaninglessness as an excuse for their own lack of principles, or found in its teaching a match for their own absence of energy. I did want very much, however, to reach those who longed to find in themselves a basis for honest faith.

I couldn't help realizing that these authors were not fools. Mistaken, yes, but I had to take them seriously if I wanted readers to take *me* seriously.

I'd spent fourteen years in an environment where everyone shared the same basic beliefs. The people I wanted to help now, however, were lost in a labyrinth of false reasoning from which they could find no way out. Many of the suicides nowadays, especially among the young, must surely be the result of a system of education that mocked at faith and bred into its students a nihilistic outlook on life. The writers I studied seemed to exult in their own cleverness. In meaninglessness they found a kind of substitute faith—dry as dust, but declaring it to people who had no stomach for it satisfied their own egos. For all their brilliance, however, it lacked common sense.

By stepping back a little from it, I realized that it was not objective. Those writers were biased toward a negative belief system. If one asks questions with a negative bias, one receives negative answers. I realized I would have to discipline myself to deal with, and not to repudiate, attitudes of life-rejection. The challenge, for me, was to try to appreciate such a point of view without letting it affect my conviction of life's deep and wonderful meaning.

The great master Sri Ramakrishna used to say that if you peel onions, your hands will smell of them. Since I'd chosen deliberately—and I hoped not foolishly, in light of my devotional life—to "peel onions," I'd have to be strong inwardly. I couldn't wear protective gloves, so to speak, for I needed to "get a feel" for this uncongenial outlook. It would always be necessary, afterward, to "wash my hands" by faithful meditation and by ever-deepening attunement with my Guru.

Dr. Chaudhuri helped me greatly with my research. A well-known writer on philosophy, he suggested books that might be of help to me. One of them would lead me to another. Thus, gradually, I learned some of the principal currents in modern thought. Much of this material was, for me as a devotee, highly unpleasant to read. The teachings had already eaten their way corrosively into the fabric of modern society. I'd had training, however, in a school of wisdom that provided the answers people needed now. I must hold to this understanding, and not be affected by the corrosion of clever reasoning, though I'd have to listen with an open mind in order to tune in, as it were, to what I was reading.

First, I tackled the question of relativity. Many claimed that, since everything is relative, every definition of morality, whether serious or bizarre, expresses only beliefs, not objective truths. A university student told me that he'd lunched in a restaurant with one of his professors. The man had pocketed a spoon. "Why did you do that?" asked the student.

"Why not?" the professor replied indifferently. "Everything is relative." To him, taking a spoon didn't rate as stealing, provided one didn't define it as such. What the restaurant lost, he gained.

That story typified much of what passes for "new wisdom" today. I read what these "philosophers" had to say, rather than pushing it away in disgust as I wanted to do. I then drew back mentally, and applied the standards of common sense to what they'd written, avoiding the convoluted logic with which they teased their readers into dropping what, in an earlier era, would have been called "bourgeois preconceptions." Logic was the trap they offered, having already fallen into it themselves. What was needed now, I knew, was not more of the same kind of reasoning, based on untested premises, but the sharp axe of discrimination.

It was then I saw the rent in their fabric. Yes, of course everything is relative. Morality too is relative. This simple fact, however, doesn't mean that truth is only a concept in the brain. It is not a euphemism for chaos and fragmented values. Over-intellectuality had tricked those "philosophers" into overlooking the obvious: that relativity implies *relationship!* To accept the relativity of values does not make them a matter of mere taste or convenience.

A toy gun in the hands of a child is only a toy, but brandished, even jokingly, in the hands of an adult might give some cause for apprehension. If Jesus Christ or Mahatma Gandhi had awakened one morning and declared, "I'm tired of serving humanity! I've decided to become a millionaire," wouldn't everyone, even an atheist, say he was making a mistake? But if a sluggard made the same declaration, wouldn't everyone, even a saint, applaud his decision?

Truth is relative in the sense that our perception of it depends on our *level* of understanding and awareness. Its relativity is directional, and that direction is the same for everybody. Only God, who is beyond relativity, may be called absolute. Values themselves cannot be that. They *are,* however, universal. A mistake often made is to confuse those two words, "absolute" and "universal." Einstein related all velocity to what he called the "absolute" speed of light. Philosophers said that when it comes to moral values, there is nothing absolute to which to relate them. However, there is no need to relate them to an absolute. There is in relativity itself a direction *toward* which all try to move: happiness. There is also a direction *away from* happiness: pain. In that directional relativity, not in any fixed moral rule, values exist. In moral philosophy, the search for an absolute has been a will-o'-the-wisp. It has lured people toward something that was never there. They should have concluded long ago that the light they were seeking was another.

Heat and cold are relative. These are universal perceptions, though they affect Eskimos and Fiji islanders differently. A relativity of values doesn't imply that the only criterion of their validity is common agreement. Many basic values apply in varying degrees to everyone, for the simple reason that those values are rooted in nature, not in human opinion. To help someone in need is a virtue not because scripture says so, but for the simple reason that nature implants in us an urge toward self-expansion. We satisfy that urge toward expansion in many ways: in sympathy, knowledge, understanding. A self-serving attitude, on the other hand, is contractive, and goes against that natural urge. Even if a whole culture endorses it, the result, for its people, is general unhappiness. To contradict any impulse that is implanted in us by nature is to be punished by nature. As the saying goes, "Ignorance of the law is no excuse." To eat nails, which the human body is not made to assimilate, is to experience pain—and, very probably, death.

The writers I was studying claimed that human

beings are independent from nature—"radically free" as the nihilist Jean-Paul Sartre put it. Sartre made this the premise for most of his reasoning. How, I asked myself, could anything *in* nature be *apart from* nature? We share the planet together with the beetles! It is absurd to claim that mankind is "radically free," and then not offer a shred of evidence in support of this statement, while adding that *therefore* one can do as one likes, provided he is sincere about it. Essentially, Sartre was saying, "Mankind is radically free; therefore he is free."

The more I studied Sartre, the more I realized that *within his own frame of reasoning* he was neither reasonable, nor realistic, nor sincere. In one of the chapters of my book I unmasked him for his dishonesty. So many of the "intelligentsia" of our times take him seriously—like the people in Hans Christian Andersen's story who convinced themselves they were beholding their emperor in a new suit of clothes, when in fact he was wearing nothing. I found it no joy to read Sartre; the man was unclean. Read him I did, however—enough of his works and more than enough to get the picture, for he represented more boldly than most the widespread fallacy of meaninglessness. When finally I wrote about him, it was a pleasure to unmask his ruthless and arrogant reasoning and reveal him as an intellectual fraud. It was a joy also to think that people need no longer be caught in his snare of false reasoning and prevented from finding the freedom of their own being, as children of God.

I read books on biology also, and saw the lengths

to which "authorities" had gone to justify the claims of materialism. It was obvious they'd made an *a priori* commitment to it. The facts alone, however, in no way forced the conclusions they came to. It was painful to see that many students in this fact-oriented society of ours had leapt onto that "bandwagon," merely because the noise it made was so loud.

"Did humanity evolve more in producing a brain than the elephant in producing a trunk?" This rhetorical question was solemnly proposed to an audience whom the author expected to be in complete sympathy with his view of life. I wanted to laugh, and probably did. But I also had to take the man seriously, if I was to answer him in terms of his own logic.

And so I applied myself to the question of evolution, and pondered why students of the subject thought evolution is only a mechanism. "Evolution," I read (this is a paraphrase, not a direct quote), "is completely accidental. It is not progressive in any meaningful sense, for there is nothing toward which to progress. The process is entirely mechanical. Life is meaningless, purposeless, and unintelligent." Facts were offered in support of this thesis; thousands of them. The conclusions drawn from them, however, were as unnecessary to the facts as the belief of certain primitive peoples that thunder means the gods are displeased. Philosophers had been asking the wrong questions.

When I was a child of six, my father told me that the human race is dominant on earth as an evolutionary accident. Perhaps, he said, the birds will be the next to rule, since they haven't had their turn yet. I remember thinking even at that age that his idea was unsatisfactory, for it implied no dominance of consciousness. I hadn't the vocabulary to verbalize my reaction, but my vague sense was that life cannot be haphazard and meaningless.

Instead of denying the facts presented by biologists, as apologists for religion have generally done, I accepted them without question. Then, however, I drew back mentally and asked myself, "What does it all *mean?*" From the same facts, I realized, completely different conclusions can be drawn—and more sensible ones, too. A sheer plethora of facts had seduced too many people into forgetting common sense.

Writers claimed that there is no difference between animate and inanimate matter. Indeed, a number of famous scientists, among them J. C. Bose in India and Karl Bonhoefer in Germany, had demonstrated that the reactions of metal to electrical stimuli are *identical* to those of nerve tissue. The materialists claimed to see in such facts proof that so-called life and consciousness are without either life or consciousness. Nothing exists, they insisted, except inert matter.

I accepted their facts. I even went farther than they had, bringing several different discoveries of this nature into a single presentation which, together, became overwhelmingly convincing. Thus, I made their case more thoroughly, perhaps, than they'd made it themselves. And then—I turned it on its head! If, I said, animate and inanimate matter are the same, then instead of concluding—*consciously!*—that both are unconscious, wouldn't it be more reasonable to conclude that consciousness exists, at least latently, in them both?

This, indeed, is the ancient teaching of Vedanta!

I addressed other issues as well in my book, all of them as reasonably as I could, and never emotionally. Years later, a student from a prominent university expressed to me his spiritual doubts, which he had as a result of exposure to that kind of thinking. For my reply I suggested he read *Crises in Modern Thought.* He did so. After graduating, he became a member of Ananda.

Many of the concepts in this book had an important influence on Ananda's growth. The emphasis, for example, on the fact that there are different levels in people's ability to understand reality contrasted with the unanimity most institutions expect of their members. At Ananda there is a different rule: "People are more important than things." People also are more important than any rule formulated for their governance. As Jesus Christ put it, "The Sabbath was made for man, not man for the Sabbath." Ananda gives people latitude for development according to their own, inner light.

The work I did on *"Crises"* was important in another respect for Ananda's development. My emphasis on the evolution of *consciousness* through form, rather than on the multiplicity of forms themselves, had a major influence on everything we do. For the spirit behind what is done is always Ananda's first consideration. Of what good, we ask ourselves, is an efficient mechanism if what it produces is efficiency, but not joy?

Research took up much of 1964 for me. In that year I also made another, quite unexpected discovery: a new way of serving Master's mission. This, too, was one that SRF had not explored, and would therefore give them no competition. This discovery also proved vitally important to the story of Ananda, and contributed greatly, in time, to its success. What it concerned was music.

CHAPTER 21

I Take Up Writing Music

In the summer of 1964 I spent a week vacationing at Yosemite National Park, in California. Yosemite must surely be one of the most beautiful places on earth. By an interesting coincidence, it was here I wrote Part One of the present book, during the summer of 1996. My first visit may have been the one I made in 1964, though it's possible I'd been there once with my parents. I was deeply inspired by the solitude there, surrounded by towering peaks, majestic waterfalls, tall trees, and tranquillity—all of which I sensed in spite of surrounding throngs of tourists.

The day before my scheduled departure from Yosemite, I noticed a couple of youths sitting on the stone railing of a bridge, playing a guitar and singing. I felt in the mood for song, and asked if they'd like me to sing for them.

"By all means!" they replied—relieved, I suspected, to be temporarily unburdened of the need for carrying a tune! I had a very limited repertoire, however. I knew Yogananda's chants, and several Indian *bhajans* (devotional songs). I also knew a number of classical songs by such composers as Mozart, Schubert, Tchaikovsky, and Grieg. None of these seemed right for that setting, or for that audience. I therefore sang an old American favorite: "Swing Low, Sweet Chariot" (the only one I could think of besides "I've Been Workin' on the Railroad," which somehow didn't fit the occasion).

"Wow!" they cried. "You've got to come sing for a party we're having tonight. Will you, please?"

I agreed. Instead of the usual cocktail party scene, with people standing about politely, these people were lying about in assorted vacationing poses on a sandy beach. My young friends introduced me, and everyone sat up to listen. I sang—well, what else?—"Swing Low, Sweet Chariot." They begged me to sing another. I demurred, not wanting to admit how very limited my repertoire was.

The next day, as I was driving out of Yosemite Valley, the thought came to me, "What a wonderful way of sharing with others!" What a pity, I thought, that there weren't more songs I could sing from my heart. None, it seemed to me, expressed teachings that had any particularly meaningful message. Even classical songs described mostly the same old sentiments: disappointed love, jealousy, or hope, none of which were particularly exalted themes. *"O cessate di piagarmi! O lasciate mi morir!"* wailed—was it Scarlatti? ("Oh, stop wounding me! Oh, let me die!") Was this the sort of thing I wanted to share with others? The only possible motive for singing such nonsense would be to show off my own voice, and what good would that do? In fact, that was why I seldom sang classical songs, even though I enjoyed many of them as music. In public I'd sung a few Indian *bhajans,* and some of Master's chants. I felt, however, that it would be betraying what he had given me if I sang songs with no meaningful message.

In fact this was why, as a young man in college, I'd ignored the suggestions of many that I become a professional singer. My singing teacher in Philadelphia, an elderly woman and a true artist, had said to me, "I'm living for only one thing now: to see you become a *great* singer!" In reaction, I'd stopped studying altogether. I didn't want to disappoint her, nor the many others who predicted a singing career for me, but my heart was bent on seeking truth. It would have seemed to me worse than hypocritical to pretend sentiments that no sane person, in my opinion, could possibly feel. (I remember a famous French baritone kneeling on the platform and clasping his hands fervently while singing the *Marseillaise.* A rousing national anthem, no doubt, but, apart from being thoroughly bloodthirsty, it offended all my aspirations toward world harmony and peace.)

Still, I visualized myself while driving: going about the country, singing songs with lyrics that were *meaningful.* Would *any* lyrics, however, express the universal truths Master had taught? None that I knew of, unfortunately.

I was about to give up the idea as a fantasy when a thought popped into my mind: "I wonder if I could write my own songs?"

The moment the thought came, a melody popped into my mind, complete with lyrics. All my life, melodies had drifted into my mind and out of it again. Many of them had been beautiful. This one, too, inspired me. I stopped at a milk shake stand and wrote the song out on a paper napkin. I had played the piano for years as a boy, and was familiar with music notation. All I needed to do now was draw two sets of five lines each on the napkin, then pencil in the notes and put the words under them. What came out was thrilling. Another amazing thing was the ease with which it came, as if it had written itself. I was obliged to rein in my inspiration to get it all down.

I was on my way to my parents' home. On arrival there, I found that my brother Dick had left a Martin guitar there. He had no immediate use for it, and later gave it to me. I bought Pete Seeger's *Guitar Player's Guide* at a music store, and began earnestly studying the guitar. Songs kept coming to me, each with a meaningful and uplifting message and a beautiful melody. Like the first, they came almost effortlessly.

I sang one or two of these new songs at the ashram during the Sunday service, to enhance my message. Before I knew it, another invitation came from the Dutton Club at the Unitarian Church, asking if I wouldn't give a concert. A concert? I'd been playing the guitar only one month! It would be the sheerest madness to accept. This was a challenge, however, and I was, as they say, "up for" challenges just then. I accepted. In justification I thought, "At least this will force me to practice!"

Practice I certainly did! Unremittingly, for a whole week. Two more songs came to me within that time, which I wrote out and learned for the concert. One of them may be worth including here. It was for the

Unitarian church members themselves, many of whom were, I'd heard, atheists.

What is love? Is it only ours?
Or does love whisper in the flowers?
Surely we, children of this world,
Could not love by our own powers.

What is joy? Is it just a dream?
Or does joy laugh in every stream?
Are the clouds mindless after all?
Or is joy all Nature's theme?

"God is dead"—so men say:
Can't they see all life's His play?
Not a church binds Him as its own;
Not a creed makes Him fully known.
Foolish we, if we limit Him:
Every atom is His throne!

The "big evening" arrived. Fortunately, I wasn't nervous: I never have been in public. My view is that if I'm a fool, what harm is there in people knowing it? Meanwhile, I do my best to share what I can. I must say, however, this particular evening presented even more obstacles than I'd expected. The worst of them was that, in order to create "atmosphere," all the lights had been turned off and only a candle shone "mystically" on the mantelpiece—*behind* me! If there was one thing I desperately needed it was enough light to enable me to see the guitar strings.

The room was packed with 200 people, all of them eagerly expectant. I must admit that their expectancy, while gratifying, didn't lessen my concern. This was hardly what the new composer hopes for from his "world premiere"! I knew my voice could lift me part of the way out of the pit of disaster. And I had hope for the *bhajans* and a few chants I planned to include along with interesting and uplifting stories. My own songs? Well, perhaps the voice and the lyrics would make up for any lapse in the accompaniment.

As it turned out, the concert was a success. A young man came up to me afterwards and said, "I'm a major in music at San Francisco State. I liked your songs, but some of your chords surprised me." He reflected a moment, then added, "Hmmm, unusual!" (Yes, I thought—*very* unusual! in fact, unintentional and undoubtedly quite wrong.) Still, my "career" as a composer had been launched, in a sense.

More and more demands began coming for my songs. To try to "tune in" to the folk-style in music, which seemed well adapted to the guitar, I joined a folk music group on Stanyan Street. Faith Petric, the leader of the group, was an enthusiast for that genre, and liked my own songs. I asked her if she knew anyone who might teach me to play the guitar. "The man you need," she replied, "is Larry Hanks, if you can find him. He's the perfect teacher for you."

One evening at Christmas time, 1964, I went to Berkeley to join a group who planned to sing Christmas music informally together. I saw someone sitting alone. Suddenly the thought came to me, "That's Larry Hanks!" I went over and asked his name. "Larry Hanks," he replied.

"I'm supposed to study with you," I said. Astonished, he agreed to take me as a student.

During one of our lessons he remarked, "I like

your songs, but they lack realism. They're too happy. Life isn't like that. There's suffering everywhere in the world, and injustice. Your songs ought to take those darker realities into account."

I went home and gave the matter some thought, then decided for Larry's sake to write a blues. What came out, however, wasn't exactly what he'd had in mind. In fact, I called it, "The Non-Blues." At my next session with him we both had a good chuckle over it.

On another occasion, after a concert, a woman came up to me and said, "Well, *you* can write happy songs. You've never suffered!"

I replied, "That isn't true. It's because I *have* suffered that I've won the right to compose happy songs. What I've written isn't sweet sentiment: It's victory!"

The evening after I met Larry Hanks, I was driving back to San Francisco over the Oakland Bay Bridge when two Christmas songs appeared, full-blown, in my mind: "The Christmas Mystery," and "That Night When Christ Was Born." Late that night I stayed up, writing them down. These two, and especially the first, have long been among people's favorites. (So also, I should add, has "The Non-Blues.")

It has long puzzled me why music should come to me so easily. I'm told that song-writers and composers often "sweat blood" getting their music right. For a long time I thought I must not be much of a musician, because, for me, it seemed almost like play. In fact, I understood why people say they "play" music! I deferred to anyone who told me he or she was a musician, and tried to learn everything I could from them. Even today, there are millions of people in the world who know far more about music than I do. The only explanation I can offer for my music is that it isn't mine. I simply listen, hear it in my mind, and write it down.

The truth is, I never studied composition, though I did once take a course in composition at college, studying hardly at all and rarely going to class. It offended me to see those wonderful notes and chords reduced to mechanisms. "Here is the first inversion of this chord. Here is the second." I just couldn't think of music in that way. I would have done so, I imagine, had I known I'd someday be writing music. All I learned from that course was two rules: that parallel fifths should be avoided (in one of my songs, however, they work perfectly), and that the bass line ought, when possible, to move in opposite directions to the melody. I didn't know chords. I didn't know progressions. All I had was an ear for music. That is to say, I knew what worked, and what didn't.

As it turned out, my ignorance was fortunate. Not knowing the rules, I was forced to discover them for myself. I soon realized that the rules are all there, waiting to be found; none of them is arbitrary. Music is a language. Every melody, every chord, every rhythm has its own meaning. Not knowing the rules, I had to learn for myself not only what worked musically, but what, specifically, would say what I wanted to say. Not thinking of myself as a musician made it easier to keep myself out of the picture, and to let the music express *itself* to me. Every piece of music I wrote was something I'd first "heard." Sometimes it was there when I awoke in the morning. I found, in time, that I could even tune in to different cultures, periods of history, and states of consciousness, and receive music that was appropriate to each of them.

One morning I woke up with a melody for Edward Fitzgerald's translation of Omar Khayyam's *Rubaiyat,* for which Yogananda had written a commentary. Years later I sang this melody to a man from Iran. "Why," he exclaimed in astonishment, "that's Persian!" I knew nothing of Persian music.

Once I became frustrated with the comparative difficulty of writing lyrics, what with rhymes and the need for squeezing meaning into as few words as possible while still making it clear, and without slipping into poetic deception by writing something incomprehensible concealed behind obscure, but supposedly deep, imagery. Clarity was my primary aim, whether in teaching or in writing. On the day of my frustration (it was with the difficulty of writing meaningful but enjoyable lyrics) I thought, "I think I'll write melodies for Shakespeare's lyrics. Let *him* do the hard work!" In three days I put eighteen of his lyrics to music. They've remained popular favorites with many people.

Once I was invited to speak and sing for Crystal Springs, a girls' school on the Peninsula south of San Francisco. Nancy Ponch, who had invited me in some official capacity and had driven me down, ended up becoming my coach in lyric writing. She herself wrote songs—bad ones, I'm afraid, though I could never bring myself to say so. But she *was* good at coaching.

"Shakespeare did this sort of thing," I'd complain, "and he got away with it!" She'd offered criticism on one of my lines.

"That's fine," she replied, "but you aren't Shakespeare. Besides, there's nothing we can do about him now. He's dead, whereas you are very much alive—still. You shouldn't let yourself get away with this sort of thing. A strained rhyme may look all right on paper, but it won't work when sung. Marlowe rhymed 'love' with 'prove,' sure. And there aren't many rhymes for 'love.' Still, you can always 'shove' a word like that into the middle of a line if it's difficult to rhyme, then put something more rhymable at the end."

A trick I'd learned in my teens had been that when you have a weak rhyme, don't put it second: Put it first. Then people won't know you've chosen that word only because you couldn't find one that rhymed well.

Gradually, from songs that expressed meaning, I went on to writing music without lyrics while *in itself* expressing meaning, and the spirit of Yogananda's teachings.

To leap ahead many years, Derek Bell, the famous Irish harpist for The Chieftains, recorded two albums of my music. Cuts from these albums, as well as from others of my music, have been played by several airlines on their international flights. A group from Ananda sang at the Vatican for the Pope. And in May, 2000, a choir of more than fifty Ananda members flew to Italy and sang, in six cities, an Oratorio of mine called "Christ Lives." Everywhere they performed, they received standing ovations. One man came up to me after the concert in Assisi with tears in his eyes, and said to me in French, "I don't know a word of English or Italian. [The concert was all in English.] I'm only a visitor here. But I want you to know, I understood *every word!*"

Music, about which for years I used to ask myself, "Is this *really* a service to Master?" has become one of Ananda's most important assets. I've composed over 300 musical works, including piano and string pieces, choral music, and songs. For me, it has been one of the great joys in my life. Often, tears of joy have flowed down my cheeks as a melody or a sequence of beautiful harmonies poured through me like a mountain stream, effortlessly. How different, in this respect, has music been from writing books, which often demand great effort to make a single, subtle point clear.

CHAPTER 22

I Dive into the Water

Dr. Chaudhuri recovered from his heart attack, but asked me if I wouldn't remain teaching at the Cultural Integration Fellowship ashram and share the load of teaching with him. Thus, I continued giving Sunday services bi-weekly, and (if memory serves) at least some of the mid-week classes. Meanwhile, it seemed to me the time had come to find an apartment of my own.

Several others lived in the ashram on the second floor, as I did. They were good people, but I'd come to realize that living so near them involved me in ways that detracted from the energy I needed for my work on the book. Moreover, the residents weren't deeply involved in the spiritual life. The friendship we shared was of a social kind, primarily. I began scanning the newspaper ads for a place more suitable to my needs.

Almost at once I found one that attracted me: "Spacious five-room apartment, quiet, rose garden." The address was 220 16th Avenue, in what is known as the Richmond district of San Francisco. The apartment, when I visited it, proved charming, spacious indeed, quiet (as announced), with a beautiful rose garden just outside my back window. I wouldn't be able to use the garden, but at least I'd be able to enjoy the view.

The rent was higher than I could afford, but if God approved my choice He would somehow manage to make up the difference; I was unworried. The place was ideal.

I mentioned it to my parents. Dad, suspecting I wasn't earning enough to meet the rent, told me, "Your mother and I would like to have a place in the city where we could sometimes spend the night after an evening at the theater or the opera. What would you say to our sharing the apartment, and the cost? We'd pay half the rent, leaving the other half to you."

Whatever my father gave to one of us three boys, he gave in equivalent form to the other two. In giving me the car, for example, he'd given the others the money it had cost him to buy it. In the matter of this apartment, then, the easiest way to smooth his conscience was to make the apartment half theirs, rather than giving me enough money to make it all mine. I understood, and accepted gratefully. Actually, during the four years I lived there I think they slept in the apartment only one night.

The apartment had large, old-fashioned rooms with high ceilings, large closets, and an adequate kitchen. I turned the dining room into an office, and set up a desk there, made from a varnished plank set upon two nightstands with drawers. The days of home computers were nearly two decades in the future. My practice was to write longhand, then transfer that material to the typewriter.

I was invited to give additional weekly classes at a home in San Mateo, down the Peninsula from San Francisco. Those who attended—nine or twelve people every week—were for the most part middle-aged or elderly. I was helped financially in return, by donations left in a basket by the door. This amount averaged about nine dollars—helpful, certainly, in my present circumstances, though hardly a "windfall."

What I noticed, however, was that none of those who attended seemed deeply interested in the teaching they received from me. I was sharing teachings, I reflected, that ought to revolutionize their lives. Instead, they'd come placidly, listen placidly, and go home placidly, placidly commenting, "What a *nice* young man." For someone who longed to share the teachings with others, this fell short of being entirely satisfying.

A difficulty in teaching at the ashram was that I didn't feel that it was in the fitness of things to emphasize my own Guru and his teachings. Thus, my problem was similar, in a way, to what I'd encountered at New Camaldoli. I was, above all, Yogananda's disciple; I couldn't be satisfied with only teaching universal truths, though I was pleased to share these, too, as the basis for everything I practiced and believed. Outside the ashram, however, I could teach my Guru's teachings openly and specifically. I felt increasingly drawn to doing so.

Dr. Chaudhuri—always my human guardian angel during those difficult years—began urging me to teach Hatha Yoga, the physical branch of the meditative science of Raja Yoga. He knew I'd posed for the yoga postures for several years in *Self-Realization Magazine.* It occurred to him that I ought to include this knowledge in what I taught now—if not at the ashram, then in classes elsewhere. As a matter of fact, my Guru had often had me demonstrate the yoga postures for his guests, later serving them lunch. (Afterward, we'd sit together privately while he discussed various subjects with me, or give me personal spiritual counsel.)

The articles in *Self-Realization Magazine,* however, had never impressed me very favorably, first because they took an approach to the subject that was not spiritual, but physical. The writer, Rev. Bernard, one of SRF's ministers, emphasized how this posture helped by pressing on a certain gland, and how that one stretched the vertebrae and increased circulation—that sort of thing. I'd never voiced any objection, but I couldn't help feeling that, inasmuch as Hatha Yoga is the physical branch of the meditative yoga science, Bernard was missing the real point.

Later on, another of the monks was given the job of writing those articles. Bernard Tesnière, a medical doctor from France, took his lead from Rev. Bernard in emphasizing the medical aspect. Fortunately, he took, in addition, my suggestion of giving the articles a more spiritual slant. Particularly, he included affirmations to suggest the mental, and to some extent the spiritual, influence of each posture. I wasn't wholly satisfied with the way he handled the subject, either, but at least it was a step in what I considered the right direction.

Tesnière and I had a falling out (from his side, not

from mine) during the time of my first troubles with Tara, my last year in India. I don't suppose he knew what I was going through, though he may have heard I was in official disfavor. It was interesting to me, however, to observe how, when the tides of karma flow strongly in any direction, everything else in one's life seems to flow in the same direction. Thus, several people without SRF connections found cause for outrage, during that period, at some of the simplest things I said or did. Whatever it was, I seemed to meet with disapproval from someone. I decided there was nothing I could do about it; I must simply wait for the storm to blow over. Thus, I got on the wrong side of Tesnière also—sadly, from my point of view, for he was a friend. (After my dismissal, of course, all my fellow monks vanished from my life in fear for their own salvation. They probably thought that if something like this could happen to their head monk, who among them was safe?)

Dr. Chaudhuri seems to have been forever pushing me in the right direction. And I seem to have been forever resisting his loving efforts. I've mentioned his insistence on my getting back into lecturing. I've also mentioned his pushing me in the direction of singing, which he did with their invitation to me to sing at the Gandhi function in October 1962. When I recorded the first album of my songs, *Say "Yes" to Life!* in 1965, he kindly wrote the following praise for the backliner of the jacket: "Kriyananda has a voice that enthralls, and a vision that ennobles." I had resisted his prompting that I begin lecturing again. As for music, it was years before I could really believe it was a service to Master to write it. And now I resisted Dr. Chaudhuri's repeated urging that I teach Hatha Yoga. He was right again, of course. (How often I've thanked God for the friendship he and Bina extended me!)

Fortunately, my "No" is rarely absolute. Usually, people's suggestions remain with me while I ponder them. If, after I've thought about them, they seem good, my "No" becomes a "Well, let's see"; then, finally, a "Yes." I say this because my reputed stubbornness in SRF was one of the points Daya Mata raised against me at the time of my dismissal. At the time I thought, "Look at all the people who say Yes to her, then do nothing. I, at least—once I've weighed a suggestion and can put energy behind it—have always carried it through to completion." My purpose at this point in the book, however, is not to "beat a dead horse," but only to say that, at Ananda, I have always made it a point to look at what people actually do, not merely at what they say. As the well-known saying goes, "Actions speak louder than words."

Anyway, in the matter of teaching the yoga postures, I prayed to Master with an open mind, and all at once realized how very much the postures could assist in teaching the meditation practices of Raja Yoga, especially to beginning meditators.

How many times in my life guidance has come from my Guru, even as it came to the disciples of Lahiri Mahasaya (his guru's guru), and to the disciples of his own guru, Swami Sri Yukteswar. Yogananda wrote in *Autobiography of a Yogi* that Lahiri Mahasaya guided his disciples in the writing of commentaries on the scriptures. "Please expound the holy stanzas as the meaning occurs to you," he would tell a disciple. "I will guide your thoughts, that the right interpretation be uttered." Yogananda continued, "In this way, many of Lahiri Mahasaya's perceptions came to be recorded, with voluminous commentaries, by various students."

Thus, too, what I have taught and written in my life has been, very often, the inspiration of my Guru. I claim no credit for it. In the present case, he had often had me demonstrate the yoga postures for his guests. Though he never actually taught me the postures, it was as if he communicated a certain awareness of them as I practiced them. I could feel him guiding my understanding now, as I went more deeply into each pose and tried to relate it to the meditative aspects of Raja Yoga. This guidance grew steadily clearer. No book that I know of explains the postures in this way, but the system that came to me is completely in harmony with the ancient teachings and with the teachings of Paramhansa Yogananda. It has come to be known as "Ananda Yoga."

This system is generally recognized as a main branch of Hatha Yoga teaching in America. It helps not only those who seek physical well-being, but has been used also by psychiatrists and others in helping people to achieve mental equilibrium. Above all, it has helped those seeking assistance in their meditations. Many thousands have benefited from "Ananda Yoga." I must again underscore, however, that it is my Guru's system, not my own. Everything in it is derived either verbally or by inner inspiration from his guidance.

My own interest in this system was, as I've implied, for its usefulness to the teaching of meditation. I wanted to devote more energy now to teaching my Guru's practical yoga science, and not only to sharing his philosophy. Dr. Chaudhuri, seeing my hesitation, which was due to SRF's insistence that those teachings were their monopoly, insisted, "This is what you received from your Guru. It would be wrong not to share it with others." He was right.

Thus, I began teaching classes more widely in the San Francisco Bay Area. To meet expenses, I charged $25 for six evenings of weekly classes for those students who wanted both Hatha Yoga and Raja Yoga, and $15 for those who took only one series. I would begin the evening with yoga postures, followed by a short break during which students could eat a light snack, if they'd brought one. Last came the Raja Yoga class.

These courses were popular from the beginning. By the time I finished this phase of my life and moved to Ananda, I was getting an average of 300 students a week and receiving enough income to purchase and begin construction at Ananda.

My firm policy was to refuse no one. If a person couldn't afford to pay, I encouraged him or her to give back energy in some other way: for instance, by bringing cookies for the students during the break, or setting up chairs for the Raja Yoga class afterward. I knew that many other teachers—in Scientology and in Transcendental Meditation, for example—charged very much more for their instruction, none of which could be compared to Paramhansa Yogananda's teachings for depth, clarity, and practicality. They ignored the need for devotion altogether and followed the "New Agey" trend of emphasizing egoic omnipotence, to the virtual exclusion of Infinite Consciousness. No consideration, however, induced me to raise the price. I knew, for instance, that if I charged more certain students would place a higher value on what I taught, but I didn't want lack of money to be a hindrance for others. Moreover, I wasn't seeking rich students; my goal was to help all. I was aware that some people would value *less* what I taught because the price was low. Indeed, I knew (and had it demonstrated to me, subsequently) that some people would take advantage of my generosity. I wasn't interested in their response. My concern was to remain faithful to my Guru and to my own conscience. I wanted to serve people without personal benefit to myself. At the same time, I knew people in our culture would take the classes seriously only if they paid *something* in return for them.

In time, I became a recognized part of the San Francisco "scene." For San Francisco during the 'sixties was the place where many national movements got their start, while others received their major impetus there: the New Age movement; the Hippie and the psychedelic movement; the Hare Krishna movement; the War Protest movement (centered across the Bay, in Berkeley); the Commune and Back-to-the-Land movement. Ferlinghetti and the beatnik poets were already thriving in the North Beach district of the city. Zen Buddhism had a major, perhaps even its main, energy-center in the city. San Francisco was, and was becoming increasingly so, the center of a whirlpool of energy that covered all of America, and indeed the world, embracing an extraordinary number of "New Age" movements. Perhaps this was why the Divine Mother placed me there.

I was never a part of any of these movements, however. The guidance I sought was within, not in popular opinions or acclaim. Still, I was very much a part of the new wave of consciousness that flowed from San Francisco at that time. Even the fact that I started Ananda at that time, when the movement toward forming communes was at its height, was a sublime coincidence. Ananda was simply the fulfillment of a dream I'd had since the age of fifteen.

Everything I did at this time was from within: not in response to the social ferment around me, but guided by what I felt from my Guru. In this sense, I was always an outsider, never "meshing gears" with those who gave the scene its accepted definition. Yet for all that, I *was* part of the scene: the odd man out who, in the midst of social ferment, held a steady course.

Interestingly, many of the waves generated during those times have subsided and disappeared, but Ananda, and the teachings I absorbed from my Guru and was sharing with others have continued unchanged, calm, ever-increasingly influential in the lives of many thousands.

CHAPTER 23

"New Age" Movements

It now became necessary for me to relate to the world more realistically. No longer did I have a monastery as a home base, nor brother monks to give me spiritual support. Virtually every influence to which I was exposed, monks would consider worldly because motivated by a desire for ego-affirmation.

I'd already dived into the uncongenial waters of scientific materialism for my research on *Crises in Modern Thought.* Now I found myself exposed to another aspect of materialism, less concerned with justification, whether scientific or philosophical, and more instinctive. Its first, unexamined impulse was to think first of oneself. "The stalwart kinship of selfish motive," a sage describes it in *Autobiography of a Yogi.* This definition of the basis for human unity, however, is not wholly satisfying for me, for though most human beings are indeed selfish, it is exactly their self-involvement that separates them from one another. The basis for human unity, as Paramhansa Yogananda shows repeatedly in his book, is our common, deeper-than-conscious need to know God, our higher, not our egoic, Self. In relating to others, then, I must do so with the "ulterior motive" of awakening them to a recognition of their basic need for divine love and bliss.

Obviously, I couldn't achieve that end in any overt manner—for instance, by staring soulfully into their eyes! What I had to do first was learn to see them as they saw themselves. Only then—and only maybe—would it be possible to encourage them to higher levels of Self-recognition. I needed first to comprehend their values, if I was to inspire them to higher values.

Strange as it may seem, I found this adjustment difficult. Not only was I not worldly in that monastically defined sense: I was *un*worldly. Even to pretend attitudes I didn't feel would be, however, a sure way of *becoming* worldly. I'd seen this happen too often, to people who, with the excuse of relating meaningfully to others, took on those attitudes and made them their own. Daya Mata used to rib me good-humoredly sometimes for my "other-worldliness." One reason for this perhaps exaggerated aspect of my personality may have been the fact that I was born and raised in a more or less medieval country: Romania. True, I'd been sent abroad to school from the age of nine, in Switzerland and in England, but my home was in Romania for the first thirteen years of my life. At any rate, I naturally shunned sophisticated attitudes, which to me suggested "bigness" and self-importance. My inclination was to ask of life, "What does it all mean?" and, "How can I contribute to that greater meaning?"

I was attracted, at first, to various forms of "New Age" thinking, which emphasized humanity's limitless potentials. In time, however, I realized that the basis for most such thinking was essentially no different from "old-age" thinking: Both were founded on self-interest. Both, therefore, were contractive, not expansive. Even people with generous natures usually thought of themselves as the source, not as merely the agents, of any good they did. Few desired to lose themselves in divine self-expansion. For this reason I found little to uplift me in those movements. The people who joined them prided themselves on a new freedom. I never joined, for it seemed to me what they really reveled in was a new conformity.

Having rejected one set of values, they now accepted what others said their new outlook should be. They felt a need to belong, and were more comfortable with vague precepts than with clear thinking, which they associated with logical rigidity rather than with the crystal waters of intuitive perception. Vaguely, they knew that deep insights are attained by feeling, not by the intellectual convolutions of reason, but they confused those insights with fuzzy thinking. The vaguer a statement, it seemed to them, the greater the chances that it might hint at a deep truth.

I remember a stern letter I received from someone to the effect that, if I wanted to relate to today's youth, I must learn to appreciate their music. In fact, I felt no attunement with their music. Its heavy beat conveyed to me only this message: "Ah wanna get *mine,* an' ah'm sure gonna get it!" I did make an effort to relate to others on another level, but I couldn't accept their way of perceiving what they considered truth: "Wow, man, that blows my mind!" "Clarity" was my motto: "clarity above all." At first I wondered if maybe they knew something I didn't know. In time I realized that their "knowing" was only affirmation, buttressed by cloudy principles and wrapped in an aura of infallibility. They prefaced every statement with, "I *feel* . . . ," as though any "feeling" at all merited the respect due to true intuition.

This was a new society to me. I'd spent fourteen years in a monastery, where contact with the "outside world" was minimal. I remember once, during a Sunday sermon at the SRF church in Hollywood, making some comment about "boogie woogie" music, which was popular during the 'forties. (I'd never had much attunement with that music, either.) A member of the congregation came up afterward and said teasingly, "Don't you know it isn't 'boogie woogie' any more?"

"Are you serious?" I asked in surprise. "What is it now?"

"Rock 'n' roll!" she replied.

"Well, well!" I marveled at my own ignorance. "How long has this been going on?

"Why, rock 'n' roll has been famous for five years!" she, too, marveled at my ignorance. And in such matters she was knowledgeable. Her husband had played the trumpet for Charlie Barnett, one of the "big bands."

Years later, I related this story to my cousin Bet. "Really, Don!" she expostulated. "You wouldn't want people to think you *quaint!*"

Well, I spoke good English. And I could drive a car. Of course, what I'm really saying light-heartedly is that in fact I've always been rather an outsider—by inclination, not because of social ineptitude. Trends and fads have always been meaningless to me. In my opinion, to go out of one's way to be "stylish" is a sign of lacking one's own standards of taste. Of course, it wasn't I who was on the outside, for I was centered in the search for an inner truth. It is worldly people that live outside their magic inner circle. They, not those who seek God, are the true "outsiders."

Divine vision, my Guru wrote, "is center everywhere, circumference nowhere." Most people dance, puppet-like, at their periphery and view all things in terms of a multiplicity of non-existent circumferences.

The research I had been doing for *Crises* had acquainted me with one of the worst aspects of worldly consciousness: the denial of consciousness altogether. That aspect of materialism which I now encountered was an affirmation of consciousness, at least, and even of higher consciousness. "New Agers," hippies, and most others who affirmed this higher consciousness (often after taking psychedelic drugs) declared that love is the only truth. I completely concurred. They believed, as I did, in human perfectibility. This was the generation of "flower children." Yet in their very belief I detected, in time, the seeds of delusion. Without the fine thread of guidance from a wise guru, I realized, no one can escape the labyrinth of ego-consciousness. Nowadays, many people scoff at the need for a guru. They project onto those who are truly wise their own desire for power and importance. Their presumption betrays them. This pride was present also, though less stridently, in the softer hippie generation. The fault wasn't theirs. Without the inner guidance of a true guru, no one can escape the endlessly tricky mind.

What the "flower children" emanated was a sort of woolly sentimentality. While declaring they loved everybody, they seemed unable to share this feeling except with those who, like them, were "high" on LSD or some other hallucinatory drug. As I got to know them better, I wondered whether some of them wouldn't feel as much love for the beautiful color, red, from a cut on a person's arm without considering the more abstract issue of his pain. It was an esthetic "feeling": passive, subjective, and drawing to itself while giving nothing in return. Especially what it didn't do was offer itself to God, and to the Divine in others. To please God wasn't, with them, an issue. Being coddled by God, or by something, was all they seemed really interested in. Like every "New Age" movement I've ever encountered, they sought enlightenment without opening themselves to the light of God's grace. Their openness showed no devotion.

I was present on two or three occasions when everyone in the room, except me, was smoking "grass," or marijuana. While I felt kindly toward them (they'd invited me as a friend), I couldn't help being aware that there was a negative force in the room.

At first I was attracted by all the talk of love. Many of the words used seemed right. What I came in time to see and feel around them, however, was wrong. Fortunately, many of those who had been attracted, as I had, to the good side in this movement ended up leaving it, and joining Ananda, where the blessings and guidance of a true guru, Paramhansa Yogananda, are actively sought and experienced.

I was attracted also by the hippie attitude toward non-attachment. What they emphasized was freedom. Yet in time I realized that freedom, to them, meant independence from the way *others* saw and did things. If they grew beards or let their hair grow long or wore scruffy trousers or long dresses and almost-as-long bead necklaces, it was in conformity to what their own set were doing. Had they done otherwise, they would have been frowned upon by their peers even as society in general frowned upon them—and for no better reason.

I was also, for a time, on the fringes of the Hare Krishna movement. This movement began in the Haight-Ashbury section of San Francisco, the heart of "hippiedom." Swami Bhaktivedanta had been invited there from India, and I, nostalgic for the devotional Indian scene, used to attend his gatherings. We enjoyed speaking Bengali together, and he gave me, in consequence, special attention. I found inspiration in chanting the *Maha Mantra* with him: "*Hare* [pronounced ha-ré] *Krishna, hare Krishna, Krishna, Krishna, hare hare! Hare Rama, hare Rama, Rama, Rama, hare hare!*" I confess the manner in which the young people around him chanted, bouncing their bodies about and stamping their feet like tribal warriors in a ritual dance, was too boisterous for my taste. It expressed none of the sweetness of devotion, but appeared rather to be a way of letting off emotional steam. *Maha Mantra* itself, however, had inspired me ever since I'd heard it sung every morning, years earlier, by a strolling band of devotees outside our ashram in Baranagor, near Calcutta.

Swami Bhaktivedanta (or Prabhupad, as he became known to his followers) was a Hindu fundamentalist: emotional in his faith rather than philosophically deep. He asked Dr. Chaudhuri and me to join his movement, but of course we didn't. As we commented smiling to one another later on, one doesn't expect philosophic depth from the beliefs Swami Bhaktivedanta held. He worshiped Krishna as God, and visualized Him literally as he is depicted in poetic allegory: blue-skinned, and playing the flute. Dr. Chaudhuri and I were nonetheless grateful that Swami Bhaktivedanta was bringing Indian devotional chanting to America. This was a wonderful gift.

One evening, the swami said something surprising to me:

"Ramakrishna was a fool!"

"How can you say that?" I asked.

"He was an impersonalist!" Bhaktivedanta used this term to designate someone who believes in God's Infinite Consciousness.

"But," I replied, "he was also personal in his worship. He prayed to the Divine Mother, especially."

"There you have it!" the swami scoffed. "Krishna, not the Divine Mother, is the Supreme Godhead."

"But Sri Ramakrishna also worshiped Krishna," I persisted. Sri Ramakrishna had demonstrated that all spiritual paths lead in the end to God. I was growing worried lest Bhaktivedanta give Hinduism a bad name in America.

"Is that so?" he replied. This too, evidently, was news to him. He paused a moment, then continued his assault: "Ananda Moyi Ma is a fool!"

"Swamiji, what are you saying?" I demanded.

"She, too, worships the Divine Mother."

"Many times I've chanted *Maha Mantra* with her!" I exclaimed.

Looking back now, I wonder whether someone hadn't spoken to him about the chapter on cosmic consciousness in *Autobiography of a Yogi.* Perhaps he'd have liked to denounce Yogananda, also, as an "impersonalist," but didn't want to risk offending me too blatantly.

I couldn't argue with an old man. In fact, I don't believe in arguing at all. I recalled my Guru's saying, "Fools argue; wise men discuss." Bowing silently, in respect for the higher teachings he, unfortunately, misrepresented, I left the room, never to return.

Years later, Alan Ginsberg, the "beat" poet, told me, "Swami Bhaktivedanta spoke to me shortly before he died. 'Where have I gone wrong?' he cried." Bhaktivedanta had accepted uncritically the fundamentalist belief that anyone who chants *Maha Mantra* will be purged of all sin. He'd accepted as disciples all types, confident that the chant alone would purify them and make them saints. Chaitanya himself, the great founder of *Vaishnavism* (the movement Bhaktivedanta represented), declared, "*Harer nam, Harer nam, Harer name* ***Kaivalyam*** ("God's name, God's name, God's name *alone* [brings salvation]").

Chaitanya, however, taught philosophically unsophisticated people at a time when their need was for personal devotion to God, and not theological clarity (as had been the case earlier, in the times of Swami Shankaracharya). He knew that, in any case, God's grace would lift them out of ignorance if they loved Him. God's "name," however, cannot be uttered by human lips. It is, as my Guru explained, the cosmic vibration of AUM—or, in Christian terminology, the Amen, or Holy Ghost.

Bhaktivedanta also made a big thing of the concept of "disciplic succession." It is true that a guru sometimes passes on his "mantle" to his chief disciple, as I often heard Paramhansa Yogananda declare he had done to Rajarsi Janakananda, and as the Bible says Elijah did to Elisha. These transferrals of grace, however, diminish in power over successive generations after the death of a great master, unless personal communion with God is maintained as the highest priority. Bhaktivedanta, whatever the merits of his claim to represent a direct line of succession, was born centuries after Chaitanya, though Chaitanya himself was a great master.

Alas, the "Hare Krishna," or ISKCON, movement soon became affected by bigotry, intolerance of others, and a belief that if anything benefited their organization, whatever it might do to others, it was right and good in the eyes of God. This attitude is, unfortunately, a feature of many religious institutions. Bhaktivedanta disciples developed institutional arrogance, viewing their lives for God in terms of profit, prominence, and self-importance. They forgot that their guru's teaching encouraged the virtues of humility and service. Poor Prabhupad! He was a good man, and well-intentioned. So also were many of his followers—though not, unfortunately, those who determined the basic spirit of the movement. His fault was only that his wisdom was lacking in depth. In this deluded world, who can really fault anyone for that? Some of his followers acquired, or came to him with, negative and even anti-social tendencies. Bhaktivedanta himself, however, was a sincere man.

It is a common delusion in religion to believe that rituals and chanting will do all the work, purifying the soul without comparable emphasis on attitude and on inner communion with God. Paramhansa Yogananda used to say that meditation is to religion what experimentation is to science. Without it, results are haphazard and unsatisfactory at best.

I was a part of the "New Age scene" of those days, though I remained on the outskirts of it. Perhaps some people identified me with one setting or another. I sought in all these expressions of God's play the role He wanted me, specifically, to play.

I remember one evening sitting on the stage of a large auditorium with Swami Bhaktivedanta, Alan Ginsberg, and other "leading lights" in the New Age movement. We chanted for, and with, hundreds of young people, while lights played erratically on the walls, floor, and ceiling as well as on the audience, which swayed to a heavy beat of its own that rocked the very walls. This, too, was an expression of God's play—but how many saw it as such? The noise and chaos created a wall around those hundreds of egos.

I remember another evening also, when I and two well-known teachers from India were on a dais before a room full of devotees. The scene was a kind of reenactment of the devotional play between guru and earnest disciples, the latter teasingly asking questions to which the teachers replied, again teasingly, out of their "wisdom." A pleasant spirit of camaraderie pervaded the room. It wasn't the game of "one-upmanship" one so often encounters when different teachers are in a room. Too much of the banter, however, came from an attitude of, "O wise ones, grant us enlightenment!" I was uncomfortable in this role. "This isn't for me!" I thought. "I'm interested in *sharing* with others, not in being looked up to by them!" I was often exposed to this sort of situation, but did all I could to emphasize that the spiritual teacher's role is to serve others, not to be served by them. My great Guru set this example, and was great especially in his self-effacement before the greatness of God.

At one such event I found myself seated on a stage with teachers from various traditions—Hindu, Christian, Jewish, Sufi, Sikh—all of us seated in a row like "crows on a fence" (as I later commented to friends) before a full auditorium. Most of those up there with me displayed only one aim: to be heard. For myself, unless I was asked to speak I remained silent. I felt as much out of it as—to borrow a phrase from the British humorist P.G. Wodehouse—"a cat at a dog show." Finally, seizing a moment when everyone's eyes were closed, I sneaked out to a nearby restaurant, where a good friend, Jay Levin (whom I later gave the name, Prahlad) and I had a good meal. (This was, I learned, his birthday.)

And so went all my attempts at finding a niche:

toward failure and alienation, not toward discovering new peers and new ways to serve God.

A song of mine expressed my feelings at the time:

I've passed my life as a stranger, Lord,
Roamed far in foreign lands:
Far, Lord—far too far!
Only he who knows he's far from home,
Only he, Lord, understands.
Only he who knows he's far from home
Feels the earth, and understands.

Sometimes a stranger did take me in:
Then love I thought was near:
Love, Lord—only a dream!
As the winds upon the desert sand
Whisper hope, then disappear:
As soft winds breathe on the desert sand,
So love sighs, then disappears.

Sometimes a child laughed, and I did pause,
And dreamed of joys at home:
Joys, Lord—only a dream!
For what joy is there without Your smile?
Empty, like the ocean foam!
For what joy is there without Your smile?
You're the sea; all else is foam.

How long must I be a wanderer, Lord?
You know where I belong:
You know, Lord, yes, You know!
Home is where my Lord's sweet presence is:
I've grown tired of strangers' songs.
Home is where my Lord's sweet presence is:
Bless me, that I hear Your songs!

Those were not easy years for me. I had no "spiritual bodyguard," as Master described the company of fellow monks, for protection. "Environment," he used to say, "is stronger than will power." I was stubborn in my discipleship to him, and in my daily meditation, but most of the people I met considered me an unknown quantity. I wanted to reach and help everyone, whether "of" or not "of" the world. I was trying to attune myself to their needs and attitudes, in order to awaken them to their spiritual nature. Outwardly, I appeared more or less like others, dressing as a swami only for special events. Many women, not unnaturally, saw in me their natural "prey." (I remember one attractive lady emerging into the living room of her home from its inner apartment during my visit there. Completely naked, she chased me about the room until I finally managed to make good my escape!)

Women were, however—again, not unnaturally—a temptation for me. Or perhaps I should say that what attracted me in them was their feminine energy. Basically, that energy—kind, compassionate, embracing—is a manifestation of the Divine Mother principle, which is untainted by ego-motive. I was as yet unable, however, to rise above a longing for human love. And I had nowhere to run for protection. The only solution, it seemed to me, was to keep loading the other side of the scales with devotion and with service to God in others.

Master had once told one of my brother monks, "I don't ask you to overcome delusion. All I ask is that you *resist* it."

Inner resistance was, I eventually discovered, a matter of—even mentally—withholding water from the plant. After years of sometimes-despairing effort, I saw the fulfillment of my Guru's promise. By his grace, that energy ceased to hold any appeal for me. Divine love, I realized, is all-sufficient to the heart's needs, and is free, moreover, from egoic limitation. In its human expression, on the other hand, sweetness and compassion can turn just as easily to vicious rage and vindictiveness—like the moods of Mother Nature herself.

The good side during those days, for me, was that yoga was "in," and there were many who wanted to learn it. The competitive aspect hadn't yet entered the picture; there was a spirit of sharing, less of appealing to people's egos, *from* the ego. The hard edge of so much of what passes for yoga nowadays was less in evidence. People seemed relatively open to the deeper and more devotional aspects of this spiritual science.

I remember a lady in Sacramento who enrolled the second time around in my meditation course. "When I took these classes the first time," she confided to me, "I was interested only in the yoga postures. I thought they'd make a good conversation piece for my weekly bridge club! But you know, this stuff's *serious!* I want to learn more about it."

And so, people came for a variety of reasons. More and more, however, they sought guidance in their inner life. Even that exuberant "Lady Godiva," having finally found herself a husband, became a devotee, and sometimes visited Ananda after it was built.

CHAPTER 24

Crystal Clarity

An almost universal denominator of thinking during the 'sixties was a tendency deliberately to cloud one's ideas in a sort of impressionistic haze. This style of self-expression may have derived from Zen *koans*, but it fitted admirably a decades-old practice in the arts. I, by contrast, did my best to make my ideas as simple, clear, and "realistic" as possible.

Yet it wasn't that I subscribed necessarily to realism in the arts. To clarify this apparent anomaly, I should explain that whereas I like impressionism in art, if it is good, I also like realism, if it is good. I am not, however, in favor of *pointless* realism or *pointless* impressionism. A brick building, to take an example, is something with which all of us are familiar. What point is there in painting it just as it is? When it comes to philosophy, however, and even more so to mystical truths, the subject is known to few people. To be as simple, clear, and "realistic" as possible is, in this case, a virtue, assuming it can even be managed. To cloud the subject deliberately merely renders it opaque.

Paramhansa Yogananda did something no one before him, to my knowledge, has ever done, in describing with extraordinary lucidity the state of cosmic consciousness. His poem "Samadhi," especially, is a masterpiece in spiritual literature. Not for him the vague, "mind-blowing" mysticism of Western legend, as in the apocryphal story of the Himalayan sage who told a Western seeker, "Life, my son, is a rainbow." (To that remark, in the story, the seeker exclaims, "You mean, I've come all this distance, braved steep mountains, snow, ice, and driving rains only to find that life is nothing but a stupid rainbow?" The "sage" replied anxiously, "Y-y-you mean, it *isn't* a rainbow?")

Art, too, ought to convey some kind of interaction, I believe, between the person seeing and the thing seen: some impression the brick building has made upon him; some hope, or even sadness, he may have felt in looking at it. In this way a painting, though two-dimensional, can add not only the illusion of having a third dimension, but can produce an *actual* third dimension—of consciousness. How well the impression is conveyed demonstrates the artist's skill. How spiritually *valid* that impression is demonstrates his wisdom. His depth of wisdom determines also his greatness, or his shallowness, as an artist. Even sadness, though usually a negative state, may suggest aspiration toward higher things and be, therefore, spiritually valid. Spiritual validity is what lifts a person toward Self-realization, instead of depressing him and increasing the hold delusion has on his mind.

Ultimately, the criterion of clarity must be determined by one's *feelings,* and not only by the intellect.

If an allegory is wholly literal, like an algebraic equation, it may please the intellect but will hardly satisfy the heart. What satisfies the viewer of a work of art is, above all, that which awakens in him a sense of intuitive soul-recognition.

The clearer the intuition, the clearer the heart's feeling. And the clearer the feeling, the more strongly it resonates with inspirations of wisdom. The intellect alone, lacking intuition, can never achieve true wisdom. For if reasoning begins with a wrong premise and one lacks sufficient clarity of heart to *feel* that it is wrong, he may devote his life to following a false trail, as modern philosophers have done who devoted their lives to "proving" that life is without meaning. The world, unfortunately, contains many intelligent idiots.

What I sought, during the chaotic 'sixties, was intuitive clarity. Many people, I realized, were seeking intuition but not clarity. For me, clarity would come not as a result of laboriously thinking, thinking a thing through to a logical conclusion, but of attuning myself to my Guru, from whose deep, intuitive wisdom flowed ever-fresh revelation. Most of the people with whom I came in contact, because of their lack of clarity, decided it was simplest merely to claim insight, then clothe their utterances in abstract verbiage to stun others to silence.

"Life is a rainbow."

"Oh, wow! that's *heavy,* man!" (What did it matter if it meant anything?)

The Zen teachers in Japan had honed to a fine art the technique of clothing deep insights in enigmatic declarations, penetrable only with the keen blade of developed intuition. Yogananda used this technique, also. For example, if he saw that a piece of advice wasn't getting through to a disciple, he might deliberately make some utterly implausible statement with the only purpose of cutting through that person's rational defenses. In the ensuing stillness of mind, an opening appeared through which wise counsel could then penetrate.

The goal in this kind of teaching is to quiet the reason and open the mind to intuitive insight. The important ingredient here, however, is intuitive insight itself. Unless the teacher has such insight to convey, silently even, the disciple will receive nothing. If he mistakes vagueness for wisdom, he may be impressed, but he will not be enlightened.

There was a lot of muddy thinking going on in the 'sixties. Indeed, lack of clarity was a thread running through the whole tapestry of the Twentieth Century. It manifested itself as pretension in art, in literature, in philosophy, even in religious teaching. I thanked God for the blessing of a true master—not only for his simple, direct, and deeply insightful words, but for the attunement with his consciousness that I found myself developing, helping me to penetrate the dense ideational fogs around me with the searchlight of clarity.

Years later I gave our Ananda publishing house the name, "Crystal Clarity, Publishers." Clarity seems simple and obvious enough once it is achieved. Achieving it, however, can be a challenge. Many people undervalue it. And few there are who achieve it.

I had no interest in "blowing people's minds," as the expression was in those days. Many people, perhaps for that very reason, accepted with a shrug what I said in lectures and in songs. They wanted something "deep"—that is to say, incomprehensible.

Such woolly-mindedness was rampant among those who dreamed of starting "New Age" communities. Somehow they thought the only thing necessary was a parcel of land, and bands of pot-smoking hippies floating on waves of "love" and wishful dreams. Apart from their lack of clarity, they had no devotion to God, nor dedication to a down-to-earth spiritual life.

For myself, I had been pondering how to create a successful community since I was a boy. I, too, had left God out of my reckoning at first. It was on meeting Paramhansa Yogananda that I discovered the right direction for my dream. God had been the missing ingredient.

There is an allegory from the life of Krishna. Once, when he was a baby, his foster mother Yasoda wanted to tie him to a bedpost so she could be free to get on with her chores. The string was too short, so she fetched another and tied it to the first. Still it was too short! She added more string. No matter how long the string, it remained too short for the job.

At last she understood what she'd been doing. No one can bind the Infinite! Most people try to do so, with dogmas and definitions of truth. They conduct their activities without a thought for God, the Sole Doer. Yasoda, recognizing her error, folded her hands and prayed to the Supreme One in that tiny form,

"Please, dearest Lord, permit me to tie you!" At last she was able to do so.

Communities were being attempted throughout America during the 'sixties. Most of them failed—mainly, I believe, because of that "missing ingredient": God.

One thing that devotion to God accomplishes is that it opens the heart to love. It also opens the mind to wisdom. People's worst problem is that they enclose themselves in little boxes of self-will. Most "New Age" thinking concerned itself with creating newly "packaged" ego-games. I wrote a song to address this tendency. (Not a misty reference in it to rainbows!)

I had a little box when my Lord made me,
And in that little box I did put a tree—
A pony, a teddy bear, a bright green sled:
Everything around me that my eyes did see.

How can a little box ever hold a sled,
A pony, and a tree—puzzles your poor head?
It can't, of course! But in a tiny baby's mind
The mighty world becomes a little box, instead!

Well, as I grew older my box grew, too:
Held airplanes and ships and a birch canoe,
And schoolbooks, a foreign trip, and college proms,
Good times, and friends aplenty—yes, and also You!

But somehow in this box would only fit one school,
One family, one country, and one social rule:

And certainly one church, for only my way's
right,
And anyone with other ways is just a fool!

Well, so I used to think, but now I must confess
At judging fools I wasn't any great success!
Truth somehow lived without me, though I called
it mine:
What box could hold the world? It's just—
preposter-ess!

Even my father enjoyed this song!

The important thing is to remain open to the truth, whatever it be. Of special importance to openness are humility and a lack of pretense (especially toward oneself).

One of my favorite compliments, though possibly it was meant differently, was one I received at the Zen temple in San Francisco. This was years after the founding of Ananda, following a ceremony to install Richard Baker as the new *roshi,* or head priest, of the temple. Richard—Dick, I called him—was a friend of mine and was, in fact, as you'll see in the next chapter, the person through whom I acquired the first land at Ananda. The present concerns a conversation I had with a young woman outside. We'd been talking several minutes when she asked me my name. I told her.

"Kriyananda!" she cried in astonishment. "But—you're famous!"

"Well, maybe," I replied. "But why the 'but'?"

"Why, all the famous people I've known seem important!"

I hoped she meant "*self*-important."

Buddhists claim not to believe in God. Generally, however, they do believe in openness, and humility, and compassion. With these attitudes, whatever God there be must surely be pleased, as He is with sincere devotion (I think even more so with devotion, however, since love for Him sublimates the ego altogether). The important thing, for the seeker, is that his or her *attitude* be right.

I once visited the Zen center on Page Street, in San Francisco. The sincerity of the residents was obvious. True, they lacked that ingredient of faith in God, but they were sincerely committed to an ancient truth, and I could see that, as a group, they were thriving.

I was astonished, however, to see them all so solemn. Why, I wondered? Could it be due to their concentration on *"hara,"* as that center in the body is known, located in or near one of the lower chakras? Such a downward direction of concentration would naturally have a depressing effect on a person's consciousness. To Zen students, yoga practice, with its primary focus on the upper chakras, separates one from the "concrete" realities of life. Attunement with the lighter aspects of truth, however, gives power over even the concrete ones. For matter is itself only a condensation of light and energy.

Love is the first ingredient in a community's success. Can there be spiritual love, however, without joy? Without both love and joy, surely judgment and intolerance must enter the scene, sooner or later. Judgment, whether of others or oneself, is discouraging, and keeps one from rising in inner freedom.

Dick Baker explained to me the Zen approach to action. He said one shouldn't do anything until one has mentally perfected what one intends to do. I disagreed with him. Perfection is achieved first in the mind, true, but it requires doing one's best, also, with the tools at hand, and thereby clarifying one's understanding.

A foremost disciple of Yogananda, Yogacharya Oliver Black in Michigan, would occasionally voice criticism of Ananda for its shoe-string life-style—a valid comment, during our "tepee city" beginnings. "Do they have to live in poverty?" he asked. He himself was a rich man; I was not. At Ananda, we did what we could, then determinedly kept growing from there. Yogacharya Oliver, on the other hand, never succeeded in creating a community, though he tried. A few months before his death he wrote, complimenting me on Ananda's success. He then asked my advice on how to create a community himself. By this time he was in his nineties. I admired him for still dreaming, but what chance had he, at that late stage in his life, to fulfill his dream?

To return to Buddhism, I have met joyful Buddhist monks. They expressed love, also. I think their belief in a higher consciousness must at least resemble another person's belief in God. For in their belief system they open themselves to higher guidance, and to the infinite wisdom and love that are associated with God. I still say, however, as Brother Bhaktananda (a fellow disciple) has declared: "Devotion is the *only* thing."

Today, humanity is trying to redefine a universe

stripped by science of all traditional definitions. It is a time when people need a bridge to new ways of thinking and looking at things. People in the "New Age" movements have perceived this need intuitively. They err only in imagining they can *create* a New Age. The truth is, whether people like it or not, we *already are* in a new age! If nothing else, we've been pushed into it by science. The fundamentals of a new age lie in the very discovery by physics that matter is not the solid substance it was once imagined to be: It is energy.

Swami Sri Yukteswar, Yogananda's guru, explained that this insight has come because new waves of spiritual energy are entering the earth's atmosphere at this time from the cosmos, and making people more sensitively aware of higher levels of consciousness, and of subtler levels of reality. There occur cyclically, Sri Yukteswar said, vast movements within the galaxy that affect human enlightenment. Our planet is on the rise, now, toward a higher state of awareness.

This book is not the place for a discussion of this teaching. I've treated the subject at some length in other books. A brief treatment of it is contained also in *Autobiography of a Yogi.* The point here is that the human will is incapable of *creating* a new age. A truth, as Yogananda said, can only be perceived. The essence of the new age, which we've already entered, is a greater awareness of energy as the underlying reality of the material world. This awareness of energy affects every aspect of our lives. It will produce greater flexibility of thought, and ever-greater clarity. Rigid definitions, whether in religion, morality, art, or even the standards of social comportment are being undermined. They will not, however, be destroyed. What people need is to *experience* values of all kinds in a new way. The vagueness of hippie and "New Age" thinking in general was only a premonition of another, much greater clarity to come.

I myself sought clarity, not refuge in beguiling vagueness. One result of my commitment to clarity was an invitation by a Christian radio station, KFAX, in San Francisco, to give a half-hour show weekly in order (as the station manager put it) to attract the younger generation, many of whom were no longer listening to their programs. The show continued for more than five years. Not long after my first radio show in San Francisco, I also began one in Sacramento. Later, another radio station scheduled me in Pasadena. At this time, I was forced to sacrifice all three programs to concentrate on Ananda.

In search of clarity of another kind, I used also to travel south to Ben Lomond, near Santa Cruz, California, where a group called Bridge Mountain held programs that were slanted differently from what I was accustomed to. They involved students rather than only lecturing to them. I was intrigued, and wanted to draw from what they did any benefits I could for my own teaching.

Thus, another world opened to me: the self-help or "self-actualization" movement. Students in the classes would make surrealistic drawings supposed to express their inner fears, anxieties, and motivations. I had no fears that I was aware of, but the leaders claimed that everyone harbors such psychological complexes.

I remember telling a member of the staff, Pat Kutzner—who for a time was my secretary, after Bridge Mountain closed—that I'd never known my parents to have a falling out. "That can only mean," she replied dismissively, "that one of them is suppressing a lot of frustration!" Well, I'd seen no evidence that this was so. Nor had anyone I'd ever known. My father's droll explanation for the harmony between them was to say, "When my wife and I were first married, I told her I would make all the important decisions in our marriage. Since then," he concluded with a grin, "there haven't been any important decisions to make!" None so important, anyway, as to come between them.

I went along with what was taught at Bridge Mountain, however, because it seemed a good place to learn an aspect of what was in vogue those days.

That was also the time of "Primal Scream" therapy, and other methods of venting suppressed frustrations: "letting it all hang out," as the expression was, that people might regain the uncomplicated freedom of their primordial nature. One of these methods was to scream like a demented animal. Those were also the days when people met for "honest confrontation." They'd pair off, face each other, and announce "honestly" just what bothered them about one another. It was all meant to relieve them of inner tensions. What it really did, of course, was *induce* tension. I never saw people purged of animosity by these treatments.

At Bridge Mountain we threw wads of mud at a board to vent our anger, thereby, supposedly, releasing it from the subconscious. I tried to join in the fun, though in fact I couldn't think of anything to vent, not even anger against SRF. It seemed to me this approach was all wrong. I wanted, however, to learn what people were thinking and doing to improve themselves. The leaders at Bridge Mountain made kindly excuses for me. No doubt, they seemed to feel, I'd dig up something from my subconscious eventually, and discover the boiling cauldron I'd been suppressing. For my part, I thought I might learn a few ideas for conducting classes involving students instead of only lecturing to them. Eventually, I realized that in fact I was involving them already, in a subtler way. What I did, and still do, was tune in to them spiritually, and commune in my spirit with their spirits. People have often come to me after a lecture and thanked me for clarifying a problem they've been having. I've never discouraged others, however, from seeking ways to involve students in the learning process. Basically, Bridge Mountain's idea in doing so seemed good to me, even though I still consider the emphasis on releasing subconscious repressions a mistake, generally speaking. All it does, according to my observation, is *affirm* one's own negative tendencies.

In 1966 another opportunity came my way. I was invited to teach a cultural program for the Peace Corps. A hundred young men were to go to India; they needed preparation for the experience. I was delighted at the thought of helping them to become cultural ambassadors. I myself had long contemplated the need for such a program.

Alas, the young men themselves were mostly interested in weekend binges at the local bars. India, to them, held the prospect only of being a rousing adventure. After some time, they complained that what they wanted from the cultural program was information on such efficient matters as five-year plans—information they would find of minimal use in the Indian villages. Since this was their desire, however, I scouted around for people who could give them what they wanted. It was not easy for me, for I'd put my heart into helping them to become cultural bridges. I let them know, however, that if any of them wanted what I had sought to share, they could come to my room after hours and we'd chat together. Gratifyingly, about twenty-five of them came regularly. I heard from some of them, later, that those gatherings had helped them really to appreciate their Indian assignment.

An advantage accrued to me from this assignment: The pay was good. All of it went toward the work I was slowly developing. First, I printed books to make what I was attempting better known. Then I bought land for Ananda.

The books I published first were a small book of aphorisms, *Yours—the Universe!*, and *Yoga Postures for Self-Awareness.* I also printed a small booklet, mostly as a means of earning money for Ananda, *The Book of Bhrigu,* which I'd written years earlier.

As it turned out, Ananda's time was rapidly approaching.

CHAPTER 25

Land Ahoy!

It was January 1967, when I first heard of Richard Baker. Soon thereafter, by an interesting coincidence, I also met him.

I heard of him from Jeannie Campbell, the receptionist and general secretary for the print shop where my first three books were printed. I had lively discussions with Jeannie, a dedicated Zen Buddhist, on the differences between Zen and yoga. She also gave me a running description of developments at Tassajara, a retreat being built by the Zen temple of San Francisco in the mountains near Carmel, California. During one conversation, I told her of my wish to find land for a retreat of my own.

"Say," she cried, "why don't you contact Dick Baker? He's the president of the Zen Center here in San Francisco, and is in charge of building Tassajara. If anyone would know about available land, he would."

I dutifully jotted down his name, but delayed trying to reach him. I suspected that this lead, like so many others before it, would lead nowhere. My latest failure in that respect had been a recent trip to Missouri. A visitor had come one day to my apartment to tell me about a college campus she'd seen advertised in her home state: "A hundred and ten acres," she said excitedly, "with several large buildings, and all that for only ten thousand dollars!" It seemed fabulous indeed. In fact, as things turned out, it *was* too good to be true.

From Kansas City this friend drove me to the little college town where the property was located. It was, as she'd said, beautiful. It was only ten acres, however, not a hundred and ten, and selling for a hundred and ten thousand dollars, not a mere ten thousand. A bargain nevertheless, but a great deal more than I could afford to pay. Considering in addition its distance from San Francisco, where I'd built my little base of operations, it was, as far as I was concerned, indeed a "utopia" (the ancient Greek word for "nowhere").

A week or so after that suggestion of Jeannie's, however, I visited a small picture-framing shop in North Beach with four paintings of mine that I wanted to hang. I was obliged to wait while another customer was served. This man was speaking to the proprietor about a parcel of land he and several friends were thinking of buying as a place for retreat. Unable to resist this entree, I said that I, too, was looking for something similar. At this point, during a still-casual conversation, the visitor produced a map of the proposed property and spread it out on a table. "I'm still looking for a few people to buy into the property with me," he said, "provided their ideals are harmonious with my own."

Had this looked like a common real estate deal, I

might not have been so interested, but this one definitely seemed worth investigating. "What is your name?" I inquired.

"Dick Baker."

The very person Jeannie had said I should look up! Evidently he and the shopkeeper were friends. The property was one of several that had been offered to the Zen Center as an alternative to Tassajara, in case that land proved too expensive for them. Partly to check out alternatives, and partly because he also wanted a place of retreat for himself and his family, Dick Baker had inspected all the proposed properties. Of them all, his favorite was this tract. It consisted of 172 acres, and was located in the foothills of the Sierra Nevada Mountains, near Nevada City, California. It had been offered for only $250 an acre: inexpensive for California, and in fact only half the normal price of land even in this remote area. Dick had figured he could swing the deal if he could find six others to go in on it with him, dividing the land into twenty-four-acre parcels. He said he planned to visit there in the early spring, and would be glad to have me come along.

In late March or early April, I joined a group of them: Dick Baker, Allen Ginsberg and Gary Snyder (both of them well-known "beat" poets), Richard Wirtheimer (an attorney), and a young woman who'd been assigned to write an article on Allen Ginsberg for *The New Yorker* magazine.

We stopped at Nevada City for lunch, where we ate at the kind of place one sometimes hears described as a "greasy spoon" restaurant—the sort that, during the nineteen-forties, used to advertise "booths for ladies." Although the only vegetarian in the group, I made out somehow. Lunch finished, we drove the twenty-something miles north to see the property.

The drive took us well into the countryside. The last three miles were dirt road, some of which had been scoured by hydraulic mining and looked like a moonscape. The last quarter mile was the "driveway" entrance to the property. Deeply rutted—some of the ruts more than a foot deep—from the rains and snows of many winters, it was impossible to drive any further. We parked and walked.

The altitude at the top was 3,000 feet. The air was fresh. The property was wooded, gently rolling, and serene, giving onto views of distant, snow-capped Sierra mountains. I went off by myself to "feel" the land. The impression came to me strongly that the particular portion I was walking had been blessed already by our Gurus. It had an eastern exposure, especially attractive to me as a yogi. As the latecomer to the group, however, I would be the last in line to choose. Fortunately, the others all felt drawn to the western part of the land. My selection had the views.

I ended up getting three "lots" in all, in the section I'd felt guided to buy. Gary Snyder bought a fourth lot; Allen Ginsberg, a fifth; Dick Baker, the sixth. Each one had just the piece he wanted. Changes occurred later in the arrangements, but I kept my parcel, which I paid for in April. I planned to begin construction that summer and autumn, with the help of a few friends.

In May 1967, I had an interesting experience. I'd

been teaching a series of classes in Rancho Cordova, a suburb of Sacramento. Three of the students invited me to a dinner at one of their homes. They also invited a friend of theirs, Ann Armstrong, whom they introduced to me as a well-known psychic, and said that she'd done amazingly accurate readings for each of them. I sang one or two of my songs after dinner, following which there was a lively discussion on various topics, mostly concerning what I'd been teaching. Ann Armstrong invited me afterward to her home on Norris Street, in Sacramento, where she and her husband, Jim, lived. The Armstrongs were the owners of Beers Books in the heart of the city, the main—perhaps the only—metaphysical book store in Sacramento. Shortly after my arrival, Ann asked if I would like her to do a reading for me. Considering it a harmless way of passing the time, I accepted with pleasure.

We entered her interview room and sat facing each other. She took each of my hands in one of hers, and closed her eyes. Instantly, both of us went into a superconscious state. I could hardly move. Ann spoke slowly into a tape recorder.

"As I took your hands," she said, "I suddenly felt your soul. It's a deep soul, a wonderful soul. God has blessed you in many ways. He has given you a beautiful voice, and fingers able to bring out lovely music from a musical instrument; a clear understanding; inspiration. You have much to give.

"The time has come, now, for you to take the next step in your life. There is much you have accomplished, but it is time for you to establish a center, where you can bring to a focus what you've accomplished so far, that you may move on to the next phase. All the doors are open before you. The ground has been prepared. It's as though this next phase is just waiting to receive you.

"And yet . . . and yet . . . I sense an obstacle. I sense hesitation on your part. Now, why? . . . The word I sense is 'pride.' It's as if you're afraid of developing pride if you take on this new responsibility. You want so much to be humble, and you're afraid of losing your humility. But you *are* humble. In trying to preserve your humility, you reject faith in your ability to serve more completely. It's as though you were poised, now, between two alternatives, asking yourself, 'In what ways ought I to be humble, and in what ways, proud?'

"I see you as this little child. It's a beautiful child. But you see, within this child there is also majesty. I see you bowing in your mind before the great ones, and of course it's good that you should do so. But see you not that you, too, are a great one? You need to understand that pride, too, has a place in your life—not pride in yourself, but in your victories. You need to claim them as your own. For they are rightfully yours.

"I see you in robes of majesty. But you will not be able to grow further if you reject what is your own. By rejecting it, you obstruct your further development. You must be proud: not for yourself, but in the greatness that God has given you. You must accept it. Only then will He be able to bless you with more.

"It is time now for you to put down roots. It is time

for you to establish a center. I feel that this land you've acquired is right for you at this time. Your fear is that it may limit you, that it may hold you back, but you need at this time to establish a plateau for the further work you have to do."

After more along the same vein, she asked if I had any questions. I inquired about SRF, and about Tara.

"Yes, I sense obstruction there. It's as if they're jealous of you. [speaking of Tara:] You see, when she's confronted by someone as open as you are, it bothers her. It makes her insecure."

There was much more, but the essence of it was as I've written. I found what she'd said most interesting both in practical and in metaphysical ways. On the one hand, she was perfectly right: I did have difficulty in understanding in what ways I should be humble, and in what ways I should feel secure in what I'd been given. Humility is a virtue, as we all know. Negative self-affirmation, however, is not humility, and can obstruct achievement. My tendency had always been to belittle the very things people most appreciated in me, in an effort not to claim credit for them personally. Master himself had sometimes scolded me for this tendency. For not only is it a common tendency for people to take others at their own self-evaluation, but self-belittlement can also prevent further accomplishment. As Master once said to me, "There should be neither superiority nor inferiority complex."

All my life, since meeting him, I have reflected on the things he said and did, and have gained wonderful insights in the process. Now, I recalled a story he'd told from his younger days in Ranchi, India. He had commissioned a well-known artist to paint a portrait of his param-guru, Lahiri Mahasaya. Unfortunately, the outcome was not satisfying to him.

"How long did it take you to master your art?" he asked the artist. Ever seeking to help people to grow spiritually, he wanted to help this man achieve deeper levels, artistically.

"Twenty years," replied the man.

"Twenty years, to convince yourself you could paint?" Master marveled.

This reply, given to an artist of established reputation by someone the older man had every right to consider a mere boy, seemed impertinent. "I'd like to see you paint as well in *twice* that length of time!" he retorted angrily.

"Give me a week," the Master replied. The other, considering this simply an insult, left in a huff. Within a week, however, the Master succeeded in painting a better portrait than his own. The artist was invited, and, on beholding it, had to acknowledge that it was an improvement.

This story seemed to me worth pondering in the present context. My own way of doing things had been almost the opposite of what Master had advised. "The only thing I want," I told myself, "is God. Nothing else matters." This would be a good attitude, no doubt, if my duty in this life were only to be a hermit. Master, however, had told me repeatedly I had "a great work" to do. Was it right in this case to retreat bashfully from success in that role? Success and failure didn't matter to me, but surely I must do conscientiously whatever life gave me to do.

Ann was saying I should be proud of my accomplishments. She'd made it clear that she didn't mean I should be proud *of myself,* but only that I should accept what I'd done as having merit, and not deny or reject its value. There was much truth in what she'd said. My very inclination to dismiss her advice was, to me, an indication that I should ponder it deeply. Pride, for example: It was true I'd undercut my own achievements by belittling them. Moreover—strange irony!—some people had seen in that very effort an indication of pride. Yet I knew also that I was right in not giving them much importance.

Was it, I asked myself, self-confidence that made people successful? Or did self-confidence only come as a result of success? If it came as a result, it was fragile and temporary and could evaporate after any serious set-back. Confidence in the true Self, however, depended on nothing outward, and could remain rock firm. On the other hand, if even confidence based on outward success was necessary for achieving further success, then perhaps I needed more of it in order to serve God more effectively, according to what my Guru had said he expected of me.

Certain things he had told me made me wonder if I was missing some important insight. He had tried, on more than one occasion, to get me to take my role more seriously. Sometimes he even scolded me for not fully accepting it. On the other hand, he had complimented me on my humility. One time he had told me with firm conviction, "You will *never* fall due to ego." How, I often asked myself, can I remain humble if I accept anything I do as important? I was convinced that nothing I could do—nothing any human being can do—really matters. This whole world is a delusion. What are we, in the greater scheme of things? Certainly I felt more comfortable with the thought that nothing, including myself, has any importance at all.

This self-interrogation lasted for years, and proved both an aid and an obstruction in the development of Ananda. For our members, especially our ministers, have naturally absorbed their attitudes of discipleship from me. On the one hand, the humility they display is beautiful. There always has been, as well, a tendency at Ananda not to thrust its accomplishments upon the public's attention. As a result, obvious opportunities for reaching people have been overlooked. Sometimes I think that Ananda is one of the best-kept secrets around.

I once hosted a dinner at a restaurant for several well-known public figures. This was in the late 1970s or early '80s. I'd been invited, with others, to participate in a gathering to discuss intentional communities. I was the only one that evening who represented an actual, functioning community. Most of the others were well-known, but not specifically in that field. Paolo Soleri hoped to get a community started based on his architectural concepts. Paul Solomon had convened the gathering to present his own plans for creating a community. Peter Caddy was the co-founder of Findhorn, but had established it as a training center, not as a community; moreover, he no longer lived there. Barbara Marx Hubbard was an enthusiast on the subject, but hadn't actually built anything. The general attitude toward me, rather to my surprise, seemed to be, "Well, so, what have *you* got to share?" I was included only marginally in their "important" conversation. I remember that occasion not with indignation, but as the reminder it gave me of the far greater importance of humility. I enjoyed the evening. A question dangled before me, however: Was my willingness to accept their lack of interest in my accomplishments a sign that I was not conscious enough of the importance of what I represented?

For myself, I felt fine about it, but I wondered whether, in God's eyes, my indifference didn't contain a hint of irresponsibility. For I believed intensely in the importance of Paramhansa Yogananda's mission, his teachings, his communitarian ideals, his very place in history. I was afraid only of pushing myself forward as an instrument of his mission. Tara's scathing condemnation of me had unquestionably influenced my thinking in these matters. I sensed, on the other hand, that her words were projections of her own swelling ego. Still, I asked myself, was it not an exaggerated consciousness of self that made me even seek obscurity? How subtle, and innumerable, are the traps the ego can set for us!

Gradually, over years, I resolved this dilemma to my own satisfaction. Ann had been responding to certain questions in my own mind, and had, I believe, perceived some of the answer. I realized in time that I'd been obstructing the flow of inspiration by my tendency to belittle myself. Instead, I should simply accept inspiration gratefully, without referring it back, even in denial, to myself as the instrument for it.

To accept confidently what flowed through me—sharing it mentally, however, with God—was not ego-involvement. Master had told me repeatedly, "You have a great work to do." Rajarsi had said also, "Master has a great work to do through you, Walter. And he will give you the strength to do it." More and more I realized that it was, indeed, from higher inspiration that I received my answers and solutions, often in the small details of my life. It was not necessary for me to deny my accomplishments. They *were* valid. The truth was simply that they weren't my own. The more I removed myself from the scene, the more I found that I could succeed at whatever I attempted. The test was not to care how other people perceived it; not to mind if they misunderstood; not to crave acceptance by anyone. I found God's glory more enticing, more satisfying, more powerful than anything human. Even if no one accepted what He gave me, the loss was theirs, not His! And certainly not mine.

In my Guru's guidance and grace I could be proud indeed—proud not in an egoic, but in a divine way. It was, I realized, this awareness that he had always sought to cultivate in me.

In this thought, however, the word, pride, remains unsatisfactory to me. It has its place, but it is also a word that can be distorted unless its true meaning is constantly clarified. Why not another word: *delight*?

Delight can apply also to a hermit's life. The more unity we bring to our vision of life, and the more we can broaden our understanding to embrace apparent differences, the deeper, surely, will be our wisdom.

Whether we serve God outwardly in some way, or inwardly in meditation, we still serve Him by offering our thoughts and energy into His river of love. Pride conveys a suggestion of responsibility for the preservation of an image, or position. But whose responsibility is all this, anyway? God's, surely, not our own.

What I've come to feel is, rather, the sheer delight of serving Him in any way that He wants. There is the same divine joy in gazing at a flower as in writing deep spiritual commentaries. Both are matters of self-giving.

The thought of a hermit's life as being passive would be unacceptable to any true hermit. It is a life of mutual rejoicing with and in God. Thus, God could give me no greater work than to share whatever I have to give—with Him, above all, and secondly with Him through others who long to escape the pain of spiritual ignorance.

CHAPTER 26

Domes and Self-Expansion

Our first need was for water. I didn't want a repetition of the story of the city of Fatehpur Sikri near Agra, India, constructed before anyone checked to see whether water was available. (There wasn't any, and the city had to be abandoned!) Herb Radel, a local water diviner from Nevada City, was recommended. He found a stream underneath the property, and correctly estimated how much water it would supply. Soon we had a well and a water tower.

Our next need was for buildings. In 1961 in India, for what came to be known deprecatingly in SRF as my "Delhi project," I'd meditated and sought inspiration for the best shape for a temple. A building's shape exerts a subtle influence on people's minds. Square or rectangular buildings, which nowadays are still the norm, seemed to me to box in thought and inspiration. Flat ceilings seemed to press down on the head and oppose expansion of the spirit. The energy emitted from the human head, round on the top, seemed reflected unevenly from the usual ceiling. Rounded ceilings, which correspond to the shape of the head, seemed to reflect energy back harmoniously.

Pyramidal shapes, considered from the standpoint of energy, draw the mind upward and help to give it focus, increasing its power. Years later, I was fascinated to learn that razor blades retain their sharpness longer if they are kept in pyramidal containers. Much information has come out more recently on the energizing influence of pyramids. When I visited Egypt and meditated in the pyramids, I vividly sensed their spiritual power.

It seemed to me, however, that for meditation the ideal form is the dome. I'd seen domed cathedrals, but always their domes were high up, as if to suggest heaven, not the sky of our earth. Their very loftiness implied a future beatitude and peace far removed from the sweat and strain of earth life. A dome would be ideal, I thought, if it came down on all sides, like the sky, to eye level.

In San Francisco, years after my "Delhi project," I visited the Morrison planetarium in Golden Gate Park. While waiting for the show to begin I was happily enjoying the peaceful atmosphere, when suddenly a group of about thirty school children rushed in and arranged themselves in the seats all around me, squirming and giggling. I was entertaining thoughts of moving when I noticed that the children, one by one, stopped squirming and were becoming silent. It seemed to me indeed that the shape of the dome was inducing their stillness. I was glad to remain where I was.

As a further comment on the influence of the shapes of buildings, during my months in Arizona a friend recommended a book to me by Joseph Epes

Brown which described the philosophy and world-view of the Sioux Indians. I was amazed to see how closely their view corresponded to the cosmic vision of the ancient seers of India. I was struck also by the emphasis the Sioux placed on living in harmony with the world around them. This emphasis stood in marked contrast to their reputedly warlike nature. Yet in fact, by defending their land against foreign invasion they were acting in accordance with teachings in the Indian scriptures, also. The Bhagavad Gita says that it is righteous to fight in self-defense.

The Sioux built tepees to correspond with the round horizon. The steep height of their tepees had something of the soaring quality of the Egyptian pyramids. And the openings faced east whence, they claimed, "all good things come." How similar this idea, too, to the teaching of yogis that one should meditate facing east to harmonize oneself with earth-circling energies of spiritual awakening and wisdom.

The Navajo Indians also built rounded dwellings, called "hogans." The entrance of a hogan, too, was placed eastward, and for the same reason. The hogan is squat-shaped, rather than dome-like, as if expressing satisfaction with the earth rather than upward aspiration and expansion. If the Sioux were as warlike as one reads, it is certain the Navajos were peace-loving. Could the shapes of these dwellings have had any relation to their attitudes?

Aspiration and self-expansion are important attitudes in meditation, in addition to peace and harmony. For all of these reasons, the dome shape seemed to me ideal especially for a temple. I had wanted a temple in such a form for my Delhi project. Now, I hoped to repeat the concept at Ananda. Most of our first buildings were domes. Years later we were able to build a true dome at Ananda Assisi, in Italy. This beautiful structure, "the Temple of Light," has become well known in a land where people resonate with artistic expression. Perhaps domes will become acceptable in America someday also. They are suitable especially for temples, though I can see homes, too, constructed in that shape. The obvious difficulty with a dome residence is that furniture, as we know it today, is built to accommodate straight walls and rectangles. Joseph Epes Brown said, however, that the Sioux believed evil spirits gather in corners. This is, I imagine, a metaphorical way of saying that corners create an inharmonious vibration.

Everything one does reflects one's philosophy of life. Buildings, too, ought to be expressions of a conscious philosophy. The more uplifting the philosophy, the more attention should be given to the forms that express it. On this point I disagree with Frank Lloyd Wright, who said a building should reflect its environment. A mindless relationship isn't enough. A building should also express the relationship of *people* to their environment, and the energy they *project* outward to it. Wright's concept seems to me limited by its emphasis on abstract considerations—a sort of "art for art's sake" attitude that doesn't take into account the part played by human consciousness in every act of creation. I'm told, in fact, that his homes aren't even comfortable to live in.

I remembered how often Yogananda quoted the

suggestion made to him by an architect: "Immortalize your teachings in architecture." The Master agreed with him. A spiritual teaching ought to be clothed in a form that expresses the consciousness it seeks to inspire. Yogananda had designed gold-leafed lotus towers, which may be more attractive on the outside than most domes—though Ananda's dome in Italy is a notable exception—and are ideal shapes for enclosing an inner dome.

This, then, was what I had envisioned in India: A dome enclosed within the lotus shape designed by Yogananda. During Ananda's beginning, of course, I was forced to be cost-conscious (as, naturally, I'd have been also in India, once I faced the problems of actual construction). I still hope that Ananda will someday be able to test the idea of a gold-leafed lotus temple, based on our Guru's original concept, along with my idea for a dome on the inside. Whether a lotus would be too imposing over a large dome, however, is a question to be considered carefully when the time comes to consider this idea seriously. Meanwhile, the Ananda temple in Italy expresses much of this concept, and very beautifully, with its transparent cupola on the top shaped in the form of a closed lotus. It is especially lovely when the cupola is lit from inside.

The first domes I put up at Ananda were, I admit, a very awkward first step in this direction. At least, however, they *were* a step.

For me, the dome symbolizes above all what I deeply appreciate in the teachings of my Guru: their universality. When certain of the nuns at Mt. Washington tried to persuade Rajarsi Janakananda, SRF's second president after Yogananda, that the Master had wanted his organization established along more sectarian lines, Rajarsi replied with a hint of distress—the only such hint that I ever heard from him—"But what I've always loved about his teachings is their universality! I've liked the way he embraced all religions as one in God." The nuns, however, insisted that Master had decided at the end of his life to change all that. Rajarsi, perhaps realizing how things would go anyway, evidently decided to give harmony among the disciples top priority. Therefore, he said nothing further. I was present on that occasion, however, and felt that the nuns had taken something that I knew Master had actually said, but had gone beyond his intentions. What they insisted on reflected, rather, a personal bias.

Master often made the statement: "SRF is not a sect." Tara quoted his statement to me once during a conversation, then remarked dismissively, "Well, we *are* a sect!"

When Master named his church a "Church of All Religions," he did not mean to endorse eclecticism. Rather, his wish was to stress the oneness of truth, based on the universal ideal of Self-realization in God. Unfortunately, that name was dropped in time, as sectarianism became increasingly emphasized.

Paramhansa Yogananda once told Dr. Lewis, his first Kriya Yoga disciple in America, "Remember, Doctor, no matter what you or I do, this work will follow a certain pattern, ordained by God." He must have been referring to mass karma. Master himself, in letters to Rajarsi, had expressed dissatisfaction with the way things were going. In one letter he questioned whether it wouldn't be better simply to raze the organization and start over. "Of course," he ended, "it's too late for that now." In another letter he wrote, "They will have to go their way, and I will go mine." To Daya Mata he once exclaimed, "How you all will change the work after I am gone. I just wonder, if I were to return in a hundred years, if I'd even recognize it!"

He stressed to Daya, however, the one thing that could prevent his organization from going the way of so many other religious works. "After I am gone," he said, "only love can take my place." I quote his statement a little sadly, for it was not with love that I myself was treated. Other disciples, too, have been treated harshly, though none of them, perhaps, so ruthlessly as I.

I do not want to belabor the personal aspect of this matter. Deep and important issues are at stake. The question to ask is: Are Master's universally embracing teachings to become enclosed stuffily in rules and rigid policies? Can it be true, as many SRF monastics actually believe, that Paramhansa Yogananda expected his organization to replace the Catholic Church? That thought seems preposterous!

In 1990 in Fresno, California, I said to Daya Mata, "Master predicted that Self-Realization will someday be the religion of the world. He cannot possibly have meant Self-Realization Fellowship, Inc.!"

"That . . ." Daya paused significantly, then continued: "is your opinion."

As if there could be another opinion!

Self-realization is a state of consciousness, not an organization. Self-realization is an attainment toward which all religions aspire, whether consciously or unconsciously. What end could be served by re-institutionalizing the religions of the world? The need at present is to affirm the universality of truth itself. Can any good end be served by creating *another* super-church?

The non-sectarian, universal aspect of Yogananda's teachings is emphasized by the dome shape. The temple I wanted to build at Ananda was intended primarily as an expression of this ideal; its *raison d'être,* therefore, was more than esthetic. I saw it as a form of architecture for the future, but also as an expression of the philosophy I believe humanity will embrace in the future.

Symbolically, however, Ananda's domes were destined to have to struggle for a "place in the sun." Ananda itself has faced, and, I suppose, will continue to face, the opposition humanity reserves for new concepts. It seems strange that this should be so, for Ananda is based on communitarian principles that were established long ago in India, and also in America by the early Pilgrim Fathers.

Partly because I'd dedicated Ananda to a universal truth, and to a system of belief different in some respects from the evolving policies at Mt. Washington, the community has been treated also as a threat by SRF. They are convinced that they *own* the teachings of our Guru. I'd seen a fiercely protective expression in Daya Mata's eyes years earlier, when Mt. Washington Estates was threatened by fire. That same protectiveness flared up in her anew as she contemplated my "audacity" in offering people an alternative to the official interpretation of the teachings. Who was I, she and all of them demanded, to think for myself? It was precisely this independence that they'd found so outrageous in me years earlier. It was not, however, that I was independent in the sense of *wanting* to think differently from them. Far from it. But I felt that I had to be true to my own understanding. How, otherwise, could anyone grow spiritually? In their eyes, however, since I'd been a disciple "only" three and a half years, what was I but an interloper? This thought is one they have often reiterated. Of course, I'm still a disciple, after fifty-two years! I might have quoted back to them Yogananda's own often-repeated statement that length of discipleship is not the determining factor in questions of spiritual merit. "The last shall be first," he often said, quoting Jesus Christ. He'd put me in charge of the monks when I'd been with him less than a year. He'd told me, "You have a great work to do, Walter," when I'd been with him very little over a year. That he intended this "great work" to be out on my own has become clear to me over the years, for within the organization no effort was spared, especially after Daya Mata became president, to force my thinking into line with their own—a direction I was constitutionally incapable of following. To try to justify myself on this question of how long I'd been with him has always seemed pointless to me. In fact, there are only two other disciples still living who were with him very much longer than I: Daya Mata and her sister, Ananda Mata. St. Paul, on the other hand, never even knew Jesus personally. Yet his understanding of the teachings played a crucial role in their formulation for posterity. SRF representatives even told inquirers that I'd had no personal contact with Master. When such reports reached me, I thought, "Isn't truth *true*, no matter who utters it?"

Tara once declared to me, after I was put on the SRF Board of Directors (I was still in their good graces, then), "In an organization, no one has a right *even to think* except the members of the Board of Directors." She was so much senior to me that I didn't feel I should voice my disagreement. I was sure at the time, however, that this attitude could not possibly prevail. Unfortunately, it did prevail. Perhaps Ananda will help—again, in time—to restore the openness that once prevailed there. SRF has, in fact, followed many of Ananda's leads, although this fact would never be admitted!

The U.S. Government, in addressing a similar need, has broken up many a monopoly. Generally speaking, the parent company has benefited, at least in the long run, from the "fresh air" this move allowed into the field.

For my part, I've never desired to oppose SRF. I repeat, I cannot help seeing truth as I sincerely see it. Harmony, however, and not opposition, is for me a vital principle.

Daya claims that her insistence on SRF's monopoly is "a matter of principle." I don't agree. No *thing*, however noble, can be a principle. Kindness is a principle, but not the specific acts expressed by kindness.

Principles are abstract; they cannot be limited by examples of them. Jesus expressed this truth when he said, of someone whom John had rebuked for casting out devils in his name, "Forbid him not: for he that is not against us is for us." (Luke 9:49)

On the other hand, *un*kindness is not a principle. Even if justification for unkindness is sought in the name of protecting a noble cause, it also betrays a spiritual principle. For the scriptural injunction against violence concerns *violent attitudes.* Unkindness is an attitude. It is an act of aggression, not of self-defense. It is an offense against karmic law deliberately to try, in the name of higher loyalty of any kind, to destroy a person's faith in God and in himself. Above all, to betray a fellow disciple is to dishonor the fundamental commandment Master himself gave to his disciples: love.

It has taken many years of persecution, and of determination on SRF's part to destroy me and Ananda, to get me to address these issues. Long and long in the name of peace I remained silent. Now I feel that, in the name of truth, I must speak out.

In April of 1967, when I bought our first property, I still dreamed of co-existing with SRF in loving harmony. At that time I was forty years old. Life, it is said, begins at that age. The birth of Ananda did, in fact, mark a new beginning for me. I hoped during this next phase to re-establish harmony between me and my brother and sister disciples. For I deeply believed in such harmony. I would even day-dream of being welcomed back by them with open arms, going to each of the monks in turn, as I had done before my last departure for India, greeting each one lovingly, and being so greeted by each of them in return. Evidently, this was never to be. To my deep sorrow, the rift has only widened over the years. What generates it is an attitude of self-righteous anger against me.

A year previously, in 1966, a student had brought a friend of his to my apartment in San Francisco. I was just then preparing a mailing to go out regarding my classes. Pressed for time, I asked them if they'd like to help me stuff envelopes. They willingly agreed.

This new friend's name was John Novak. The very manner of our introduction seems in retrospect to have been symbolic, for, in time, John became my "right-hand man" in service to Master. Later, I gave him the spiritual name, "Jyotish." When I retired from active leadership in 1998, I appointed Jyotish as the spiritual director of Ananda.

John—Jyotish, as I'll refer to him from here on—shared my and Master's philosophy of universality. In some ways his universality was even greater than mine, for while I recognized the need for practical application of spiritual principles, he tended sometimes to see practical needs as an affront to the principles themselves. (Such differences of temperament only enrich the colored tapestry of life.) For well over thirty years, he has been among my most loyal and dearest friends, sharing with me the struggles and growing pains of Ananda, and my perception of it as one of the most exciting and important ventures of modern times.

Jyotish enrolled in my classes. A year later, he helped me also by teaching a few of them.

The first question I put to myself at this time was, "Can a dome be constructed without spending astronomical sums of money?" Even purchasing the property had been, for me, a major undertaking.

Another student and friend of mine, Karen Leffler, suggested I look into "geodesic domes," a design by Buckminster Fuller. (I was to share the lecture platform with "Bucky" several times, years later.) Karen and I drove to a site in Marin County, north of San Francisco, where she'd seen one of these geodesic domes. Esthetically and philosophically, I found it rather a disappointment. Still, it *was* a dome, and didn't look all that expensive to construct. Buckminster Fuller's design required the binding of flat triangles together in such a way as to present the illusion of a hemisphere. The building was sturdy; indeed, it was an engineering marvel. What I didn't so much like about it was that it attempted to achieve roundness by means of straight lines and flat planes. This seemed to me an esthetic contradiction. Still, given my perennially under-fed bank account, I recognized the need for compromise.

With Karen Leffler's assistance, I located a company that made and sold geodesic domes. They were tool designers, not artists, and their structures rather resembled toadstools in a book of nursery rhymes. It was far from what I really wanted. In fact, I decided these domes represented just too much of a compromise. In the end, however, I had to go back to them.

Another friend of mine, Charles Tart, a professor at U.C. Davis, showed me a geodesic dome he'd been constructing in his back yard. "Sun Dome," this structure was named. He'd taken the idea from an article in *Popular Mechanics,* as I recall. Inexpensive, and easy for amateurs like me to construct, it offered a ray of hope where, so far, I'd seen none. I grasped at it as eagerly as a drowning man at a straw—and, alas, as unadvisedly!

Easy the Sun Dome may have been to construct, but cutting one-by-one-inch struts to the correct angle, assembling them into triangles, then covering them with plastic, took months of labor. Having waited years, I was determined to build my retreat that year, if possible.

Jyotish helped me. So did a number of other friends. Jyotish also filled in for me by teaching occasional classes when work at Ananda kept me from returning to San Francisco. Pat Kutzner, my secretary at that time, wrote to me in exasperation, "Am I to resign myself to an attitude on your part of total irresponsibility?" (She hadn't bargained for Ananda when signing on to help with my correspondence. In time, in fact, Ananda ended up exasperating her so much that she did, literally, resign.)

I had an interesting experience one day concerning the efficacy of Yogananda's "energization exercises." I was stapling plastic sheets to their triangular frames. The staple gun was stiff, and was, besides, large for my hands, which are small. (My shoe size might be described as an "oriental" five-and-a-half.) A woman working with me needed both hands to make the staple gun work at all. The job required the use of only one hand, however, while the other held the plastic to the triangle. I had driven in about 500 staples when all at once it seemed to me I would not be able to squeeze out even one more. Mindful of winter's relentless approach, however, I told myself sternly, "You *must* finish this job!" With every ounce of will power, I sent energy to my hand muscles as one does when practicing the energization exercises, and managed to squeeze the gun—just barely—one more time . . . then just once more . . . then—ouch!—a third time. By about the tenth squeeze, for each one of which I had to force myself to the utmost, I suddenly found I could continue without effort. I probably drove in another 500 staples that day. At the end of the day I was as full of energy as I'd been in the morning.

My co-workers and I finally got the dome up. The last triangle was about to go in; after that, supposedly, the dome would stand firm. Until then, however, its stability was precarious.

Just then, a strong gust of wind swept up from the valley below. The entire structure collapsed. All that remained was a jumble of matchsticks and plastic, littering the wooden platform.

Refusing to give up, I set out immediately to replace the broken pieces, reassembled the unbroken triangles, and stapled them together once again. Weeks later, the new structure was up. In all fairness, it was more beautiful than anything we have constructed since. Its delicate struts were an esthetic delight. Keats was wrong, however: Beauty is not necessarily truth, nor is truth beauty. The "Sun Dome" proved a snare and a delusion.

I didn't realize that it had been designed to rest

undisturbed in the fenced-in enclosure of a back yard, protected from the mildest spring zephyr. Up on Ananda's hilltop, the winds of late autumn can get up to sixty or seventy miles an hour. My beautiful dome-house, before the onslaught of our first storm, simply disintegrated. I walked away and didn't give it even a backward glance.

It took me days to summon the courage to try a third time. This time, after cutting and assembling more struts, I screwed them firmly to large metal plates. "Now," I thought, mopping my brow, "the wind can't possibly rip them apart."

It didn't have to. I knew nothing of air's power to lift a hemisphere, as it does the wing of an airplane. I returned to Ananda after several days of classes, eager to get in a little meditation there before the winter came.

On my arrival, I found pieces of dome draped artistically over the surrounding bushes. Worse still, since this time the triangles had been screwed so firmly together, every strut was broken. There was nothing to do but recognize defeat, and accept it calmly.

I sat down on the bare platform, and—perhaps surprisingly—had a joyous meditation.

To me, this failure was a sign that I must build a temple for many others first. My own home could come later.

The birth of Ananda

(above) Dr. Haridas and Bina Chaudhuri, my guardian angels after my dismissal from SRF

(left) This photo was taken of me in 1965. It helped to promote my first music albums.

(below) A campsite at the Seclusion Retreat in 1967. We began holding weekend retreats here in 1968, after the first buildings were constructed.

(above) Here I am performing *mayurasana*, the peacock pose, on the beach at Sausalito, California. This was part of a series of photos taken for the first edition of *Yoga Postures for Self-Awareness,* published in 1967.

(left) I perform a Vedic fire ceremony before the Sunday service at the Seclusion Retreat in 1971. Seated behind me, left, are Jyotish and Asha. Asha, though not mentioned in the book, is shown on the back cover cheerfully clearing away the debris after our devastating forest fire in 1976. Directly behind me are Seva and Jyotish's wife, Devi.

(below) At the Seclusion Retreat, 1970. I am singing Indian bhajans accompanied by the Indian tanpura.

(above) I teach a class during a weekend program at the Seclusion Retreat in the early 1970s.

(right) A class at the Seclusion Retreat. After the first temple burned down, classes were held out of doors, or in the common dome.

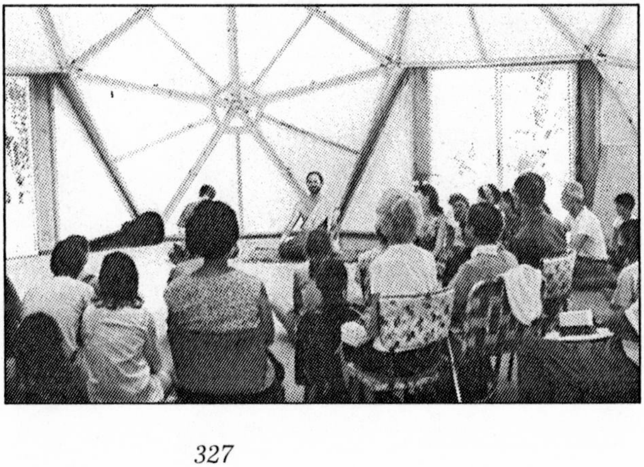

(left) Overview of the Seclusion Retreat domes. The temple is the new, white structure, right. It later collapsed under the weight of a heavy snow.

(left) My home and the view from it, 1974. This, the original structure, was later expanded and became part of Crystal Hermitage.

(below left) Chanting with a group on the deck of my dome in the early 1970s. This is the group that recorded the album, *O God Beautiful.*

(below right) Inside my dome in 1976

(right) Seva, whose name means "service," was one of the first people instrumental in creating Ananda.

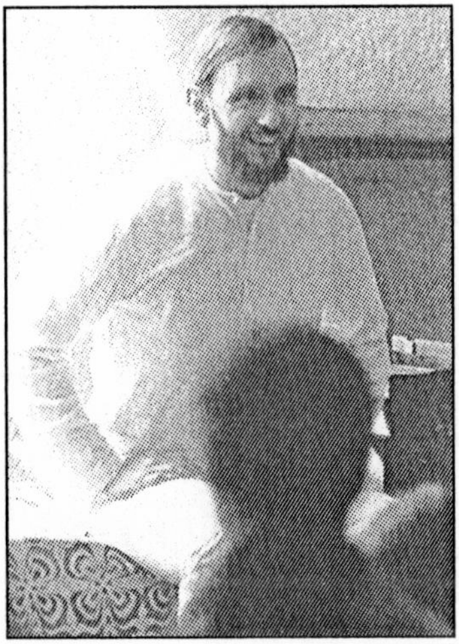

(above left) Jyotish giving a class at the Seclusion Retreat in the early 1970s

(above right) Here Jyotish and I are on our way to India in 1974. "Jyotish" means "inner light." He has been my right-hand man since Ananda's beginning.

(above) A group of Ananda members went with me on two nationwide tours in 1978 and 1979 to spread Master's teachings.

CHAPTER 27

Ananda Retreat

My first thought had been to let others come and build near me. Matters didn't turn out so simply, however. This step would have meant, for most people, a major commitment. To me, the commitment seemed quite simple, but then, they hadn't been through years of mental and spiritual preparation for it as I had. In fairness to my friends, moreover, they didn't lose interest, as others had done so quickly when I was fifteen. These ones, at least, were ready to ponder the proposition.

Putting myself in their shoes, I realize now that the decision can't have been easy for any of them. There were other challenges involved than a mere change of life style. For one thing, even if people saw anything in me that inspired faith, I always made it clear to them that I didn't want a personal following. I hoped that those who came would be, or would become, followers of Paramhansa Yogananda. Complicating this expectation was the fact that I refused to make claims for myself as a disciple. I never "talked down" to others or reminded them they should listen to me because I was older and more experienced than they, or because I was a direct disciple who had known Yogananda and been trained by him personally. If sweet reason can't prevail, I thought, I won't claim superior insight. And if they can't see the truth for themselves, I will attempt only to sway them with reasons they should be able to understand. To respond to their challenges in such a way as to strip them of all defenses would, I felt, be both cowardly and unfair. I had already seen that such comportment not only silenced well-meant objections, but effectively suppressed creative thought.

I spoke well of SRF. If anyone asked me, I answered frankly that I was not in SRF's good graces: that, rather, I was *persona non grata* at Mt. Washington and in their churches. As I reflect back now, I realize that the inducement I was offering people to join Ananda wasn't much. SRF's headquarters were in southern California, relatively nearby. Daya Mata herself had been outraged by the fact that I'd moved to my parents' home in Atherton. She'd accused me: "You've settled practically on our front doorstep!" Anyone could travel easily from northern California to Los Angeles and personally check my bona fides. And anyone who went there could ascertain, as I told them they would, that no such bona fides existed. No one I knew, moreover, was in a position to declare from years of experience that I was trustworthy, honorable, and sincere.

One might ask, whimsically, whether I actually *wanted* to make membership at Ananda difficult. It seems to me now that what helped me most was SRF's utter certainty that I would fail anyway at whatever I attempted. It was also a help that some

SRF representatives spoke of me so heatedly. No fair-minded person likes to hear people berated emotionally. In fact, people who knew me even superficially couldn't believe the accusations against me, particularly since few of those accusers were willing to be specific. Some who *were* willing resorted to outright invention: "He absconded with the organization's funds"; or, "He left in a huff because Daya Mata told him he couldn't start a community." Most of the accusations were vague: "If you *only knew* what he did!"—this, said with a shocked expression. And when anyone asked for particulars, the answer was the same: "Oh, if you only knew!" In fact, my most aggressive critics had no real explanation to offer. They themselves had been as aghast as I at my fall from grace. Officially, the policy was tight-lipped silence.

I wanted the members of Ananda to be devotees of Paramhansa Yogananda. In time, I asked them also to look upon themselves as his disciples. I refused to pretend anything. My desire was to serve Master, not to do him a disservice by claiming a false relationship to him or by pretending to be in SRF's good graces, nor by talking against his organization.

The first question in people's minds, naturally, was, "Who is this Kriyananda that we should listen to him?" I never answered that question. Rather, I let them answer it for themselves, on the basis of what they saw and experienced in their association with me.

These conditions for founding Ananda as a community were unquestionably daunting. Almost more daunting, however, was my first formal attempt at interesting people in the venture.

I held a meeting in my apartment, inviting friends who I thought might be interested. Others came, uninvited, claiming the right to be involved because they were interested. The presence of these people, some of whom I hardly knew, was far from helpful except in the negative sense that it gave me some idea of what I was letting myself in for.

"How do we know you're on the level?" demanded one.

"If you start something this big, you'll forget all about your ideal of serving humanity."

"I know a teacher from India who got so involved in building such a place that he lost his inner peace. Today, he's a MONSTER!"

"Think of it, everyone. If Kriyananda really wanted to draw us into this thing as partners, *why didn't he call this meeting sooner?*"

The only thing to do at this point was serve tea and cookies.

The meeting was not a total disaster, however, for it convinced me that I must explain my concepts in writing. Mere talk, with people bursting in and declaring their own ideas on a subject I'd been pondering since I was fifteen, would prevent any clear picture from emerging of what I had in mind.

I left for the property, accordingly, and stayed there in a tent for one week. There I went over the notes and reflections I'd gathered over many years, and arranged them into coherent order. I took long walks, hammering these ideas out in my mind as though I were a mental blacksmith, then polishing them till they shone. As I worked over my concepts, I wrote them into a book, *Cooperative Communities—How to Start Them, and Why.* On returning to the city, I published this book in a loose-leaf format, and offered it to people who were interested in the idea. I then gave them time to reflect, before broaching the subject again.

Interested persons, I realized, needed also the reassurance of something concrete, something already happening. One of the obstacles to starting any new venture is usually that it requires people. If one hasn't money, one can't hire them. How then can they be attracted? Most people want to see a thing actually functioning before they'll put energy into it.

The best way to begin under the present circumstances, I decided, would be first to create a meditation retreat, where people could visit and get a feeling for the place and for the sorts it attracted. By creating a spiritual vortex of energy, a retreat would, above all, clarify the principles on which Ananda would function as a community. Ananda is 180 miles from San Francisco. This distance too was a daunting factor. Still, it was the best I could offer.

I had reached the conclusion, by means which the tactful reader will no doubt view with surprise, that I was not cut out to be a carpenter. Nor, unfortunately, were any of my friends. However, my classes were by this time earning a fair amount of money. Donations also were starting to trickle in. I now had, including stocks my father had given me over the years, about sixteen thousands dollars—enough, I decided, to hire professional help.

I still wanted geodesic domes. The only company I'd found that made them remained that tool manufacturing firm, whose domes had reminded me of toadstools. I bowed to the inevitable. At least these were something I could afford.

Joan Forest, a friend from Bridge Mountain, recommended as foreman for this job the man who had built her own home. The man assured me he could finish the project in two weeks. He wanted two other professional carpenters to help him. Friends of mine worked with him also, at reduced wages. And a number of local high school children agreed to work for a dollar an hour. Even these low wages added to $1,000 a week: to me, a fortune. Worse was to come, however. Two weeks passed, and even the foundations were not completed. The project took two and a half months in all, not the two weeks promised. Long before that time, I ran out of money.

I'd hoped to get a bank loan to meet emergencies. At my own branch of Bank of America, however, the loan officer refused to give me even a penny. This was a major blow. Five buildings were under construction: a temple; a common dome combining a kitchen, a dining room, and a living room; a bath house for men and for women; an office-cum-reception center; and my own home. It was imperative that these buildings be completed before the winter storms. Instead, the foreman and one of his professional helpers walked off the job. The third one remained with us, but I still had outstanding bills in the amount of thousands of dollars. Completion of the construction was to cost me, in the end, another $12,000.

I persuaded my creditors to accept partial monthly payments. Happily for me they agreed, since I'd always been prompt in my payments. Even so, the least I could get them to accept totaled $2,500 a month, for five months. This was a staggering sum, especially when one considers that the dollar in those days was worth a great deal more than it is now.

I was screwing up the courage to face this predicament, when Hills Flat Lumber Co., the firm that had sold me all my lumber (except for the pre-fabs), placed a lien on the property. Pardini, the owner, had, like the others, expressed willingness to accept partial monthly payments, and I'd been adhering to our agreement faithfully. Why was he now breaking his word? Anyway, I now learned what a lien was! Years in a monastery had not prepared me for certain things.

In addition to those monthly payments, I had all my usual expenses: apartment, car, correspondence, class promotions, travel to and from the classes, food, and so on. Years in a monastery had not prepared me for these things, either!

Or had they? Knowledge alone could not have helped me over this hurdle. The only thing that works in a real crisis, I've discovered, is faith in God. I plunged in, did the best I could, and placed the outcome firmly in His hands.

More students than ever enrolled in my classes. Friends also helped generously, even nobly. Every month, though sometimes with very little to spare, I met every commitment.

Some time earlier, I'd been teaching at North Point, an apartment complex in the North Beach district of San Francisco. A young woman in the class had attracted my attention. Her eyes were unhappy. She seemed to be thinking, "What is this life all about? Why does it seem so empty and meaningless?" She was, I felt, in real need of spiritual understanding. Her name was Sonia Wiberg.

In time, Sonia dedicated herself, as Jyotish had done, to serving Master with me. In the evenings, while I was giving classes to earn the money for Ananda's development, she would come to my apartment and typeset *Cooperative Communities—How to Start Them, and Why.* I had a "C" model IBM typewriter—nothing fancy, but usable for the purpose. She would carefully count out the "numerical value" of each letter—five points for every "m," one for every "l"—and the spaces before typing in each line, in order to make the right margin as straight as the left one. Thanks to her, the book appeared at last in a suitable format for bookstores. It wasn't high-class in appearance, but people who were interested in the subject began buying it in increasing numbers. In time, this book actually became a classic in its field—if only because in that field it stood alone! No one else, to my knowledge, has ever addressed this subject specifically in a "how-to" manner.

When Sonia moved to Ananda in 1970, I gave her the spiritual name, "Seva." Her presence there—steadfast, regular, and always cheerful—was crucial to Ananda's early development. She had been the acting office manager at Rex Allen Associates, an architectural firm in San Francisco, and had brought them out of indebtedness into solvency.

In the fall of 1968, however, she was still not certain as to her directions. She and a friend of hers, Arlene, faithfully attended my classes. When Seva (as I'll call her from now on) heard of my financial straits, she offered to lend me $2,000. A man in Texas, also, the owner of a guitar store, kindly sent me a donation of $1,000.

I'd hoped my father would help, but he considered the venture unrealistic and would have nothing to do with it. In fact, none of my relatives had any faith in the venture. Even my mother described it teasingly as "land fever." One relative by marriage denounced the venture as "hair-brained." Another, a successful businessman, pontificated at length, whenever I gave him the opportunity, about my need to get my feet on the ground. Generally, in fact, anyone with experience in the world treated me as though I were a child, touchingly unsophisticated and naive.

Meanwhile, I received a letter from Leo Todd, the lawyer for Hills Flat Lumber Company, informing me that if I didn't pay off my entire debt within two weeks, they would foreclose.

I telephoned Pardini. "Well, Don," he replied defensively (I'd made the mistake of thinking we were friends), "you see, a person has to be practical." What, in his vocabulary, did "practical" mean: greedy? I'd been honoring our agreement. Worldly people, however, don't always think in terms of honoring their word, or of being generous, or simply honorable. "Look out for number one" is their motto. I prayed that Ananda would be an inspiration to others to seek high-minded alternatives to cut-throat business wheeling and dealing. In fact, it has been gratifying to see how many business people have benefited from Ananda's example of concern for others.

"I don't know anything about an agreement!" raged Leo Todd when I visited his office. "Show it to me in writing." To him, evidently, as to Sam Goldwyn in Hollywood, verbal agreements aren't "worth the paper they're printed on." On further inquiry, I learned that foreclosure would in fact take another two months before the final papers were signed. Meanwhile, I had no idea what to do except slog along, clinging to my faith in God.

Later that week, I was in the home of some friends in Palo Alto showing color slides I'd taken in India. I didn't mention my predicament; to do so would have seemed inappropriate to the occasion. Afterward, however, as I was getting into my car, a young man came out of the house and approached me.

"I like what you're doing," he said. "Would you allow me to give you a donation?"

"I'd willingly accept anything you care to give," I replied. Probably, I thought, he'd give me five dollars, or maybe ten. Instead, he wrote out a check for $3,000.

I telephoned Mr. Pardini that evening and said, "I have the money you want, but I won't pay you until you've incurred all the legal fees you can. Recalling your demonstration of greed, I'll just wait till the last moment before I pay you what I owe."

"Gosh, Don," he replied, "if you pay me now I'll give you a big discount." He'd dug a pit for me. Now he fell into it himself: a classic karmic retribution!

My bank account at the end of that month, after paying what I owed Pardini, stood at $1.37.

The name of the young man who had so miraculously come to my assistance was Tom Hopkins. Tom later lived for a time at Ananda. I have always kept a special place for him in my heart. His help during those critical times was a priceless memory of God's grace.

I sincerely believe that one of the reasons God helped me during those difficult times was that I never compromised my principle of serving others. If anyone wanted to enroll in my classes but hadn't the money, I let him come anyway. I asked only, as I always had, that he return service in kind by setting up chairs, or by bringing snacks for people to eat during the breaks.

God tested my sincerity. One evening a young woman student announced, "I won't be coming to your next class, as I'll be flying to New York to visit my parents." Surprised, I responded, "Then you do have money?"

"Oh, yes" she replied, "I have it for things I consider worthwhile." How should one reply to such a deliberate insult? I simply let it go. To me, the important thing was that my own heart be free.

On another occasion a couple told me casually that they'd just spent fifty dollars on books. This was what they'd said they couldn't afford for the classes. Again, I made no protest. It was for my own conscience, above all, that I held to the principle of placing service to others ahead of personal benefit to myself—even if, as was the case here, the benefit would have accrued not to me, but to Ananda.

Within the bounds of integrity, however, I did what I could. I even sold a prized astrological bangle, of nine gems, which I'd worn during all my years in India. I got $2,500 for it, through Gleim's Jewelry in Palo Alto.

By the end of 1968, by God's grace, the retreat was built and was very nearly paid off. People were beginning to "rally round the flag." The time seemed right to think seriously about building the community.

I'd already dedicated Ananda in August 1968. The domes weren't finished, but people nevertheless came, especially on weekends, sleeping in tents or in sleeping bags under the stars. We had strolling *kirtan*s (singing joyously to God) at dawn, classes in the open air, and group meditations.

Three or four hardy souls remained there through the winter months. The crisis had passed with God's grace, and with my Guru's help. I had been a little upset with God, I confess, that I, who had never wanted money, should have been forced to devote so much of my energy toward earning it, and for so many months. My gain, however, was far more than the money I earned. Most of all, it was spiritual. I'd grown in inner strength by doing what I'd had to do despite every obstacle, even that of intense personal reluctance, and I'd done it for God.

Tara had scoffed at my "Delhi project" during our meeting in New York. "Don't you know," she sneered, "that to create anything this big takes spiritual power?" She might have added, "or bulldog determination, and a willingness to sacrifice everything."

Many people in my position would have taken these difficulties, which seemed insurmountable, as a sign that God didn't want the project to succeed. A common attitude, especially in that era, was that if one decides to go out shopping, but trips lightly over a carpet on his way to the car, that mishap is a sign that God doesn't want him to go out. I'd been given my share of such advice by well-wishers, all of them wanting to be helpful. If my stubbornness in pursuing victory can inspire anyone who faces difficult situations in life, let this be the lesson: If you feel strongly in your heart that you have something you must do, be guided from within if that feeling is one of calm, inner certainty. Don't look outside your Self for guidance. For at that point, omens—and let's face it, as omens go, tripping over a carpet isn't very impressive!—are rarely signs from heaven. Signs should be sought, if at all, while the mind is still uncertain as to the rightness of a course, not once one has fully committed oneself to it.

Most of the great achievements in history, beside which my little victories were small indeed, have come in the face of all-but-impossible odds. Victory's laurel goes not to the faint-hearted, but to those who are willing to lay their very lives on the line.

CHAPTER 28

Hidden Influences

As I reflect how I breasted the waves in towing Ananda to shore, I realize that those efforts were, in a sense, a repetition of what I had put into the "Delhi project" in my efforts to obtain the Indian government's approval. There, too, I had faced obstacles that seemed, and that everyone agreed were, insurmountable. Those obstacles were overcome by determination, hard work, God's grace, and my Guru's help.

It would be interesting to ponder here the karmic patterns in both episodes. My own attitude in both was essentially the same: I did them to serve my Guru. In India, my hope was to make him better known. In America, I wanted to launch his "world brotherhood colony" idea. As far as my underlying purpose was concerned, there were no differences; each effort seemed to me appropriate to the existing need. As far as I could see, I was the same old fellow: determined, yes, to finish what I'd put my will to, but otherwise non-attached. I demonstrated non-attachment, to my own satisfaction at least (if not to Tara's), by my instant willingness to abandon the project when I learned that the Directors were not in favor of it. (I regret, however, that I took so hard

Tara's judgment of my motives. The difficulty with having to satisfy one's superiors is that it is easy to confuse their reactions with God's inner smile of approval, or lack of it.)

My own view of things was the same. The only difference was that, in getting Ananda started, there was no one above me with other priorities. I was my own boss, my one-man "board of directors," free to follow my inner guidance rather than wait and check every move against the judgment of others. Such freedom has both advantages and disadvantages, which can be judged best from the consequences. If my "Delhi Project" caused outrage at Mt. Washington, their reaction was nevertheless still subjective, and not necessarily related to what I was actually doing. General outrage might have told a different story. Had my efforts produced disharmony elsewhere, for example among the Indian government officials, matters might have been less favorable to me. However, they hadn't. Even Prime Minister Nehru was pleased with the idea.

What raises these questions again for me now was a fact I learned only later: In 1968, while I faced those challenges of Ananda's construction, Tara Mata suffered a massive stroke. Barely able to function, she lingered for two more years, and then left her body. An SRF monk, Brother Turiyananda, who was in charge at the SRF Lake Shrine in Pacific Palisades, told me that she had said, "I know this happened to me to teach me compassion."

I was unfamiliar with her personal tragedy, and regretted it when I learned of it. For in spite of everything, I loved her as a friend, and still do. She deserved everyone's sincere respect, for her deep spirituality. Worldly people have narrow ideas of what it means to be spiritual. They little realize how subtle, and how hard to avoid, are the snares of delusion.

It is easy to attribute to more than coincidence the fact that her stroke occurred the same year that I put up the first buildings at Ananda, and dedicated Ananda as a retreat and intentional community. Tara was no doubt furious to learn of these developments. She had been outspokenly determined to destroy me, at least as a disciple. She tried to encompass that end by one massive stroke. Was it so strange that she herself should suffer a massive stroke on receiving news of my rise?

In the 1950s Tara told me, "Master said I would live a long life." I murmured sincere gratification. We were friends at that time. "Yep," she continued happily, "I'll have all the time I need to finish editing his books."

It was known to all of us at Mt. Washington that Master liked and trusted her editing work. So many former editors had intruded their own ideas into his writings. There's a saying in Italian, "*Traduttore è traditore*—to translate is to betray." The same might be said of editors. Tara, however, had shown herself faithful to his thoughts and teachings.

He had given Mrinalini Mata—again, as we all knew—the job of editing his lessons. Had he given anything to me in this respect? Well, he had said, "I predict you will be a good editor someday, Walter."

He had also said, "Your work is writing and lecturing." Anything else?

I believe, but cannot state with certainty, that he said my work would also be editing. My position as editor of his own works, however, is less clear. When he went to Twenty-Nine Palms in 1950 to work on his scripture commentaries, he took me with him, saying in front of the monks, "I asked Divine Mother whom I should take with me, and your face appeared, Walter. I asked Her twice more just to make sure, and each time your face appeared. That's why I am taking you." So I was there, somewhere, in the divine will with respect to editing, but he never explained to me just where, or how—or when.

At Twenty-Nine Palms he gave me the job of "editing" his *Rubaiyat of Omar Khayyam* commentaries, and also his commentaries on the Bhagavad Gita and the Bible. I have put "editing" in quotes, because, obviously, he didn't really expect me to edit at that time. "Work like lightning," he told me, "but don't change a word." Possibly this paradoxical instruction meant only, "Don't change a single concept." I'm disposed to think, however, that he really didn't want me to make any changes at all—that is to say, to do serious editing. In any case, it didn't matter. He was testing my spiritual attitude, primarily.

I was only twenty-three at the time; my skill with the pen had yet to be honed. Moreover, I was still relatively new to the teachings. He was happy to find in me a desire to tune into his wisdom, rather than intrude my own ideas. I think he was preparing me for the future, realizing that he himself had little time left to live. (Again and again he remarked in those days, "Work like lightning. There is no time to lose!")

Tara had said to me in the mid-'fifties, "I'll have all the time I need to finish editing his books." Daya Mata was the new president then, and although Master had told her not to let Tara become involved with people, Tara herself, being Daya's senior in years and in the work, and being in any case forceful by nature, intruded herself more and more into institutional decisions and management. In the process, she neglected more and more her own duty.

I am forced, here, to intrude my own perception of some of the facts. I want you, the reader, to be aware that I am doing so, that you may judge my perception for yourself and compare it to what are indeed, I assure you, facts. But please don't let frankness on my part offend you, for though people think it unseemly "to speak ill of the dead," Tara's contribution to Yogananda's work will become a significant part of history. It might be unseemly to say, for example, of someone in Napoleon's army, "He was a bad soldier," but it would be essential to say it of Napoleon, were it true. I bear Tara no ill will, but it is, I think, important to tell the truth *as I see it,* even while admitting to myself, above all, that, because I was a participant in those events, my understanding may be biased. I shall do my sincere best to be fair. And, I repeat, I have no personal grudge against her. I still like and respect Tara, and recognize the important role she played in my own service to Master.

Tara was highly advanced, spiritually. She had had deep experiences of God. It seems to me, however, that she permitted pride to influence her. For I'd noticed increasingly over the years a tendency on her part to correct not only Master's words, but also the meaning of those words. This tendency is not unusual in disciples, some of whom may think, "I believe in the Master as a man of God, but in practical matters—well, he seems to me a little innocent, sometimes!"

Tara once said to me with a chuckle, "Even when he was William the Conqueror [who he told us he'd been in a former life] he never mastered the English language!" Thus to underscore his need for her editing seemed inappropriate, though it was not, in itself, highly significant. (Friends do sometimes like to "let their hair down" with one another, and don't want to feel they must weigh every word before speaking. Sometimes they say even more than they really mean.) Of course, English didn't exist as a language at the time of the Conquest. It was the conquest itself that led to what is known today as "Middle English," by introducing French into the mixture of Saxon, Scandinavian, and indigenous languages.

A later statement of Tara's to me, however, *was* significant: "Well, we *are* a sect." Those words contradicted Master's oft-reiterated statement in public, "We are not a sect."

In my opinion, Tara developed the arrogance common to craftsmen in their field. She once told me, "I can make anyone react exactly as I want him to, simply by the clever manipulation of words."

I remember Master speaking of a change she had made in just one word from *Whispers from Eternity*.

It was in the poem, "God! God! God!" His complaint was, "Every time I write 'I will drown their noises by loudly chanting . . .' she changes *noises* to *clamor*." I confess I myself liked "clamor" better, though I see now that, while it is more literary, it lacks the color-tone of "noises." Now I prefer "noises" because it expresses Master's "vibration" better.

This is a small point beside the fact that she went ahead and re-edited the entire book. In that same poem Master had written, "I will whisper: God! God! God!" Tara changed it to "I whisper: God! God! God!" Evidently she reasoned that, since he always whispered to God, there was no need for him to affirm, "I will do so." Her version didn't take into account, however, that the poem was intended for the inspiration of spiritual seekers; it was not meant as a purely personal statement. The poem had been received by Master, while lecturing, from St. Francis of Assisi, whom he lovingly called his "patron saint." Tara's omission of that word, "will," gives the line a peremptory sound, not sweet and encouraging.

This, still, is a minor matter compared to the changes she made throughout the book. She made them years after his passing. In its new format it had too much of her own peremptory vibration. And she actually had the audacity to write a preface to this new edition, thanking "the editor" in Yogananda's name for her laborious work. Years before then, Tara had described to me a different "authorization" altogether. (Master told me himself, incidentally, that *Whispers from Eternity* was the only one of his books he'd edited personally. To me, this work has always seemed a literary jewel.) Tara, on the other hand, though skilled as an editor, was not a poet. She lacked the feeling for sound and "color" in words, and for how to insinuate colorful images into literal passages. When pronouncing Master's boyhood name, Mukunda (pronounced "Mookoondo"), for example, she made "u," and also "a," sound like the *u* in "but," thus: "Muhkuhntuh," with also a hard "t" instead of a soft "d." Perfectly normal, of course, for most Americans, but suggestive of something that she herself readily admitted: The sounds of words didn't mean much to her. A poet needs to relish the music of words. To Tara, they were mere "beasts of burden" for her ideas.

"I told Master," Tara said in this context, "that I'd like to try my hand at editing *Whispers.* He approved of the idea. 'Oh, *would* you?' he said." Tara related this exchange to me after his passing. If the job of editing *Whispers* had already been done by the time of his death, permitting him to write the preface for that book, she would not have quoted that far more meager endorsement in justification of her plan to work on the book. Yogananda passed away in 1952. Tara's version of "Whispers" came out in 1958. What can be said of that preface, except that Tara herself composed it, long after his death?

Hers was a complex nature, not easy to understand, and more difficult still to explain. On the one hand, I admired greatly her deep devotion to our Guru. She showed not the slightest consideration for anyone else, but where Master was concerned she was one-pointed in her loyalty. At the same time, she felt relaxed enough in that devotion to disagree with him openly when she felt the need, and that disagreement did not always seem to me impersonal. I appreciated her frankness, and took it as a sign of her sincerity. Still, it worried me sometimes when she disagreed with him on points that I knew were, to him, important.

One of these points was his enthusiasm for "world brotherhood colonies." She laughed outright, once, in conversation with me at his "naiveté" concerning this concept. (She didn't use the word, "naiveté," but her tone of voice implied it). Once she said to me, "You wouldn't *believe* all the copies he had us type out of a community proposal for Henry Ford, hoping to interest him in the idea!" I have already mentioned how, when he first acquired Mt. Washington Estates, Tara's comment to him was, "Now your troubles begin!"

The organization had meant nothing to her in those early days, except "trouble." She once said to me, "I used to think Master had come to America to gather up a handful of disciples, after which we'd all go back to India with him and meditate in the Himalayas." To her, serving others spiritually was meaningless. I don't see this as a fault, necessarily. The hermit's calling is a wonderful one. Master, in fact, sometimes described her as "my hermit."

For her, however, granting this facet of her nature, to take on the unnatural responsibility of involving herself in organizational matters after his passing had to have, and did have, disastrous consequences. Even her attitude toward the books he wanted her to edit became, gradually over time, cavalier. She once told me, "What do they need with more books? They have all the books they need, to find God." Master was distressed when I reported her comment to me, in 1950, "I can't possibly get out his Gita commentaries by the end of this year." Partly, I think, his distress was because he saw that more was involved than a delay of six months. Forty years passed before those commentaries appeared in book form! This was twenty years after Tara's death. Meanwhile, she interfered with everything, even hinting to me that she felt Daya Mata had betrayed her by not implicitly obeying her "instructions" on organizational matters. In fact, as Tara told me, "People say that Daya and I run the organization. Well, it's true. We do." And she let slip once in a Christmas card to me, "To the first vice president of SRF/YSS from the second president." I first thought she meant, "from the second *vice* president." In time, however, I came to realize that, even if that were a mere "slip of the pen," it expressed her real meaning. She was not given, moreover, to slips of that kind.

Tara was enough opposed to Master's community idea to remove it, in the late 1950s, from his official "aims and ideals." The explanation for this change, and for many others that have been introduced into his books and organization since his passing, is, "He changed his mind toward the end of his life." I know for a fact that he did not change his mind on those communitarian ideas, though I was given this as the reason why I should not have started Ananda. My natural reaction, then, was to think, "Even if he *had* changed his mind, the fact that he always spoke so strongly in favor of it *has to* mean, *at the very least,* that we cannot consider communities a *bad* idea." SRF's directors were not interested in starting communities, but why were they so anxious to prevent *me* from starting one?

Tara's character was amazingly decisive and forthright. In practical matters, however, she sometimes reminded me of a cartoon by George Price years ago in *The New Yorker:* A plane rising from the runway; in the foreground, an austere, dowager-type lady posed sternly at the top of the embarkation staircase, her forefinger pointed upward commandingly to the sky, while a team of airport personnel push the staircase frantically toward the already-departed plane. Tara was like that woman.

Her bold declaration, for example, that Disneyland had to fail because it had been opened on the dying moon, was something she told me when Disneyland was already one of history's outstanding success stories. She, however, having made that declaration years earlier, stuck by it resolutely. "What a pity!" she said. "All that money they poured into that project!" Disneyland remains today, after more than forty years, an outstanding success.

Daya Mata said to me after Tara's death in 1970, "Master told Tara to give up her involvement with astrology. She disobeyed him. That's why she fell."

That's why she fell. It is possible for even highly advanced souls to fall. Master once warned me, "Remember, you will not be safe until you reach *nirbikalpa samadhi.*" Tara was advanced, certainly, but I do think she fell. On the other hand, I don't think it was a major fall. As I see it, she has yet to develop a quality she herself said she lacked: compassion.

Many of Tara's statements were drastic. As opinions they might be refreshing, but as policies they were often devastating. She never thought of spiritual work in terms of giving service to spiritually hungry souls. To her, all that mattered where people were concerned was to keep them from diluting the teachings. She saw our Guru's work in terms of the control it exerted over others, not of the hope, comfort, and understanding it brought them. Thus, she imposed on SRF the dictum, "In every situation, ask yourselves always, first, 'What is best for the work?'" This, she said, must be the guiding principle. And so it became.

How was it possible for one person to exert so much power? By being powerful, herself. No one could gainsay her, if only because she wouldn't allow anyone to. I myself was always aware that, much as I liked her, we would someday come to loggerheads. Our perception of Master's mission was, on certain issues, far apart. When the crisis arose between us, I was helpless: 12,000 miles away in India. Tara engineered my dismissal, and persuaded the other directors to accept her will, placing Daya in a position where Daya finally screamed, as she herself told me, "All right!" Tara then insisted that the two of them meet me in New York—a safe 3,000 miles away from Los Angeles—and hand me my "walking papers." No one came to my support. I can't imagine anyone daring to do so. I was given no opportunity to speak in my own defense.

Tara lambasted me for my supposedly "atrocious personality." I never could understand her meaning, for I've always been popular with both strangers and people I've known for many years. The explanation is ordinary and quite simple: I like people. Tara must have projected onto me her own personality, for she herself bullied others. It was natural that she should consider me a bully. According to her, I'd bullied the officials in India and forced them to relent. Of course, they held all the cards; I couldn't have forced them if I'd tried. Tara, however, thought nothing of bending others to her will. As I said, no one could stand up to her. In fact, few people could even stand her! If I myself found her forthrightness refreshing, it was because I knew she loved Master and was completely dedicated to him. Her inconsiderate way of treating people, however, was demonstrated on many occasions.

Time Magazine once published an article about Master. She took exception to something in it, and wrote the editors a stern letter taking them to task. Then she fairly dumped onto them the entire set of Master's books. I can imagine the editors thinking, "Oh, dear, does she really want us to sit down and pore over all that material, and then ask ourselves, 'Now, where did we go wrong?'" She could have taken lessons from Dale Carnegie in "how to win friends and influence people"! For it never occurred to her even to think how others might react.

When she decided to get *Autobiography of a Yogi*

out from under the control of Philosophical Library, its first publisher, she waged a campaign of the sort she must have imagined I waged against the Indian government. I never got all the details of this campaign, but from what she told me later she did everything to coerce those publishers into doing what they definitely did not want to do.

What I've always done, by contrast, is try to find ways in which others *will benefit from* my proposal. Tara, with her "direct onslaught" mentality, considered this duplicitous, but in fact I really do have others' interests at heart. If I see that any proposal of mine might not be of mutual benefit, I drop it immediately.

So, to return to the question of karma: In India, my methods had been directed with the same energy that I put into starting Ananda in America. I didn't coerce anyone. On the other hand, I didn't let anybody coerce *me.* Despite considerable opposition (not the least of it from my fellow disciples), I stood firm. As Mother put it years later, "You stuck to your guns." I didn't try to persuade anyone, whether with "slick" or with any other sort of logic; if people attacked me, I simply tried all the harder to embrace them in the good that I was trying to accomplish. It has never been my way to attack; I simply stand up for what I believe. Even as a child, the occasional bully was discomfited to discover that, though he was stronger than I was, he couldn't subdue my spirit. Nor did I ever begin those fights.

Very well, then, but what about the question of karma? Was it my karma to lose in the matter of that

"Delhi Project"? Interestingly, it may actually have been my karma to win. Neemkaroli Baba was a well-known saint in India, who became famous in the West after Ram Dass's book, *Be Here Now,* was published. Neemkaroli actually spoke to a friend of mine in New Delhi about my Delhi ashram, and predicted, "It will come up." This is the Indian way of saying, "It will happen." His word was generally considered infallible.

Again, I had actually been given a prediction in *The Book of Bhrigu,* about which I published a short report in 1967. That prediction had been specific, and fairly elaborate: "His father will name him James." (My full name is James Donald, but no one in India knew my first name.) "He will be born in Romania, and will live in America. He will meet his guru Yogananda at the age of twenty-two, and will receive the name, Kriyananda." Of my work in India, the prediction said, "He will build an ashram in the city of D-, on the banks of the river Jamuna. Its fame will be glorious, and will thrill his heart." It seemed to me that, as they say, "All systems were *GO.*" Even Prime Minister Jawarharlal Nehru had walked the property, and had given the project his approval.

Why, then, the disaster that followed?

The ways of karma are endlessly fascinating. God's will can alter any karmic dictate, within its own established parameters. And the masters, working in harmony with the divine will, can change karmic directions for their disciples, concerned as they are with their spiritual development.

Consider the "Delhi Project" and its resulting

dispute between Tara and me. On the one hand, Master had told her she would live long enough to finish editing all of his books. She suffered that massive stroke, however, at the age of sixty-eight, and died before, or soon after, she turned seventy. Hers was not a long life. I think it was cut short because she disobeyed his will—not only, as Daya told me, by continuing to practice astrology, but for the qualities which that practice brought out in her. Specifically, it increased her tendency to see people as "types," rather than as souls struggling to reach the light. She told me, for example, "You are the lone wolf type." A nonsensical assessment! *Lone?* Well, I've always needed to see things honestly, instead of accepting others' opinions just because they were "politically correct." But, again: *lone?* When I was a young man on vacation, within a week of my arrival in any new town I already knew half the population as friends. *Wolf,* then? This too didn't make sense. I made a point of never even asking for favors.

So—was my personality really so "atrocious"? Or, perhaps, was it my karma to be judged so harshly by her?

If we think in terms of Master's work, and not of personalities, a clearer picture emerges. What did his mission pressingly need? An organization, only? Some of the SRF monks have said, "Master was sent to America to start a monastery." Is this a realistic summation of his great mission?

In Ranchi, when he was young, he started a school for boys. In America also, in 1925, he tried to start a school at Mt. Washington, but dropped the idea when he couldn't find enough parents responsive to his educational ideas. Throughout his years in the West he also kept urging people to found communities—"world brotherhood colonies" as he called them. In addition, he wrote a booklet of practical guidance on a purely mundane subject, *The Law of Success.* He wrote another one, *Scientific Healing Affirmations,* to offer help on another mundane matter: physical and mental well-being.

Most of his chief disciples, contrary to the claim that he was sent to found a monastery, were married or had been married at one time. A few names spring to mind: Rajarsi Janakananda, Yogacharya Oliver Black, Señor Cuaron, Sister Gyanamata, Dr. Lewis, Kamala Silva, Sister Meera, Durga Mata—and, indeed, Tara Mata herself. Yogananda's param guru (guru's guru), the great Lahiri Mahasaya, was a householder. Yogananda's guru, Swami Sri Yukteswar, had been married before he became a swami, and had a daughter. That Master wanted to establish a monastic order in America goes without saying, but his mission went far beyond that concept.

The school he started in India, and the one he tried to get going in America, are indications, surely, that he had other hopes for the work. The community he tried, albeit unsuccessfully, to found, about which he spoke every time he got a chance, is surely another indication of his non-monastic hopes for the future. His booklet, *The Law of Success,* is not a mystical treatise designed for the edification of renunciates, but was written—based of course on spiritual principles—for anyone who aspired to succeed. His

Scientific Healing Affirmations is for everybody, and not directed specifically toward monks and nuns. Another book of his, *The Science of Religion,* is intended also to help everyone; it presents a fundamental law of existence to inspire people everywhere to shun lesser fulfillments and seek their highest fulfillment in God. All of these books are spiritual in the broad sense that they help everyone to live a better life. They were not designed specifically for people dedicated to the monastic calling. Yogananda spoke publicly, besides, on many other "mundane" topics, such as how to succeed in business, how to be a good marriage partner, how to develop common sense, how governments can achieve truer, spiritual ends.

In short, his mission was universal. He spoke of the underlying oneness of all religions. He spoke of incorporating spirituality into daily life. He described the ideal government of the future. He spoke a great deal, in fact, about the future, explaining how this new age of energy would affect everyone, and urging people everywhere to work toward world harmony, in keeping with the needs of this age. In his last speech at the Biltmore Hotel (at which I was present), on the evening he left his body, he pleaded with governments to pool the best of their countries' accomplishments and not to be deluded by false patriotism and selfish national ambition. He spoke of oneness, cooperation, universal love, good will and kindness to all.

I would say that Paramhansa Yogananda was a prophet for the New Age. Monasteries? yes, but far more than that. To me, he spoke of the renunciates as unencumbered workers in his greater cause. He wanted everyone to strive toward unity with God, but his mission was to raise the consciousness of the human race, not only that of a few monastics. Indeed, he also decried monastic arrogance, which sometimes tends to view non-renunciates as "second-class" human beings. We see today that monasteries everywhere are empty. A new way of life is needed. Until there is a return *in the home* to spiritual principles, there will be no widespread spiritual renaissance anywhere.

These are the fundamental needs of our times: not the withdrawal of a few spiritual seekers from society at large, but the *reformation* of society itself.

In pursuit of universal upliftment he even spoke, in private conversation with me, of certain inventions he had inspired, or in one case discovered among practices in India and elsewhere. One invention he told me about was to place the gear shift of a car on the steering shaft, instead of in the floor. He mentioned how he and two students had driven into Chicago (or Detroit) with this new gadget. He even said he'd introduced the concept of covers on toilet seats. And he taught people how to extract gluten from wheat by washing it. Gluten, he said, could make a good-tasting meat substitute. Thus, we see that his enthusiasm for improving life at every level was boundless.

Let us consider a still broader picture. There was a need for books on countless subjects that will inspire and guide people everywhere. Did he want everybody to live in a monastery? Was he resigned, on the other hand, to the imperfectability of worldly people? Certainly not! Books were needed on subjects that offered a new and practical, but at the same time spiritual, point of view: books on business, the arts, education, friendship, marriage, human love, success, psychology, self-acceptance, leadership, prosperity, raising children, bringing harmony to life and to relationships, overcoming harmful emotions, freeing the mind of subconscious "complexes," and countless other topics. He had told me to write books. "*Much* more is needed!" he'd said when I asked him whether everything hadn't been written already that needed writing. Many more books were needed. Schools were needed. Communities were needed, where householders and sincere seekers at all stages of life could live in harmony together, seeking God. A whole new approach to living was needed. Openness to new, better ways of thinking was needed to bridge old ways to new ones. Yogananda had seen that I, with my creative energy, was just the kind of person to entrust with this aspect of his message, especially because of my faith in the high potential of his teachings. My peers scorned me for my very expansiveness. Master never did so.

What would have happened, had I remained in SRF? For myself, I'd probably have died of ulcers brought on by lingering frustration. For Master's work, these things would have had to be explored in the future by others who never knew him, and who came to his work with an already-formed mind-set of their own—people who weren't in tune with him as disciples, let alone knowing much about him as a man. Anything contributed by such persons would almost certainly dilute his original impact and message. Yogananda's mission *needed* a Kriyananda. Had the "Delhi Project" been accorded the joyful approval it merited by SRF's directors, I'd have happily worked under them. I'd have worked there happily anyway, because I was living for God, but I doubt that I'd have accomplished much. And I'd surely have felt I wasn't giving of my best. It was they, not I, who forced my dismissal. Their mind-set, however, was not expansive. Had they approved my ideas—and increasingly, over the years, I'd seen they rejected them—they'd have done so for no better reason than to "pacify" me. Whatever I accomplished would have been hardly a tithe of what I knew in my heart Master wanted of me. In short, for the sake of Master's greater mission, my dismissal was necessary.

What, then, about such predictions as Neem Karoli Baba's, that the "Delhi Project" would "come up"? It didn't happen at that time, but is this to say it never will? Who can tell? That story hasn't yet happened, but. . . .

I came to Master near the end of his life. It was then, especially, that new ideas were needed. Other disciples had come, long before me, to support him in his mission. My job, and also my nature, impelled me to look ahead: to serve him not so much directly—though it thrilled me to do that, too, when I could—as through service to others. This was what he himself wanted of me. It was what I, too, felt inwardly guided to do. That he approved of my attitude signaled his own broad-mindedness. He hadn't come on earth to complete, but to initiate. He said I had "a great work to do" because he saw not only my desire to push his work forward after his lifetime, into the new age of energy, but to do so in close attunement with him.

Everything I have done has been as his disciple. I have prayed earnestly to be guided in his footsteps. I have taken no major decision without first asking, "What would *you* do in this circumstance?" I have meditated on the episodes in his life; on his words, actions, and reactions; on his very facial expressions and tone of voice—trying always to understand, "What would *you* do in this circumstance?" I have also tried to remember things he said and did that might contradict the guidance I felt. For my sincere desire has been not to let myself be fooled by desires or personal inclinations. His will, and his will alone, has been the polestar of my life.

Could I have done all this in the atmosphere of doubt and disputation that had attended my efforts when I was in SRF? Answer that question for yourself. For me, I am satisfied that it is answered.

CHAPTER 29

Community Beginnings

I had to get a permit from the Building Department before beginning construction at the meditation retreat. At the Building Department I learned that I also needed a permit from the County Health Department. Hal Cox, the Superintendent there, placed us in the category, "church camp." Had we been categorized otherwise, we'd have needed a further permit (something I didn't know at the time) from the Planning Department. Being a church camp spared us more bureaucratic red tape, and, probably, the need to spend more money for the project than I even had.

I'm sure many people have lamented the regulations that force them to spend considerable amounts of money simply to be able to begin earning money—or, as in my case, to be of service to others. If only there were a way for people—young people, especially, starting out in life—with little capital but with lots of energy, ideas, and enthusiasm to launch a project without the burden of bureaucratic restrictions. I wonder if this isn't one reason some people, anxious to serve God, have gone off as missionaries to far-off places like Africa. In less developed countries, these restrictions are at least few or non-existent. People can devote their energies in more worthwhile directions.

Spring of 1969 arrived, and people began arriving at Ananda in slowly increasing numbers. A few came as families. I intended to build a community eventually, away from the retreat. God encouraged me in this intention by sending us a few particularly noisy children at the outset. Meditations in the temple became a brow-furrowing background to gleeful shouts, angry accusations, and bitter tears over which no one had the slightest control.

One couple, Ray and Burma Harilla, arrived with their small daughter, Cici. They were a sweet and unassuming couple, but Cici definitely was a Presence. I remember Jyotish telling me, "I was sitting on my deck one morning, when Cici approached it from the side. The top of her head barely reached the level of the deck. Disdaining the obvious solution of climbing the steps, she studied the problem a moment, then said, 'Hmmm, looks tough. I guess I'll have to give it my FULL BLAST!'" Everything Cici did was FULL BLAST.

Children's restless energy at a meditation retreat is a dubious blessing, and Cici had ten times as much energy as the average child. That we needed other land, and soon, was becoming more obvious every day.

At that time, and for many months to come, I continued teaching in the cities. I was therefore able to come to Ananda only on weekends. A friend of mine in Sacramento, Dr. Gordon Runnels, learning that we needed more land, mentioned a property he'd heard about from a real estate agent friend of his. "It's in your general area, I think," he said. Our "general area," however, included places as far away as Auburn, fifty miles south of us. I shelved his news mentally, thinking it wasn't time yet in any case to take on another venture.

The first week of June, however, I received a letter from Dick Baker, who was in Japan. He had heard of an influx of people at Ananda, and somehow got the impression that I was building a town! Distressed, naturally, he reminded me that the property we'd bought together was intended for seclusion. "Please," he wrote desperately, "do no more construction until I return from Japan in the fall. We can then meet and discuss these things."

Not many people had come yet, but, in fact, if a community was to begin at all, spring, not autumn, was the time to do it. The delay Dick wanted couldn't have come at a worse time for us. God's ways of forcing us to move forward, however, are not always those we ourselves would choose.

Dick's letter arrived on a Friday morning. "Divine Mother," I prayed, "help me to find a solution! I don't want Dick to regret having included me in his venture. On the other hand, I can't control who comes to Ananda. What am I to do?" I was about to leave San Francisco for another weekend at Ananda. Accompanying me was Sandy Miller, a student and friend who had expressed interest in the project. (Married since then, her name became Sandy Ross. My father and her husband, Ed, became friends.)

On our way to Ananda, we stopped at Gordon

Runnels's office in Sacramento. Another friend of Dr. Runnels stopped by. As we waited for Gordon, this man told me he was a real estate agent, and took the opportunity to speak about what he called "the hottest real estate buy I've ever seen." I began to realize that this was probably the man Gordon had spoken of. From Gordon's description, I'd surmised that the property was unlikely to be very near Ananda. My doubts increased when this man said it was "somewhere north of Auburn," which made it seem almost a suburb of that town. Out of politeness only, therefore, I asked if he had a map he could show me. He pulled one out of a pocket and spread it on a table.

The map was of Ananda's exact area! Things all at once looked promising. The property he pointed to was only six miles from Ananda Retreat. With Dick Baker's letter lying heavy in my pocket, I asked, "Would you care to show it to me?"

"When would you like to go?"

"Would this afternoon suit you?"

"I'm free," he said. "We could leave now." The three of us drove up that afternoon. Gordon, unfortunately, had appointments and couldn't join us.

"The owner of this land," said the agent, "is a Mr. Sylvester. He has terminal cancer, and is anxious to settle his affairs as soon as possible. He's had most of the property subdivided into forty-acre parcels. It isn't even on the market yet, but already the guys in the office are fixing to place options on some of the parcels for themselves, and are getting their friends interested."

In the fading daylight, we walked over some of the most beautiful countryside I have ever seen. I asked him, "Could you hold a few of these parcels for me over the weekend?" I told him which ones I wanted; they amounted to most of the property.

"I can certainly give it a try," he replied.

The down payment for those pieces came to $13,500—an unthinkably high sum, especially considering that I'd have to raise promises of loans or donations over that weekend. "If God wants us to have it," I reasoned, "He'll work everything out."

I've never been one to attract wealthy donors, perhaps because of a deep-seated aversion to letting anyone think he owns me. I knew many people, however, and a number of them had at least a certain amount of money. I sat down and made telephone calls. By Saturday morning, less than twenty-four hours after getting Dick Baker's letter, I'd received promises totaling $13,500.

I phoned the agent. "To play it safe," he said, "I went into the office at two o'clock this morning and took the listings you wanted off the board. It's lucky I did! When the office opened today, five or six of the fellows came and pleaded with me to free up at least one of the parcels. By getting those promises of help so quickly, you've snatched the land right out from under their noses."

Thus, we obtained Ananda Farm—not so far away from the meditation retreat that both couldn't have the same identity. Interestingly, most of the original promises of assistance fell through. God had other ways of raising the money when the down payment actually came due. For the time being, however, those first promises gave us the confidence we needed to proceed.

The farm purchase had a particularly touching sequel. I'd been sorry that this good fortune should have been ours as a result of someone's misfortune. Later, I happened to meet the former owner's doctor, Robert Hume. Dr. Hume, speaking of Mr. Sylvester's cancer (which he said had indeed been terminal), told me it had vanished quite marvelously after we acquired the land.

By an interesting coincidence, Dr. Hume's wife was the daughter of family friends of mine in Scarsdale, New York. Their residence had been on the same road as ours, Claremont Road. We'd lived at 13 Claremont before moving to 90 Brite Ave. How many threads weave themselves into the tapestry of a person's life! I'd again met her father, Harry Gibbon, in Patna, India, at the airport. I was seated at a table chatting with friends, wearing the orange robe of a swami. I had let my hair grow long, and had a beard. Thus I was, or so one would have thought, quite unrecognizable to someone who hadn't seen me since I was a teenager. This man came over and said, "Say, from your voice you sound like one of the Walters!" Mr. Gibbon was retired, and acting as a consultant for some firm in Bombay.

Harriet, their daughter—another thread!—had had a crush on my brother Bob when she was seven years old and he, eighteen. "When I grow up," she asked him, "will you marry me?" He took her childish "proposal" lightly, of course. "Sure," he said, smiling off-handedly. A few years later, however, when he married someone else, she took it very hard. "You promised!" she wailed bitterly. Harriet must have been eleven at that time.

Dr. Hume became my doctor for a time, until he and Harriet moved away. After that, we gradually lost contact with each other.

Ananda began in truth as a community with the purchase of Ananda Farm. On July 4, 1969, we signed the papers that committed us to buying it. Now began a population explosion that we nearly didn't survive.

The news spread by an amazingly efficient grapevine that a new "commune" was starting up and wanted members. People began arriving from points north, south, east, and west! One afternoon alone there were seven cars parked in our driveway, full of people eager to join. We did manage gradually to sift through this landslide of humanity and select from it a fair number of viable candidates. It was a slow process.

Strange as it may seem, comparatively few of my hundreds of yoga students ever became residents of Ananda. Most of those who came now had never studied with me, knew little or nothing about me, very little (if anything) about Paramhansa Yogananda or his teachings, and were in no way interested in fulfilling Yogananda's or my communitarian dreams. They came because "communes" were the vogue, and it seemed to them an easy and comfortable way of avoiding worldly responsibility.

This "mass migration" raised several important

questions. We did indeed need numbers, for without them it wouldn't be possible to develop anything on our several hundred acres of land. We also needed help with the mortgage, which amounted to $1,750 a month—a large sum in those days. I had no intention of compromising my ideals, however, and therefore had to establish a few guidelines.

Though I wanted as few rules as possible, I'd already decided on two as essential: no drugs, and no alcohol. The anti-drug rule concerned hallucinogenic drugs, of course, not medications. Most of those coming were of the hippie, hallucinogenic drug culture. They couldn't even understand why I would want such a rule. Many assumed I meant only, "No drugs on Ananda land"—perhaps as a legal protection. But wasn't what they did off the property their own business? It took some time to persuade them that joining Ananda meant a personal commitment, not a casual excuse.

I'd seen at Mt. Washington how a surfeit of rules can destroy the spirit, as Master had warned me when I organized the monks there. For a time, notices were posted almost weekly on our bulletin board from the main office, informing us of a stream of new rules, regulations, and procedures. When I organized the main office, after Master's passing, it was to streamline and simplify matters, not to impose rigid controls. Other people, however, had welcomed my reorganization with the glad cry, "Finally we're getting *organized!*" Happily they added to the momentum, going from simplicity to ever-increasing complexity, imagining they'd found in the organizing process itself the key to efficiency! I myself felt that all they were producing was an ideational labyrinth.

At Ananda, faced again with the need for bringing order out of chaos, I determined to depend not on rules, but on the creative exercise of common sense.

For I wanted everyone to have the freedom to grow in personal understanding and ability, and not to have decisions imposed on him or her from above. Only thus, I felt, could Ananda grow vigorously, instead of slowly losing its first momentum. From the beginning, the decision-making process was kept as close to the "grass-roots" level as possible. People who were involved in a project were given an active say in whatever concerned them. We also permitted people to introduce a personal style into their activities, rather than force them all into the same mold.

I determined on certain guidelines, also, for myself: Never coerce; never "pull rank" on anyone; win others to a view by letting them convince themselves, rather than by overwhelming them with reasons, or with my own conviction. Naturally, my enthusiasm did count for something. Without the yeast of strong leadership, Ananda would have come out a flat pancake. Strong leadership, however, means *leading,* not *driving.* It means having the inner strength to be patient with others, to absorb the blows of opposition, to be completely fair to everyone, and never to play favorites. What I tried to do was inspire a kindred enthusiasm in others rather than impose on anyone my own enthusiasm. I let others think things through for themselves, without pressure from me. If I saw that someone was agreeing to a proposal only to go along with me, I let the matter rest until I saw that he or she really did agree. Tepid support, I've always felt, is almost worse than no support at all, for when it is put to the test it often fizzles out, generally when you most need it.

If I called a group meeting, I tried to give people on all sides of an issue a fair hearing. However, I kept the reins of such meetings in my own hands, never allowing discussion to descend to a verbal free-for-all. I did my best to get people not to think in terms of what they themselves *wanted,* but rather to ask, "What is right? What will benefit everyone?" Inwardly I always prayed for my Guru's guidance, that his will be my own point of departure rather than any consideration of personal feelings or biases. What I hoped to establish was a *"dharmocracy,"* not a democracy. *Dharmocracy* (rule by what is spiritually right) I defined as a community dedicated to actions leading to soul-freedom, rather than to further ego-involvement. Ego-centeredness is the root cause of spiritual ignorance, but dedication to doing God's will leads to wisdom. Ego-motivated desires are self-imprisoning, whereas desirelessness is the way to perfect freedom. Ego-attachment is bondage, whereas non-attachment is essential for those who seek true self-fulfillment.

"Ananda itself," I insisted, "is merely a thing. Don't be attached to it. Don't imagine that we'll ever create another Garden of Eden here. Ananda can never achieve perfection, for outer perfection is a delusion forever unattainable. Be attached only to doing God's will."

It helped that I gave weekly classes and devotional

services, and thereby exposed people to Master's teachings, instead of leaving them to work out everything for themselves, influenced by a heterogeneous collection of books and friends.

I insisted they work on developing solution-consciousness, not problem-consciousness. "It is easy to see a problem," I said; "a little harder, perhaps, to define it, but only by solution-consciousness will you *attract* solutions. If you want to draw attention to problems, then suggest solutions for them; don't just grumble and complain. To point out defects without showing the courage to look for solutions can paralyze people's will power. If you induce such paralysis in others by your negativity, you owe it to them, as well as to yourself, to offer practical and constructive remedies."

One time, I learned that a number of people were planning to "call me on the carpet" before the community to demand why certain things weren't being done. I forestalled their tactic by calling a meeting myself, and listing their complaints. "What," I asked everyone, "shall we do to remedy these matters?" It took the wind out of their sails! They themselves had no constructive suggestions to offer. The rest of us did what we could to remedy matters.

Actually, I paid little attention to people who were steeped in problem-consciousness. The energy it would have taken to persuade them to become constructive would hardly have brought any of them from a minus value to zero. Those who, in later years, worked with such people, from a desire to help them, found (as Jyotish once put it) that ninety percent of their energy went toward counseling ten percent of the members, and even then this ten percent usually ended up turning against the community, or in other ways letting it down.

Perfection is no mere dream: It is everyone's destiny. In terms of present realities, however, the plain truth is that few people change radically over the course of a single lifetime. The best one can do in one life is refine what he started with; he can't alter his nature drastically. When I was told recently of the arrogance and worldliness of St. Francis of Assisi as a youth, I thought, "Oh, no! He was always an innocent: exuberant, joyful, eager for experience, but never proud or selfish; never worldly in the sense of avidity for egoic fulfillment." Worldly people project their worldly attitudes even onto saints.

A wonderful thing at Ananda was the fact that, after our first rocky years, community meetings almost always ended in a spirit of harmony. I never insisted on consensus, but if people couldn't agree I generally shelved a discussion in order to give them time for further consideration. For when people sincerely seek a right solution, and not one they only desire, agreement comes relatively easily. In any case, I was not attached to the outcome. If an idea of mine didn't meet general approval, I simply dropped it. Perhaps my own lack of attachment helped others, also, to see that mere things are not really all that important.

A principle I established—one with which everyone came in time to agree—was: *People are more important than things.* In practice, this means that people's spiritual well-being is more important than anything else. If a job needed to be done, but the best person for it would not benefit from it spiritually, someone else was sought for the job. If no one was found, an entire project was sometimes abandoned.

For myself, even if an idea I presented was one I particularly liked—like architectural concepts for residences—I felt that what mattered most was encouraging people to think for themselves. For if a person's idea is squelched, even for the simple reason that it is wrong, the person may as a result feel discouraged from making further suggestions. Thus, if his suggestion isn't drastically wrong, it may be wise to remember that we learn by our mistakes, and therefore to give him a chance to prove himself. If, again, anyone came up with an alternate proposal to one of my own, even if I didn't think it was as good as mine, I often went along with it to encourage that person to think creatively and to develop a sense of personal responsibility. For more important than almost any specific project is that people develop the ability to come up with ideas for projects themselves. Moreover, I sometimes found that an idea that I hadn't considered very good turned out to be better than my own. It was good in any case, and helpful especially for me personally, to hold myself open to new ideas.

The primary goal of leadership in a place like Ananda is not to win admiration, but rather to develop leadership in others. As much as possible, and increasingly so through the years, I helped people to develop their own leadership skills, instead of making all their decisions for them. If someone made a mistake—which, as I've said, is often the best way to develop understanding—one had to consider the type of mistake, and people's *ability* to grow in understanding. To allow a person to keep on erring would be absurd. Sometimes, also, the mistake was my own for expecting too much of someone. It is better always to give people less of a load to carry before burdening them with a heavy rock.

I said it was important for Ananda not to be sectarian, but to respect other faiths, and include all broadly in our sympathies.

I also urged our members not to think of Ananda as separate from society as a whole. Our good, I said, includes the good of everyone, and not that only of Ananda. If our immediate gain means loss for someone else, it is not a gain at all.

Thus, in June 1976, after a forest fire destroyed 450 acres at the farm, and twenty-one of our twenty-two homes, neighbors phoned us excitedly to announce that the cause of the fire had been a faulty spark arrester on a county vehicle. "We can sue the county," they enthused, "and get all our money back!" I wrote the county supervisors about it, but in a different vein. "I'm sure you're aware," I said, "that Ananda was the biggest loser in the fire. Perhaps you've been worried about what we'll do about it. I want you to know that we won't be suing. We don't want to take our bad luck out on fellow citizens by increasing the county's insurance rates. Anything that harms the county will harm Ananda also, in the long run." Our neighbors sued and collected. Ananda, on the other hand, faced the real possibility of bankruptcy. Another motto of ours has always been, *"Jato dharma, tato jaya:* Where there is adherence to truth, there lies victory." We "stuck to our guns" and not only survived, but flourished.

Some twenty members (including families) left as a result of the fire. Those who asked us for help were paid, out of donations that individuals and other communities were sending us. Only after paying them off did we begin the rebuilding of our own homes.

The people who came to Ananda in the beginning were not devotees, for the most part. The word soon spread, however, that Ananda's goals were spiritual. In time, non-devotees stopped coming. I didn't force spirituality on anyone. Thus, I also didn't demand that people become disciples of Yogananda, nor that they accept him personally in any sense. These are sacred decisions, and must be left to the free will of the individual. I made Master's way attractive to people, however, by sharing with them my own devotion to it. Soon enough, people began not only coming as devotees, but with eagerness to become his disciples.

I've always found it difficult to say No to people. My solution to this difficulty was the same as when Master put me in charge of the monks at Mt. Washington: to help those who didn't belong to weed themselves out. One way I did so at Ananda was to encourage a spirit of devotion. Faced with this spirit, the "freeloaders" and nay-sayers became uncomfortable. In fact, our first need was to make clear to those who came what we were, and weren't. As long as we were unclear on our self-definition, it was easy for anyone to think he or she could decide what we ought to be. The veriest newcomer often thought, "This is *my* community. Why shouldn't I and those who agree with me have a right to determine what Ananda will be?" Negative energy, fortunately, has little cohesive power, especially when faced with positive energy.

People wanted frequent meetings to decide Ananda's future. I let them meet as often as they liked. I didn't often attend those meetings, for I saw no way they'd ever accomplish anything significant. Often, all they did was stir up useless emotions. I knew, however, that the success of a community depends primarily on *attitudes,* not on superficial questions like zoning or how much everyone needs to tithe. I also knew that when many voices are raised on every side of an issue, nothing is likely to emerge.

There was a dog at Ananda named Blue. Blue caused general consternation by chasing the deer, barking at visitors, and obstructing people in their work. Declamations were made on every aspect of this issue. Unbelievably, it took all of five years for everyone to agree that Blue should be taken elsewhere and abandoned. (Blue had strayed onto the land in the first place.) The positive side of this fascination with minor issues was that the meetings never generated more than one-horse-power energy.

My own concern was with issues of more far-reaching importance. To achieve my spiritual ends, I found it necessary to accept compromise on certain issues in the name of harmony, and for the sake of things I considered more important: especially, the creation of a core of people in whom I felt I could instill a spirit of service and devotion.

Meanwhile, therefore, I worked with those whose spirit was positive, those who wanted to build, not merely to complain.

I tried also to do what Master did with his disciples: project thought forms toward those who wanted to work with me, rather than spelling out exactly what I wanted each one to do. Thus, they were free to take an idea from me or not, as they chose, and work to make it their own instead of coming to me constantly for guidance and approval. I told them they could accept as much, or as little, of an idea as they liked. If they tuned into it, it became *our* idea, neither theirs nor mine. Thus, Ananda became *our* community, gradually, and grew in a homogeneous spirit. For the thoughts I held and projected were those our Guru gave me for our development. Sometimes it appeared to others as though I were merely leaving them to their own devices. Far from it! By tuning in to our Guru's guidance, and to my own awareness of it, they developed their own inner strength, and didn't become weakly dependent on guidance from outside themselves.

Ananda's true leaders have always been those who tried to tune in, seeking guidance primarily from within themselves. It was, I had seen, the way Master trained us if we listened to him inwardly. Ultimately, we all wanted only to project God's will for this time in history, in response to humanity's needs to which God Himself was responding.

Dick Baker once said to me, "When I die, all this will disappear. The universe has no more reality than I myself give to it. It exists in my own mind." Evidently, this thinking was a product of his Zen training, though I cannot imagine it was the teaching of Buddha. For although this philosophy crops up from time to time in human thought, it is easily demolished. It simply represents an attempt to exclude God from the scheme of things, and it forces several obvious questions. For instance: Could you, Dick Baker, write plays as good as William Shakespeare's? carve statues as good as those of Michelangelo? build bridges of a grandeur equal to the Golden Gate Bridge? compose a Beethoven symphony? sing like Enrico Caruso? Mind has produced "all this," yes: but not *your* mind, nor mine. We are merely dreaming within a cosmic dream. That One Consciousness which dreamed "all this" brought us into existence as well. The noblest thing we can do in life is to open ourselves—our hearts and minds—to the influence of His dreaming.

I didn't insist, to begin with, on people becoming disciples of Master. Bit by bit, however, they did become disciples, or else left to follow some other calling. Our rate of attrition over the years has been remarkably low. Many members today at Ananda came to us in those first years.

A suggestion was made early in Ananda's history that we close down the retreat at least for a time, and concentrate on developing the community.

"No," I said. "We need to direct our energies outward in service to others, and not inwardly only. Otherwise God will cease to pour out blessings on us. If no one else wants to serve at the retreat, I'll do it myself—all of it, if necessary."

At first, the retreat drained Ananda's coffers, returning nothing of tangible value. In time, however, it became a major income-producer for the community. On the other hand, spiritually speaking, it brought much of the energy that built Ananda.

I once remarked to my mother, "I simply can't understand a wealthy person wanting to build a beautiful home and garden just for himself and his family." Mother replied, "That's a novel way of looking at things!" And I thought, "How strange to look at things in any other way!"

After my parents died, I wanted to give my inheritance to Ananda. However, I realized that Dad especially, who had never donated a dime to Ananda, would be restless in his soul if he saw that money going elsewhere. One day he exclaimed to me in exasperation, "You've just *got* to stop giving all your money away!" I, on the other hand, would have been uncomfortable keeping it for myself. I then hit on a compromise: Build a beautiful home and garden for myself that would serve not only me, but the whole community as a spiritual center. Many hundreds, perhaps thousands, have been inspired by Crystal Hermitage (as I named my new residence). Actually, I myself rarely get to enjoy it, especially now that I live in Italy, and even at Ananda Village my work of writing and music composition requires privacy, which is available to me only in my apartment and little garden downstairs. To me, however, when I'm there, the occasional shouts of children around the pool upstairs, and the chanting of devotees in the upstairs dome, are a greater fulfillment than any sense of proprietorship could be.

Only once in Ananda's history have I allowed the thought to enter my mind briefly: "It was I who brought this place into existence!" This was one evening during our early years, when most members had only trailers to live in. I strolled past these simple dwellings enjoying the light coming from their windows, and thought, "There was darkness here not long ago! It was I who brought soft light to this place." I entertained this thought happily for a few minutes, then put it out of my mind—not with a sense of sacrifice, but in the suddenly vivid awareness that this kind of happiness, though pleasant for a time, was constricting to my consciousness. The smallest hint of ego only imprisons the soul.

Beauty, however, was important in my dreams for Ananda and in Ananda's development. Men and women played equal roles in the community from the beginning. It is equally true, however, that each sex is blessed with special gifts—not uniquely, but generally so. Women, for instance, are more naturally inclined to create beautiful surroundings. I urged the women in the community to concentrate on beautifying Ananda. Quite a few of Ananda's homes are esthetically pleasing, and nestle in beautiful gardens. Music, drama, and the visual arts play an important role in Ananda's community life. Recently, the forest land was thinned out to give it a more park-like appearance, which made it possible to plant trees in a greater variety, in locations that were carefully thought out in advance.

Enjoyment of beauty is a delight to the soul. Attachment to it, however, is a prison. Thus too with my own heart's feelings, every time they felt drawn to feminine beauty and tenderness. Even in that inspiration, thoughts wove themselves of *personal,* egoic fulfillment. For many years the fear lingered that, thus threatened, the very soul freedom for which I'd come to my Guru was in danger. Must I sacrifice salvation itself on the altar of service to him? Could God really ask of me such an enormous sacrifice? Yet, I asked myself, how can I liberate myself from sensual and romantic longings when all my energy needs to be devoted to serving this work? If only, I thought, it were possible to live in a monastery, or as a hermit, instead of having to mix always with people of both sexes! If I weren't exposed to temptation, wouldn't I, at least, gain spiritually? Could I run away? Yet this work was what my Guru had given me to do. I could see no alternative but to go on, hoping for the best, clinging with faith to his power, believing that he would take me eventually out of delusion. To me personally, the risk was agonizing. Meanwhile, I never pretended to myself or to anyone else that it was *not* a delusion, or might be in some way justifiable. At last, as it happened, I discovered that his blessings had been with me always.

Divine Mother sent me someone who satisfied a need deep within me, and brought a satisfaction that didn't depend at all on the person involved. Several times I said to her, "Nothing you do or don't do, say or don't say, can affect the blessing you've awakened in my heart. It isn't human love. It's inner completeness." She didn't remain at Ananda. For many years now, however, that sense of completeness has remained within me, unaltered: a sense of holy sweetness and beauty in which desire plays no role. Love inspires me more now than ever, but a love that embraces everything I see, every person I meet. This love recoils from confinement in any form, as a freed prisoner might from the memory of incarceration in his old cell.

It would be foolish to presume on this inner freedom. It is too sacred to be treated lightly. Helping me in this regard is a distaste even for hugging anyone anymore. Love, I feel, is of the spirit, not something to be grasped outwardly.

A disciple of Swami Sri Yukteswar's received a similar blessing. Having long suffered from an unfulfilled attraction to human love, he begged his guru to help him win release. One day, the guru told him, "Divine Mother will give you a blessing today." They were seated in a train, which was standing in a station. Another train next to theirs was just pulling out.

"Look there," Sri Yukteswar said. The man glanced across, and caught a brief glimpse of a woman, the mere sight of whom forever satisfied his human longing.

I can best express through music the feeling of holy upliftment that possessed me. Therefore I tell people, "If you want to know me, listen to my music." It is through this that people have come to understand what Ananda is truly all about. Without its influence, Ananda would not be what it is today. Books and lectures are only the outer form of the teachings. Music is its coursing blood.

One thing I have always discouraged at Ananda is anything resembling a group attitude. I remember a convent I visited years ago. The nun assigned to greet visitors addressed me in a whisper. "And over there," she said reverently, "we have our chapel, where the nuns pray daily for others. We get up every morning at. . . ."

Just then, their Father Confessor arrived with a large box of chocolates as a gift for the community. The tone of her voice suddenly shifted from one of hushed reverence to a squeal of girlish delight. This change has always stood out in my mind as showing the difference between assumed and genuine feeling. Is not God more pleased with us when we share with Him what we sincerely feel, instead of mumbling prayers to Him from within a cowl of assumed humility?

I wrote a song that has become a theme song at Ananda:

Walk like a man,
Even though you walk alone.
Why court approval
Once the road is known?
Let come who will,
But if they all turn home,
The goal still awaits you:
Go on alone!

Follow your dream,
Though it lead to worlds unknown!

Life's but a shadow
Once our dreams have flown!
What if men cry,
"Your dream is not our own"?
Your soul knows the answer:
Go on alone!

Give life your heart,
Bless everything that's grown.
Fear not the loving:
All this world's your own!
Make rich the soil,
But once the seed is sown,
Seek freedom, don't linger:
Go on alone!

Walk like a man,
Even though you walk alone.
Why court approval
Once the road is known?
Let come who will,
But if they all turn home,
The goal still awaits you:
Go on alone!

We encourage eccentricity at Ananda. At Mt. Washington, by contrast, Arne Lipovec (Brother Premamoy) used to say to me, half in appreciation and half in criticism, "You're eccentric!" I asked him to explain himself. He replied, "I don't mean you're crazy. What I mean is, you aren't centered in anyone's expectations of you. For instance, you don't hold as sacred, necessarily, the things others consider solemn and important. When the nuns wanted a new designation for themselves, in order to get away from the word *nun,* you couldn't resist suggesting—jokingly, I know—that they consider the designation, 'renunciettes,' or—with a more Indian sound—'monkinis.' That's what I mean: You aren't always reverent enough, and at times when others think it proper to be serious."

At Ananda, perhaps infected by my own light attitude toward excessive formality, people are encouraged to be simply themselves as long as they develop inward devotion to God.

I once said to Glenn Dittrich, a friend of Ananda's, that one could usually tell which spiritual group a person belonged to by his outer attitude. Many "Hare Krishna" devotees tried to imitate the Bengali accent of Prabhupad, their founder. SRF members affected inwardness by excessive solemnity, unaware perhaps that Yogananda himself had a delightful sense of humor, and would sometimes actually shake with laughter. Glen surprised me by replying, "I can generally recognize an Ananda member, also."

I wondered how he could say that, when I'd worked so hard to avoid group attitudes. "Please explain," I said.

"Well," he replied, "I find everyone I meet from Ananda to be genuine, not artificial. I find the members open to others, and willing to listen to their points of view. They talk *with* people, rather than *at* them. Moreover, I find them all very friendly. It's obvious they care for people as individuals."

Of such attitudes, what could I do but approve?

Something I avoided at Ananda was Indianizing people. This wasn't easy to do, for I myself loved the

Indian *bhav*—that is to say, its spiritual attitude. I let my hair grow long again, as it had been in India, and I gave Indian names to many of our members. Indian devotional music has always thrilled me. It generates a vibration, however, that in America is not "here and now." Wherever God places us, I said finally, there He must come to us. More and more, therefore, I withdrew from practices that took us away from our present realities. After all, we lived in America now, and were doing a work designed to spiritualize Americans, not to Indianize them. My basic goal was to inspire people everywhere to embrace a more spiritual outlook. This could not be accomplished if we created a separate identity for ourselves, and withdrew mentally from the rest of society.

I didn't push unnatural theories on our members, such as strict communal ownership, or strict poverty. Nor did I tell them they had to give everything to Ananda. Rather, I tried to help them to grow beyond the life to which they were already accustomed toward a new and better way of living. I saw to it that people received an income, which they were allowed to keep or spend as they liked. For myself, however, I accepted no salary. Seva and others tried to insist that I receive one, but whatever money I needed I earned outside the community by lecturing and teaching, and most of that money, even, went to Ananda. Thus, others developed similar attitudes of sharing, and soon thought no more of earning for themselves. It became quite the norm at Ananda, in fact, for department heads to receive lower wages than some of those working under them whose financial needs were greater than their own.

The devotee's outlook is fundamentally different from that of the worldly person. For one thing, where worldly people define wealth in terms of acquisition, the devotee defines it in terms of inner happiness. Where the worldly person defines fulfillment in terms of desires satisfied, the devotee defines it in terms of desires transcended. Security, to the devotee, is not a bank account but a sense of constant inner peace. Inner renunciation is the way to true fulfillment. The true devotee is not interested in owning anything personally. He thinks only of serving God. And he sees God as the sole Doer. To God the devotee gives all the credit for anything he or she does.

I myself naturally like people, as I've already said. I see them, however, as souls primarily, not as personalities. In speaking to them, I've always done my best to address their souls, rather than their egos. Thus, what others thought of me, or whether they even liked me, did not greatly matter to me. Of supreme importance, where my relations with them were concerned, was the reflection that all of us are fellow pilgrims on the long climb toward God. My love for them was impersonal in the sense that, basing my attitude on my Guru's example, I wanted nothing from others. My love was also, on the other hand, deeply personal in the sense that I wanted the best for everyone. I wasn't always pleasing to them, for what I wanted wasn't always what their egos wanted. My desire was to help their souls to emerge from the chrysalis of ego-attachment and soar in

Spirit. Sometimes, in the process, I made enemies. I never compromised my soul-friendship for them, however.

We made other requirements of people, partly to sift out the superficial seekers and partly to help Ananda to meet its expenses. I asked, as a condition of membership, that people pay a fee of $1,000 for individuals, and $1,500 for couples after they'd been accepted for residency. This seemed to me a minor sacrifice to make as a demonstration of one's sincerity and commitment. This is still the practice, though the amount was lowered in recent years, compensated for by the cost of training they received. We also asked people to help with monthly maintenance costs and other on-going expenses. And there was of course the monthly mortgage of $1,750. For some time I accepted the burden of paying the mortgage myself. It meant my continuing with nightly classes in various cities. It was only after a year, as people came to consider Ananda their own, that this burden was taken off my hands.

In 1969 I wrote a yoga correspondence course as a means of helping to support Ananda. The course was limited at first to Hatha Yoga, for I didn't want my lessons to compete with SRF's correspondence course. In time, however, I grew dissatisfied with the thought that what I'd written didn't wholly express my true heart's feelings. Thus I re-wrote the lessons, approaching the teachings not as SRF had done in its lessons, but rather as Paramhansa Yogananda had once approached them in classes he'd given on Patanjali's yoga aphorisms.

I moved out of my apartment in June 1969, and settled in my little house at Ananda. Soon after that, we rented a large apartment house on California Street in San Francisco, which served us as a sort of halfway house where people could live before moving to Ananda. For the rest of 1969, this apartment house was my main base of operations.

From January to May 1970, I rented a small house in the southern part of Sacramento to be closer to Ananda. For nearly a year I gave yoga classes every evening from Sunday to Friday, then drove up to Ananda. Late Friday evening I dictated my correspondence lessons while Suzanne Huntzinger (Bharati), who had been a professional secretary, scribbled industriously. This took me late into Friday night. Early Saturday morning I led a strolling *kirtan* through the grounds to the temple, followed by group meditation. Later, I gave classes for retreatants and residents. Saturday afternoon I held interviews, then recorded my weekly radio program. Saturday evening I usually gave a concert and a talk. Sunday morning there was the weekly devotional service. (It wasn't until 1986, near Assisi, Italy, that I wrote the Festival of Light, used since then every Sunday.) Sunday afternoon I drove back to San Francisco, there to begin my weekly schedule all over again.

It was a busy time for me. In later years, others could help out, Jyotish of course acting as my mainstay.

We have a motto at Ananda: "Many hands make a miracle." This truth has become ingrained in us over the years. I didn't build Ananda alone. All I did, really, was give it the push it needed. Many hands, many voices, many minds made the miracle that eventually emerged.

Thus, we also have another theme song at Ananda, one I wrote some years after the first one:

Many hands make a miracle:
Let's all join hands together!
Life on earth is so wonderful
When people laugh and dance and struggle as friends,
Then all their dreams achieve their ends.

Many hands make a miracle:
People climbing together.
Soon we reach to the pinnacle
Of every mountain peak we hazard as one:
We'll lift our hands to welcome the sun!
We lift our hands to welcome the sun!

CHAPTER 30

Karmic Patterns

I have made occasional references in these pages to the karmic threads or patterns of coincidence that run through human life. Those patterns can be discerned not only in the lives of individuals, but in the vast tapestry of history with its panorama of nations, cultures, and religions. History, as has many times been said, repeats itself, and many of its repetitions demonstrate moral and spiritual principles. They may be seen in the eventual destruction of persons or nations that seek to destroy others. They may be seen also in a continuity of regional and national characteristics. The Germanic people, for example, have always shown exceptional ability in many fields. Julius Caesar noted it more than two thousand years ago. He noted also that, as a consequence, they repeatedly rose to prominence, only to fall again because of excessive conceit.

Another example may be seen in the artistic talent of the ancient Etruscans. Their gift continued into the story of Florence and Tuscany, giving birth eventually to the European Renaissance.

One thinks too of the American Indians: independent, yet cooperative within their own nations, and dedicated to living in harmony with nature. Their consciousness must have impregnated the North American soil, for the white settlers also absorbed much of it. It was manifested in the pioneer settlers of the West, in their ability to cooperate with one another. The independent spirit of Americans is well known. And the growing interest of their descendants in harmony between man and nature suggests that Americans today may not only have absorbed that consciousness from another people, but in many cases may actually *be* those people, reincarnated. Many of them today, at any rate, express a deep affinity for the earlier Indian culture.

I have noted this phenomenon also in New Zealand and Australia: a tendency to express in new ways many aspects of the cultures they thought they'd supplanted. I don't propose here, however, to examine those similarities in detail. Suffice it to say that this was the impression I've formed on my visits there.

As for Ananda, I have often thought that the community movement, difficult as it has been to get started, would have been far more difficult to launch in any other country.

The openness of present-day Americans to new ideas made it easier, finally, for Paramhansa Yogananda to start a mission designed to bring harmony and a sense of common purpose to the world's great religions. Not for nothing is America called the "New World." Its very newness puts it in a position to accept more easily a teaching intended to lift all humanity into a new age. Perhaps, with the new-age insights that are now sweeping the world, it will be possible to break some of the fixed karmic patterns of the past.

Yogananda declared, "I was sent by God and the masters to bring back original Christianity, as taught by Jesus Christ, and the original yoga teachings of Krishna, as taught in the Bhagavad Gita." Truth never changes, but its manifestations are at the same time ever new. The Bible tells us that nothing new exists under the sun, but there is repeated re-discovery. Christopher Columbus, as people are generally aware now, was by no means the first person from the "outer world" to discover America. With America's re-discovery, however, there came an opportunity for re-appraisal: for re-affirmation of what was true, and rejection of what was false.

The karmic patterns that concern us here are those running through the fabric of Christian history, specifically. Yogananda made it clear that Jesus, in his original teachings, placed little emphasis on outer religion—that is to say, on church affiliation and church rituals. Had Jesus intended to strengthen people in their outer affiliation, he would have tried to work *with* the rabbis of his times. Instead, he challenged them outspokenly. He stated that he'd been sent to fulfill "the law and the prophets," but clearly that fulfillment didn't embrace the rabbinical point of view. He could not have intended to fulfill "the law and the prophets" in an outward, institutional way, only to contradict himself by urging his followers to establish a separate church. The fulfillment of which he spoke was the deeper teaching of the prophets: the teaching of *Self*-realization; the inner "ritual" of communion with God in deep meditation.

Paramhansa Yogananda, befitting his own mission to "bring back original Christianity," named his organization "Self-Realization Fellowship." He declared that SRF wasn't a new sect: Its purpose was only to give renewed emphasis to an important, universal principle. To him, this name signified *Self-realization for every soul through communion with God, inner fellowship (sat-sanga) with great saints and masters, and outward fellowship with truth-seeking souls.* With the obvious purpose of establishing a new karmic pattern, he sought to prevent a re-enactment of what he considered the disaster in Christian history, by founding an organization dedicated specifically, even by name, to perpetuating these high ideals.

The ancient karmic patterns, however, were already established, and powerful. Self-Realization Fellowship, in its short history to date, has already introduced many changes into his work. The founding ideals of the organization were clearly stated by Yogananda: in its name; in his "aims and ideals" (some of which, however, have already been changed); in his books; in countless lectures. His organization, unfortunately, found itself drawn by that old karma into the vortex of "churchianity." By an irony of fate, the four principal directors, loyal disciples all—Tara, Daya, Ananda, and Mrinalini—were also former Mormons, raised in a tradition of absolute obedience to a supreme bishop, whose dominance is quite as absolute as the Pope's in Rome. Does this mean that nothing can be done now to return Yogananda's work to the spirit of individual freedom he intended? I understand from certain knowledgeable people Yogananda grieved over these matters in letters to his closest disciple, Rajarsi Janakananda. He warned Daya Mata, "How you all will change this work!" Perhaps he even hinted to me of the need for "fresh blood" when he said, "You have a great work to do, Walter." Perhaps those words contained a subtle plea. For he said to me also, in May of 1950 at Twenty-Nine Palms, "Apart from St. Lynn (Rajarsi), every man has disappointed me—and *you mustn't* disappoint me!" He certainly didn't mean that all had disappointed him *as disciples.* We were talking then of the future of his work. His disappointment was that, whereas the spread of the work demanded more of an outgoing, masculine energy, no male disciple so far, except for Rajarsi, had understood the broad implications of his mission. I myself, before I was dismissed from SRF, was the only man on a nine-person Board of Directors.

To Dr. Lewis he said, "No matter what you or I do, this work [that is to say, this mission] will follow a certain pattern, *ordained by God.*" What can those words signify, except a reference to karmic patterns? For Master would never have set his will against God's will, and certainly he hoped that no true disciple would ever do so, either. God had sent him into this incarnation to change old, karmic patterns: to reinforce the bright threads, if possible, and to diminish or eliminate the dark ones. It must be understood, of course, that no one, however great, could change the whole tapestry. God Himself would never do that, for it would mean going against his own karmic law. God never treats human beings as puppets, making and remaking history without reference to their individual and national karmas. When Yogananda used the words, "ordained by God," what he meant was, "ordained by the karmic law established by God." Again, if Yogananda was sent to bring back original Christianity, and if he saw that karmic currents would actively oppose that divine purpose, he did not mean that those currents would win out. Quite the opposite! In one way or another, by one instrument or another, the purpose of his incarnation, divinely ordained, *cannot fail.*

For this is, as I said, a new age—declared to be such by our own gurus. It is an age of energy. Jesus came at a time of descent into materialism and the entrenchment of people's consciousness in solid forms and fixed dogmas. In the present age, albeit materialistic, people's consciousness of matter itself is of the underlying reality of energy. Human understanding is lighter now, more expansive, less inclined to lock everything into fixed definitions and forms.

I have often told Ananda members, "If by any chance we fail in carrying out the divine plan, God will find others to do so. If Master gave me a work to fulfill, it was not to me, personally. This is simply a mission that needs fulfilling. The advantage to our fulfilling it is that I knew him, personally. I can recall countless examples from his life that support what we are doing. And if anyone here, or if I myself, feel inclined to make a wrong choice, I can recall too many examples as possible correctives, and will always do my sincere best to abide by those examples."

Paramhansa Yogananda often remarked, "Jesus Christ was crucified once, but his teachings have been crucified daily for nearly two thousand years." In making this statement he implied not another failure, but eventual triumph. As he himself sometimes said, "The spirit I like in America is implied in the saying, 'Eventually? Eventually? Why not *now?!*'"

We live in a new age—an age of energy. Humanity is ready to embrace a new and broader understanding. As Yogananda predicted, "Self-realization will someday become the religion of the world."

I challenged Daya Mata on this point in 1990 at a meeting between SRF and Ananda in Fresno. I said, "Master cannot possibly have meant 'Self-Realization Fellowship, Inc.' He had to have meant Self-realization as a principle." Daya replied, "That's . . . your opinion." Daya's way of responding to every challenge has always been to suppress it. But no, Daya, it is not mere opinion! It is self-evident in Yogananda's mission itself. He predicted that a new understanding would in time become the basis of all religions: a recognition that the purpose of religion is the realization of the one true Self of all beings, within.

The betrayal by Judas has been treated as a unique event in history. It was by no means so. Yogananda even explained that Judas, personally, could have avoided the karmic pattern that forced him to that betrayal. Judas merely perpetuated an already-existing karma in Judaism itself, and perhaps in all religions. Jesus referred to this pattern when he declared,

"O Jerusalem, Jerusalem, which killest the prophets, and stonest them that are sent unto thee; how often would I have gathered thy children together, as a hen doth gather her brood under her wings, and ye would not!" (Luke 13:34)

There has been a perpetual struggle in Christianity between inner, soul-aspiration and egoic desire for power, control, and worldly recognition. Judas betrayed Jesus because of his desire for money and worldly acceptance. The karmic "invitation," however, to respond to these delusions was already woven into the tapestry of history. By that betrayal, the thread was woven also into that part of the tapestry which depicts the story of Christianity.

Yogananda, in saying that the teachings of Jesus have continued to be betrayed, was speaking from his realization of God; he was not speaking as a historian. His statement was born of divine insight, not of scholarly logic. He also named the betrayer: "churchianity"—distinct, as he pointed out, from "Christianity." It is institutionalism that has undermined the purity of Christ's teachings.

Judas, by his betrayal of Jesus, only gave another push to the downward spiral of delusion that was present already in Judaism. The churches added a push of their own, like runners—to change the metaphor—seizing the baton in a relay race.

One wonders how Judas fell, if, as Yogananda said, he could have avoided this destiny. What he did was open himself to the broader karma of his own people. His first thought (so one imagines) was: "The Master deserves wider recognition. It's a pity to see such a motley array of followers around him—earnest, no doubt, but hardly *Voices* to which important people will ever listen. His greatness deserves recognition by the real powers in this world." Finding Jesus unreceptive to his idea, Judas must have tried to justify it by dwelling on the importance which those powers centered in themselves. His next step, once he'd developed that mindset, would naturally have been to concentrate on the source of that power: money. The Bible calls Judas a thief. Surely he was not yet one when Jesus selected him as one of the twelve apostles. One imagines Judas thinking, during his gradual descent into delusion, "If only Jesus weren't so *unworldly!*" Gradually, his focus would have shifted from inner communion with God, which Jesus had taught him, to the value of worldly approval and influence.

Every thought form has its own magnetism. The more we invest a thought with energy, the greater its magnetic hold on us. One can be drawn into any delusion by simply concentrating on it, and investing it with energy. The satanic force is not some sly, shifty-eyed imp with horns, hooves, and a long tail. Satan, Yogananda explained, is an aspect of infinite consciousness itself. God, in creating the universe, manifested an infinite number of thought forms, each of them a vortex, itself, of consciousness and energy. Thus, each thought form generates its own magnetism. "Satan" is that force which consciously draws one into the ideational vortex of one's choice, and prevents him from releasing his awareness and letting it expand toward infinity. Many vortices are generated by human beings themselves: by their infatuation, for example, for collecting trivia such as paperweights or china figurines. The desire to accumulate, on the other hand, is universal. It draws power from infinite consciousness, narrowly focusing it in the ideational vortex of "I" and "mine." As Yogananda put it in *Autobiography of a Yogi,* "Thoughts are universally and not individually rooted."

Certain of those thought forms resonate particularly with human nature. Thus, Judas was tempted, through his fascination with outer importance, into an ideational vortex of money, power, and personal recognition. That vortex had the power to attract him, as long as he himself responded to it. Having once entered it, he was sucked downward. When its power of attraction was spent, it spewed him out again, as if out of the bottom of the whirlpool. Suddenly he recognized the enormity of the evil he'd perpetrated. Filled with self-loathing, he took his own life.

The karma of Christ's crucifixion was not only that single act of betrayal. Nor was it expiated by that suicide. The act had been foretold long before the life of Jesus. And the karma persists even to this day. What is the karma? It is that world-involving tendency to take the highest spiritual teaching, the soul's relation to truth and God, and to redefine it in such a way as to control those who believe in it.

The Church has consistently kept a tight rein on what it is pleased to call "Christian" worship. It has persecuted what it calls "heretics." It has even persecuted its saints. Thus also did the Jews, long before

Jesus, for they considered their saints (whom they called "prophets") threats to the status quo. While the saints (or prophets) were alive, they were persecuted. Once they were safely dead, their persecutors claimed credit for their holiness.

The Jews would not accept any revelation that was not already declared in their scriptures. A rabbi I met in Jerusalem said, "Even if the Temple of Jerusalem were to descend from above onto the place where it once stood, I would consider it my duty to measure it carefully and see whether it corresponded exactly to the measurements given in the scriptures."

The Christian Church, also, has insisted that there could be no revelation since New Testament times; that the final declaration of truth can be found only in the Bible. Thus, the Church avoided the need to deal with any influence that might pulverize its rigid theology. The Jews, of course, have refused to accept Jesus even as a prophet, for Judaic theology was already ossified by New Testament times. Had there been openness in the time of Jesus, there would never have been a Christian religion. Jesus himself never said he'd been sent to start a new religion. Rather, what he told people was, "Think not that I am come to destroy the law, or the prophets: I am come not to destroy, but to fulfill." (Matthew 5:17) The first Christian, as has been well said, was not Jesus Christ, but St. Paul. It is unfortunately common in this world for tradition to be built up, like a stone wall, to enclose its tenets, saying, "This much we accept, and no more." That was what Yogananda meant in saying that the teachings of Jesus Christ have been crucified daily. The spirit of Judas lives on, vitalized by the churches themselves.

Interestingly, Yogananda himself was aware of, and even valued, both sides of this issue. He was not anti-authoritarian, as one might expect from the fact that he prized inner freedom so highly. He only wanted people to give supreme recognition to *divine,* not merely to church, authority.

He showed this orthodox outlook in the way he summed up an episode that he and others of us witnessed together in an Indian movie called "The Light of India," about the life of Gyandev, a medieval Indian saint. (Gyandev is perhaps better known in India as Gyaneshwar.)

Gyandev's father had been born a brahmin. He sinned, however, against the brahminical code, and as a result was declared an outcaste. Later in life he paid the supreme penalty for his sin by committing suicide. The brahmins of his day, however, would not reinstate his children as brahmins even then, for they could find no sanction for doing so in the scriptures. Gyandev reminded them that the Bhagavad Gita states that all beings are equal in the sight of God. Thereupon the priests replied, "On this particular point, the scriptures are silent; therefore we must be silent also." Receiving this answer, Gyandev started to recite a passage from the Bhagavad Gita which declares that God is equally manifested in all beings. A priest tried to stop his mouth, placing a hand over it. At that point, a bull standing nearby finished the passage, speaking in a deep, bovine tone. The brahmins then had to accept Gyandev as a great soul indeed, and reinstated all of them, humbly stating, "Truly, it is you who are the *true* brahmins!"

Yogananda's comment afterwards was, "Those priests were right also, however, to abide by the scriptures as they understood them. Gyandev was right, but they too were right. What Gyandev did was simply give them a higher perception of truth."

Thus, Yogananda's statement that the churches have crucified the teachings of Christ by "churchifying" them cannot mean that he faulted them for acting according to their sincere understanding. What he faulted only was their narrow vision, and their determination to impose their narrowness on others. In India, this danger is avoided by the general recognition that true saints revitalize religion, and bring to priestly understanding the fresh air of direct, inner realization.

The emphasis of early Christians on the importance of Self-realization was first condemned by the Church as heretical, then persecuted, and finally, in time, buried. Writings that emphasized inner communion with God were determinedly destroyed, and "true" (which is to say, formally recognized) Christians were exhorted to heed only outer authority, and to engage only in outer ritual.

This was the churches' act of betrayal.

It wasn't until the Twentieth Century that long-buried texts were discovered at Nag Hammadi. Though scholars at first kept them from the public eye, they were obliged at last to release them. People who have scrutinized those texts declare that they reveal something quite unexpected: that the ancient, so-called "Gnostic" emphasis on direct communion with God, so long dismissed as heretical, was far more important to early Christians than had hitherto been thought. Indeed, from what Yogananda said about "original Christianity," the teaching of the early Gnostics was probably—when stripped of its later distortions—the original, true Christianity.

This is not to say that all those gnostic teachings were equally valid. It seems safe to say that, where they depart significantly from the sayings of Jesus in the New Testament, they deserve to be discarded as either suspect or, quite simply, wrong. I have frequently stated elsewhere in my writings that *the true custodians of religion are the saints.* There were Gnostics and Gnostics. Those alone were true who had attained divine insight, or true "gnosis."

Webster's Third International Dictionary, published in 1961, when the contents of Nag Hammadi discoveries were still being debated, out of sight of the public, defines Gnosticism as "The thought and practice of any of various cults of late pre-Christian and early Christian centuries declared heretical by the Church and distinguished chiefly by pretension to mystic and especially esoteric religious insights, by emphasis on knowledge rather than faith, and by the conviction that matter is evil." The *Oxford American Dictionary,* published in 1980, does not even contain the word "Gnosticism," nor any word related to it, such as *gnosis* or *gnostic.*

If we could go to Jesus himself, there would be no need to look to scholars for explanations of his "original teachings." Nor is there any need now to go to scholars for explanations of "Gnosticism," about which present-day information is in any case vague, since we have Paramhansa Yogananda's explanation of the original teachings of Jesus. For Yogananda was himself a great master. However, the issue here is not even whether Yogananda's explanation was correct. Rather, it is that, since he did explain them, his disciples have a spiritual duty to abide by that explanation.

Unfortunately, the history of his organization shows already a tendency to enclose his teachings in a straitjacket. Such indeed was the betrayal Yogananda imputed to the Christian Church! Alas, he himself said to Daya Mata, *"How you all will change my work!"*

In early Christianity, disciples who wanted a personal, inward relationship with Christ and God were persecuted by an institution that was determined to subject them to its control. The Church insisted that, if people's emphasis on a direct relationship with God were not brought under rigid control—of course, in time it was suppressed altogether—the Church would lose any say in what practices were permissible. Who, then, the Church "Fathers" asked, could be certain what the teachings of Jesus really were? The solution they settled on was to ban as "heretical" the claim that anyone could speak—as Gyandev did—with inner, God-given authority. Authority became vested in the pope. Martin Luther's Reformation caused Protestants to invest it in scripture itself. This, however, was a disastrous development, for it removed altogether the possibility of a wise, living authority, and led inescapably to the conclusion that truth depends on majority agreement. Thus, any interpretation of scripture is admissible, provided only that enough people fancy it.

SRF today has introduced a new paradigm, one very different from that which Yogananda originally—and, I should add, fervently—proposed. Surely SRF's actions, and the justification SRF offers for those actions, are identical with those of the Church, which has "crucified" Christ by insisting that it has a monopoly on Christ's teachings. The Church enforced its claim by persecuting all whom it considered "heretics." The lengths to which SRF has gone to achieve the same ends are extraordinary. SRF, too, has persecuted others in the name of "protecting the purity of the teachings."

I see some justification for self-defense, when one is under attack. I can see none for destroying people whose motives are pacific and harmonious, and who merely want to serve God as they are guided to do from within, and as they are able. Kamala Silva, for example, wrote a beautiful book of reminiscences on her life with Paramhansa Yogananda. She was denounced by SRF, not because the book itself was objectionable, but only because it was written without SRF's sanction. Many such examples might be cited. Perhaps it is enough to cite the fact that I myself was denounced without being given an opportunity to defend myself, that I had projected onto me motives I knew were not true, that my right to continue serving my Guru either within or outside of the organization was denied, and that I have been persecuted for more than forty years because I wouldn't simply turn my back on them, as most people in my shoes would have done. Their accusations against me are based entirely on the fact that my continued devotion to my Guru, and to his teachings, is an embarrassment to them. They have shown themselves to be more concerned with saving face than with compassion, or with truth.

When Daya Mata asked me to declare publicly that I'd resigned from SRF, to which request I replied, "I can't. It isn't true, and you *know* it isn't true!" she said, unbelievably, "Well, you *should* have resigned."

SRF would like to say that I have changed the teachings. In fact, it is they who have changed them, and in some respects fundamentally. Unknowledgeable people have asked us, "Why did Ananda take Krishna off its altars?" Ananda never took Krishna off its altars: SRF *added* him!

Most people are unaware of the numerous ways SRF has changed Master's work during Daya Mata's presidency. The addition of Krishna to its altars is at least understandable, since Yogananda, and Lahiri Mahasaya before him, said that Babaji *was* Krishna in a former life. Another change is less understandable: the spelling of Yogananda's title, "Paramhansa."

Yogananda himself wrote it that way. SRF added an "a" in the middle of it, thus: *Paramahansa.* Both spellings are encountered in India. The problem with that extra "a," apart from the fact that in Yogananda's printed signature it has necessitated copying another part of the same signature—a glaring forgery—is that it also forces Westerners to mispronounce the word.

For with all those "a"s staring at them, they feel the need to linger on the middle one as if gathering strength to move on to the finish. An Indian, on the other hand, sails over that "a" as if it didn't exist. That is to say, most Indians don't pronounce it at all. Particularly offensive to me personally, however, is the fact that the change, which Tara accepted on the advice of a pundit in India, showed Tara herself willing to take a stranger's word over that of her own Guru. To me this shows her inclination, already evident from other statements of hers, to belittle Master's linguistic ability, from a tendency to pride herself on her own. And this pride of hers is worrying, when one thinks of the editing she did on his works during her final years.

These are all minor points, however, relatively speaking, in view of the many and much graver changes SRF has introduced into his books, teachings, and policies. *Autobiography of a Yogi* has been subjected to so many changes that Ananda, having won from the courts (as you shall see presently) the right to republish that book, has felt it a duty to make the first edition once more available to people.

New editions contain over one hundred additions of the organization's name, many of them obviously with the particular purpose of promoting the organization. Yogananda's original references to communities have been removed as well as any hint of his enthusiasm for them. There are substantive changes in the text, such as the new statement that only SRF-approved ministers may give Kriya Yoga initiation. (What Yogananda originally wrote was, "The actual technique must be learned from a *Kriyaban,* or *Kriya Yogi.*")

A significant change appears also in a passage comparing the path of the yogi householder to that of a swami. The first edition of the book says, "To fulfill one's earthly responsibilities is indeed the higher path, provided the yogi, maintaining a mental uninvolvement with egotistical desires, plays his part as a willing instrument of God." This passage was changed in the mid-1950s (as I happen to know personally, having discussed the matter at the time with Tara). It now reads, "*Fulfilling one's earthly responsibilities need not separate man from God,* provided...."

These are examples, only, of the kind of alterations I mean, all of them intended to increase the authority of Self-Realization Fellowship in the dissemination and practice of Yogananda's teachings.

Another quite amazing change is the exclusion of at least a quarter of his poem, *Samadhi,* from the autobiography.

As for his enthusiasm for communities, SRF downplays it, actually saying (as they do, to justify so many changes), "He changed his mind at the end." Once, however, he declared during a public lecture, "Last night I was thinking so much about communities that I wasn't able to meditate! Then I chanted to God, and my mind came back to me."

Two chapters ago I pointed out the drastic re-editing Tara did on *Whispers from Eternity.* That, too, must be listed among the substantive changes SRF has sanctioned.

A word that is frequently used by SRF is "the

blueprint"—as if Yogananda had sat the directors down and dictated to them his exact wishes for the work. He did nothing of the kind! "The blueprint," he used to say, "is in the ether." The pattern "ordained by God" (as he expressed it to Dr. Lewis) remained for his disciples to work out. Even in the responsibilities he gave me personally, which were considerable, he left it mostly to me to tune in to his will and apply it according to my own ability to perceive. If I needed help, he supplied it, but his way with his disciples was to help them develop their own intuition. The so-called "blueprint," then, is simply an organizational ploy for exercising control.

In 1990, SRF instituted a lawsuit against me and Ananda, claiming it had a monopoly in its name, and the right to prevent me from quoting anything of Yogananda's (my own Guru's!) without their permission. At the present writing, January 2001—nearly eleven years since the suit was filed—the case is not yet completely over, though we've won almost everything. So far, SRF has forced us to spend some five million dollars in defending ourselves.

Could we have simply reacted to their charges by ignoring them? People occasionally ask us this question. The simple answer is, No. How we wish it had been possible! SRF took their suit to the courts of the land, demanding legal sanctions against us. To ignore them would have meant forfeiting the right to continue serving our Guru as his disciples. To submit would have been to admit publicly that they alone have the right to speak on his behalf. It would have meant surrendering any such right, ourselves.

SRF's leaders have done their best to win by bringing us to financial ruin. In the process, they have used endless delaying tactics, and caused us to spend more and more money. Every time they've lost a point, they've appealed it—ineffectively, for the most part—to the higher courts. So far, the outcome has been quite different from what they intended: They have lost the right to a monopoly on their name. They have lost their claim to ownership of Yogananda's writings. Ananda, meanwhile, has been like David fighting Goliath, for SRF is enormously wealthy, and Ananda simply is not. Still, we have so far won almost everything. But the struggle, unfortunately, goes on. Will it go further, after we win everything? Are there other ways they can persecute us? The answer is in God's hands. We are open to His will, no matter what tests He sends us.

In 1997 I wrote Daya Mata to say that the Judge had declared, finally, that he was going to give us both an opportunity now—as he put it—"to practice your own teachings! You'll have to decide these last matters for yourselves." In my letter to Daya I wrote, "Ananda has no desire to gloat over your defeat. We've no wish to declare ourselves victorious, for that would imply that you were the losers. How much better it would be if both of us could declare to the world, 'We've agreed to the following, ...' We could list the points on which we'd agreed, so that what emerged would be perceived as a joint agreement between us." This would, I said, demonstrate harmony between us as fellow disciples of the same great Guru.

Daya Mata agreed to meet us in Pasadena. It was a wonderful reunion: harmonious, loving—an outspoken recognition of the deep bond between us. Always my dream had been that we would work in harmony together, spreading Master's mission of love.

Ananda's view of the teachings, however, seems never to have been the same as SRF's. This fact was revealed clearly by what followed that meeting. Daya has always seen the teachings in terms of centralized control, whereas I have always seen them in terms of people's spiritual needs. Thus, even though our meeting in Pasadena was harmonious, SRF assumed from the love we expressed that we intended to cede back to them everything we'd gained in the case. To us, the construction they placed on our love was hardly believable.

Daya Mata said to me at that meeting, with reference to their persecution of me, "It has never been personal." Needless to say, the person being persecuted is not so easily inclined to see that persecution impersonally. Still, I know what she meant. The issues involved are, in her mind, more important than any individual's life and reputation. A dubious claim, of course, in light of Yogananda's statement, "Only love can take my place"! I'm reminded of a movie in which a lawyer comments on some villain's threat to destroy Los Angeles: "I think we need to define what is meant by 'destroy.'" Jesus Christ said, "He that is faithful in that which is least is faithful also in much; and he that is unjust in the least is unjust also in much." (Luke 16:10) The saying, "I love humanity;

it's my neighbor I can't stand!" seems fitting in this context.

The Catholic Church has used a rationale similar to Daya's in its explanation of the Inquisition, which it still justifies. A recent Vatican item in a secular newspaper in Italy praised Torquemada on the anniversary of his birth—Torquemada, I ask you! the "butcher of the Spanish Inquisition." It described him as a humble, devout monk whose only desire was to protect the faith. Nothing personal in that, of course! When Torquemada burned people at the stake, we were asked to believe that he did it in God's name, that his was an act of love—for the Church, of course, not for human beings, but anyway without animus (so the Church claims) toward the sufferers he tortured and killed. Such is the story. If one steps on an ant, the act is probably quite "impersonal." Still, one wonders how the ant sees it. SRF, however, has stepped on this particular "ant" with such grim determination that it makes the stepping itself seem directed with great and very *personal* feeling.

Is it true that SRF's persecution of Ananda has been impersonal? Hardly! Daya Mata wrote me that it has all been to defend a principle. What principle? No mere institution can be a principle! A principle is by very definition abstract. Their exercise of hegemony, too, reveals considerable personal attachment.

Much has been said and done by SRF and its members to discredit Ananda—all quite impersonally, no doubt! We ourselves, however, have had to fight for our lives. If Master had wanted the organization to be his entire spiritual legacy, I would sincerely embrace it as such, aware that my own understanding, being human, cannot but be fallible. I cannot see, however, that their claim is supported by anything he ever said, did, or wrote.

Wishing to demonstrate complete loyalty to my Guru, however, I actually offered two or three times to give Ananda to Self-Realization Fellowship. This may seem extraordinary for one in my position, but I made the offer not because I'd had any change of heart toward Ananda, and certainly not out of any sense of guilt toward SRF. Indeed, Ananda represents for me the culmination of my life's work. It might also be fairly considered a vindication and a triumph for me personally, especially in light of the things Tara said against me. I offered Ananda to SRF with the simple thought, "This has never been my work. It is Master's. If by any chance it should end up becoming SRF's, I would relinquish it gladly." To underscore my complete non-attachment I offered even to leave Ananda forever, and never give it a backward glance.

Obviously, Ananda members themselves would have had to be consulted, and their feelings taken into account. As a formal proposal, therefore, my offer was contingent on the will of others, not only on my own will. The important thing then, to me, was that I be completely willing to leave everything, if such should happen to be my Guru's will. What became of me personally thereafter would, I felt, be entirely in his hands.

Simplicity, however, is not often understood. Ananda itself has been simple in its motivation regarding SRF's lawsuits. "Whatever you want," we have prayed to God and our Gurus, "we will accept with love." Daya Mata herself led us in a similar prayer in Fresno in 1990, before the formal filing of their lawsuit. When decision after decision went against them, however, they appealed, and appealed again, then yet again. In the end they submitted the matter to the U.S. Supreme Court. Daya's prayer might perhaps have been better stated: "Master, may your will be done—provided it agrees with mine!"

The first time I offered Ananda to SRF was in 1972. Daya Mata replied then, "We'll see." Nothing happened. Later I made the same offer by letter, to which a variety of responses came from SRF's representatives, none of them positive. (Their general tone suggested that I was being merely irresponsible.) The third time I offered, Daya Mata replied, "We wouldn't want to inherit your debts." Could she possibly believe that Ananda was teetering on the verge of collapse? Disappointed at the meaning implied in her answer, I replied, "And I wouldn't want to give you Ananda if I thought you would run it into the ground!"

Daya once said to me, "It isn't the good people of Ananda I have anything against. It's Kriyananda." To me, the only thing that matters is that we have the freedom to serve our Guru's mission. SRF had raised me in the thought that the organization *was* his work. Ananda members, on the other hand, have never shared this scruple. I myself have seen from SRF's very narrowness that the scope of his mission is far, far broader. Ananda, to us now, has been and always will be part of Master's work—that is to say, of his overall mission. Our members are directly acquainted with SRF, for it is not very far from Ananda's California communities and many have gone there. I have often said to people, "Visit SRF. See for yourselves, then draw your own conclusions." Most of them have chosen Ananda, though I have not influenced them to do so. Their choice is not grudging—a sort of compromise, or necessary substitute for SRF. Many have told me, "I would never have become Master's disciple except through Ananda." Most of them add, "Their way simply doesn't attract me." In the eyes of God, I believe they are right to follow their soul-guidance. Still, I have given them perfect freedom to make that discovery for themselves.

SRF's denunciations of me have been surprisingly personal. They have denounced me to the courts as an "interloper." They have attempted to defame my character, my discipleship, my spiritual and moral integrity, my right to speak on behalf of my Guru. I'm sure they feel, however, that none of this is "personal." They have repeatedly rejected my attempts to bring unity between SRF and Ananda, but have not shown the slightest qualm about trying to steal Ananda members, or even Ananda itself, away from me whenever they've seen a hope of fomenting trouble between us.

Do these attempts reflect Master's counsel to Daya Mata, "Only love can take my place"?

In my heart, and I'm sure in the hearts of all Ananda members, there is deep love and fellow-feeling for the members of SRF: for its renunciates and lay-members alike. We deeply desire harmony with them, and would willingly forget all past hurts unhesitatingly in the name of love. If truth is needed to clear the air—and such is presently, I believe, the case—we speak it with sorrow, and with unchanging love. If by any chance their efforts to destroy us should prove successful, we would love them still. Until now, however, our efforts to win them with love have meant only a hardening of their animus toward us. I cannot but think that the consequence, for them, has been their spiritual and institutional loss.

One point stands out, however, in their efforts to undermine Ananda. If a person seeks victory by honorable means, it may be that he is merely mistaken, in which case he cannot be held spiritually culpable. If, however, he seeks victory by dishonest and underhanded means, there can be no justification for his actions. In such a case, indeed, he can only be considered dishonorable.

SRF has lied. Daya Mata herself has lied. Daya Mata has asked me, too, to lie in order to protect SRF's name. The tactics their lawyers have used, which SRF has endorsed, have been what other lawyers themselves call "despicable." This aspect of the story is so sordid that I cannot even bring myself to describe it in detail.

There is another instance, here, of karmic repetition. The early Christians are known to have gathered into small, spiritual communities—"intentional" in the sense that their members shared the same beliefs, practices, and ideals.

Why does history tell us so little about those communities? From all indications, they were successful. The inevitable conclusion, surely, is that they were suppressed along with the gnostics. Indeed, autonomous communities can only have been considered a threat by the Church in its determination to impose control on its members. It is for similar reasons, surely, that SRF is not happy with Ananda's existence.

Since communities would certainly have been inconvenient to the newly organized Christian Church, it seems probably for this reason that references to those early communities were suppressed, along with the gnostic writings. Yet what could have been more natural than for Jesus to want people to live together in communities, practicing together the teachings he had given them?

At any rate, Paramhansa Yogananda himself urged people all his life to form communities. And SRF, like the early Church, has set itself against this idea. Daya once said to me, when I raised this subject, "Frankly, I'm not interested." In 1988, to celebrate our twentieth anniversary, a group of 200 members went from Ananda to visit SRF's main centers in southern California. On the Encinitas grounds, the nun in charge, Sister Shanti, stated to a group of us, "Oh, I know, many people have tried to start communities, but none of them have succeeded." Two hundred people, celebrating twenty years of successful existence, and she could say that to us! Her very statement makes it clear, however, that SRF has no serious intention of ever starting the communities for which Master campaigned so ardently.

Yogananda himself tried to start a community in Encinitas. His hopes were not destined to be fulfilled during his lifetime, and I cannot help thinking that one reason the venture was abandoned was owing to resistance by some of his monastic disciples. Even so, until the end of his life he kept urging people to form communities. His last-known plea on the point came only four months before he left his body. Kamala Silva reported it in her book, *The Flawless Mirror,* from a conversation she had with him.

It has been my own lot to fulfill Yogananda's communitarian dream. Ananda now consists of six communities: five in America and one in Italy, with a seventh under way in Rhode Island. An ancient karmic pattern is re-emerging through Ananda's striking success story: a repetition of the trend begun long ago among the early Christians. I've pointed out SRF's attempt to freeze the mission of Paramhansa Yogananda. SRF seeks to exercise rigid control over its members, who go along with that attempt in the sincere belief that such was Yogananda's desire. His wish, certainly, was that his disciples love one another and not fight together. I myself have been "turning the other cheek" for decades. Can I continue to do so now with integrity, in the face of renewed attacks by them? Master told us not to be doormats for others. Self-respect, and respect for truth itself, demands that I defend myself and Ananda—with love, yes, but firmly.

Ananda today

(right) Crystal Hermitage today, as seen from the interior garden

(below) The colonnade, fountain, gardens, chapel, and Shrine of the Masters at Crystal Hermitage

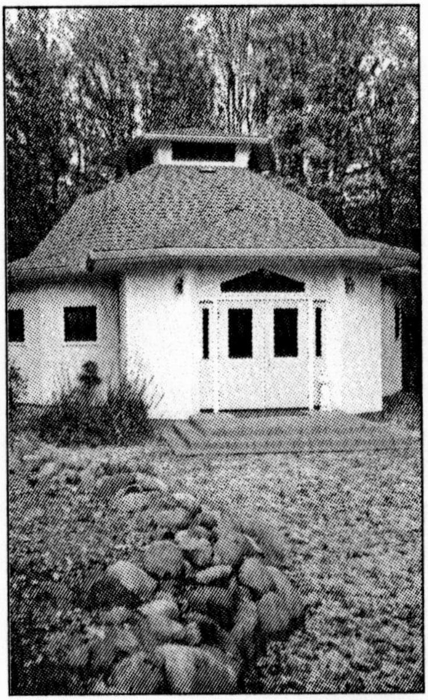

The temple (left) and dining room (below) at the Seclusion Retreat, which has maintained the vibration of the simple forest hermitage from which Ananda has evolved

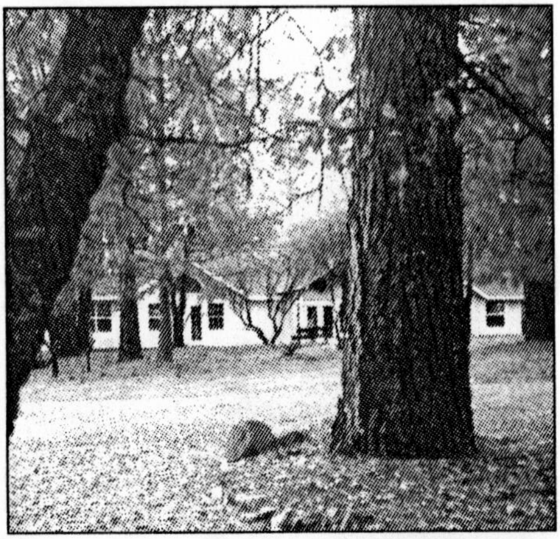

(right) The dining room, temple, and adjoining gardens at The Expanding Light, our meditation retreat

(right) A small meditation shrine dedicated to Lahiri Mahasaya, Yogananda's guru's guru, at The Expanding Light

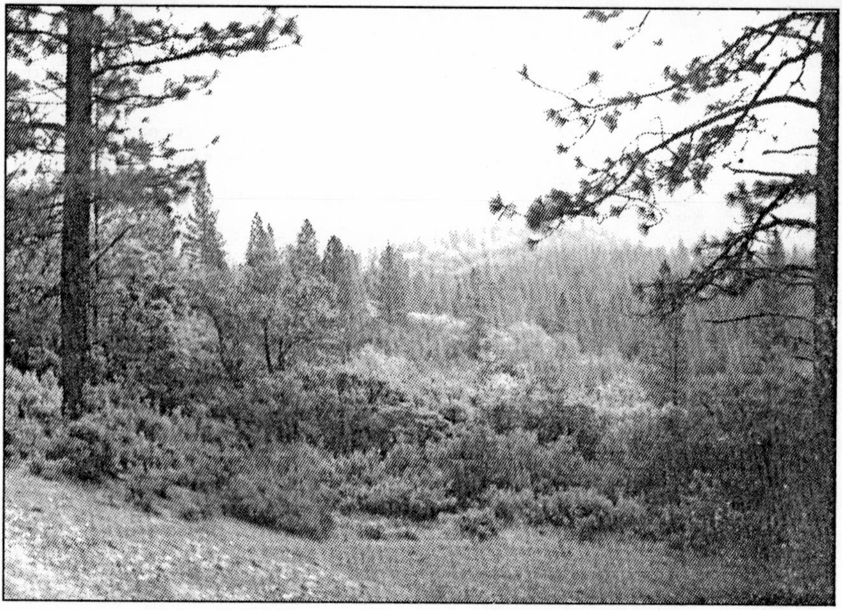

(above) The Sierra Nevada mountains, seen from the Seclusion Retreat

(above) Ananda now has a variety of single-family dwellings, large and small. (directly above left) There are also several shared living situations, such as this cluster of cottages which share a common dining room and garden.

Ananda Worldwide

(right) The Temple of Light at Ananda's international retreat center near Assisi, Italy

(right) Ananda Mandir in Palo Alto, California. Ananda also has a branch community in Sacramento, California, as well as communities and teaching centers in Washington, Oregon, and Rhode Island.

(right) Jyotish and Devi Novak, the spiritual directors of Ananda

What Ananda stands for is an attempt, paralleling that of the Gnostics and the early Christians, to simplify matters, and to center the teachings in the individual's own Self-realization. To Daya Mata, we and everyone who disagrees with her are—to quote a favorite expression of hers—"pipsqueaks." In my belief, and Ananda's, all of us (including Daya herself) are children of God, heirs in equal right to soul-freedom in Him.

Again, there is a growing insistence within SRF that the strictly monastic life is the only way to serve and spread Yogananda's teachings. Many of his close disciples, however, were, or had been, married. Suppression of non-monastic communities is another indication of a historic karmic pattern. The struggle between inner spirituality and "churchified" spirituality is being repeated in the struggle between SRF and Ananda. I myself deeply believe in the monastic ideal. I too am a monk, and, despite many attempts by SRF and its members to deride my monastic calling, I am firmly committed to it. Monasticism sets an example to devotees everywhere that the spiritual life must be founded at least on *inner* renunciation. I have, however, seen a measure of arrogance among renunciates in their calling that I heard Yogananda himself also deplore.

In about 1970, some of the members of Ananda expressed a desire to start a monastery. Though I encouraged them, it was with trepidation, for I realized that men and women living in the same community would probably not succeed in persevering in that calling. In fact, the monastery did not endure permanently, at least in that form. What came out of it eventually, however, was a new kind of monastic order including householders dedicated to the traditional monastic ideals of non-attachment, simplicity, service, and self-control. Such a community, I find, is an inspiration to people everywhere, at a time when most monasteries in the world are empty. It inspires, moreover, in a way that communities that are exclusively monastic, in the traditional sense, have not achieved, or at least are not achieving nowadays. People at every stage of life are encouraged to be devotees wholeheartedly. This pattern of life was first established by Lahiri Mahasaya. Paramhansa Yogananda approved of it, and, indeed, recommended it for most people.

I had to set the pattern myself—such, it seems, has always been my job at Ananda—for "monastic householdership." Seeing many Ananda members burdened with feelings of guilt that they couldn't be renunciates, I deliberately chose marriage for myself. This step was of course, for me, a serious risk, but I felt that I could accept the married state now without losing my inner spirit of renunciation. My marriage completely changed the community. Everyone, since then, has felt a pure dedication to God and to doing God's will. Our teachers and ministers, householders all, are the best I've encountered in any spiritual community. As for myself, God saw to it that the marriage didn't last. I am grateful for what I gained from it. I am grateful He took the burden from me. At no time, I am glad to say, did I feel any personal attachment to it. I was, am, and always will be a monk at heart above all.

Ananda has already broken many karmic patterns of the past. A new pattern is emerging instead—one of personal spiritual freedom, similar to the system since ancient times in India, where no organization tried to control people's spiritual quest. In India, far more so than in the West, the purity of the spiritual teachings has been maintained by the spontaneous devotion of sincere individuals. Above all, it has been maintained by the repeated manifestation on its soil of great saints. India's is the final, complete disproof of any claim that an organization is needed to uphold the purity of high teachings.

Ananda's, then, is a success story: gloriously so! Many thousands of lives have been changed, even by simple contact with it. I never forget, however, where that success comes from. It comes not from this simple, mere human being, but from God, and from the blessings that fill our hearts from our great gurus.

Conclusion

Everything in life necessitates cooperation. Breathing itself is an act of cooperation with Nature. Great works of genius require the work of many: those who make the tools used in creativity; a general foundation of awareness from which the individual can soar; the inspiration of others' thoughts; an appreciative audience. Would Leonardo have produced his masterpieces had no one been interested in his work? Would Jesus Christ, self-complete to perfection, have given outer expression to his wisdom had no one cared to hear him? Jesus himself said, "Cast not your pearls before swine." A need must exist before it can be addressed. Cooperation of many kinds is essential to life itself. Without it, there would be only one hand flapping, but no answering clap.

Cooperation within intentional communities can lead to madness, however, if it isn't based on a desire to cooperate with wisdom, at least to the extent that its members understand the concept.

I have tried in these pages to present the principles out of which Ananda grew and has flourished. I admit that my first expectation was that I'd tell more of Ananda's actual story: to bring it up to date with anecdotes, and to explain the lessons we learned from our tests, adventures, and interesting or amusing episodes. Fortunately, these events were mostly a proving ground for the teachings of our Guru, Paramhansa Yogananda. I say therefore that, apart from the blessing he bestowed on the concept itself, he is, in fact, the patron saint of modern communities. His frequent intervention in times of need, though subtle, has been repeatedly a lifesaver for us. Instead of writing the anecdotes that make up Ananda's history, what I have done is leave you—poor reader!—stranded on a beach. The launching of the ship, Ananda, to which I thought I was inviting you, has been delayed. By 1970, the point to which this story has taken us, the ship was still unfinished. Many events followed, some of them dramatic. In fact, I wonder whether the story can ever be told fully.

In March of the year 1970, I received a second threat of foreclosure, this one from the trustees for Ananda farm. (On the last possible day I was able to send the check in the mail!) One month later, on the fourth of July (Independence Day, of all dates!), our temple burned down. This proved in fact to be a blessing, for rebuilding it provided a means for uniting the community in a common purpose.

Again and again, miracles saved us—like the day our carpenters, building the publications building (renamed since then, "Hansa Mandir"), were saved from disaster. The roof had an unusual design, which the men couldn't carry to completion. Extensive research hadn't provided a solution for its construction. The men were literally leaving the job when a car drove up, and a man stepped out of it. "I've come from Santa Barbara today—five hundred miles!" he announced. "My purpose in coming was to ask if there's anything I can do to help you." Hope glimmered faintly. The men explained their predicament, whereupon the visitor exclaimed, "Why, I'm probably the only builder in California who knows just the technique you need for this job. It's something I learned in Canada, brought over from the Orient." With this help, the roof was completed.

We were blessed with tests also—like the forest fire I've mentioned already—and the pluck that helped us persist in the face of seeming defeat: Jyotish turning to his wife Devi, who ten days earlier had given birth to their only child, and saying, "Well, at least this fire solves the problem we've been having with leaks!"

I could go on and on. Indeed, I expected I'd do so: What a lot remains to be told! And I'd have enjoyed the telling of it. Such a book, however, might easily run to more than a thousand pages: far too long, and counter-productive to its real purpose. Indeed, the story has already been told by the explanations I've given of the principles on which Ananda was founded. Those principles tell who we are, what Ananda is, and why the whole experiment has turned out so successfully. I hope I've shown convincingly why my belief in cooperative communities is very deep. To me, they are an essential solution to the problems of civilization at this stage of history. Small, clearly thought-out, consciously lived experiments are needed as a way of working out the challenge before humanity: how to preserve human values under the onslaught of technology. I've explained basic attitudes without which, I think, no community can succeed. What would follow the telling would only be details. A plethora of them might cause the reader to lose sight of more important points.

I built Ananda on principles I'd learned through meditating on the life of Paramhansa Yogananda; after years of working with people, as head of the monks in Self-Realization Fellowship, and as the director of SRF center activities throughout the world; as the victim of ongoing attempts to suppress, and then ruin me; and as a consequence of having to deal with people's indifference to interests other than their own. One of the things I learned was the relative importance of cheerful, willing cooperation compared to blind obedience.

At Ananda, I delegated responsibility to others as much as I could. I did so partly because it takes the energy of many people to create a work of which the goal is to benefit people. Partly, too, I did so because I recognized that others were blessed with skills in which I myself was lacking. I always took care to protect, and also to further, principles of practical spirituality in keeping with my Guru's advice to me: "Be practical in your idealism." I contributed my own energy—often to the limit of my strength—while never forgetting that we are all only small cogs on life's very large wheel. Community leadership requires team effort. Success is not a one-man show.

I tried, therefore, to channel energy and inspiration *through* others, in cooperation with them, and never stood over them as "the manager," nor intruded on their free will. Instead, I tried to win them by kindly reason, and by my own sincere commitment to truth no matter who utters it.

At this point in my story, then, practicing as ever the principle of delegating authority, I leave to my companions in our thirty-four-year odyssey the task of telling what remains—the bulk, indeed—of this saga! Each of them will tell it differently, and will give his or her perspective. And so they ought to do, for it is their story and Ananda's quite as much as it is mine. The story will be the richer because I didn't write all of it myself.

There are a few points I'd like to make here, at the end of my account: a few final hammer taps, so to speak, to make sure the nails are set as tightly as possible.

One of those "nails" is a question that several readers, I suspect, will have asked: Is it necessary for a community like Ananda to be spiritual? Much thought has been devoted in modern times to finding solutions that depend entirely on human effort, without God—and without even such high ideals as love, happiness, and voluntary (as opposed to enforced) cooperation. I've written unabashedly of my own ideal: to live wholeheartedly for God. I fully realize that to say so is frowned upon in today's society. Even granting that Ananda has worked well, is there a hope that a more "normal" community can succeed?

No; frankly, I see no such hope. The reason is perfectly simple: A so-called "normal" life is *not* really normal at all: It is *ab*normal! If people live selfishly, what hope have they of clambering out of their habit-worn mental ruts? Attempts have been made, and the results always have been disappointing.

I hope you won't mind if I have a little fun here? I have a counter-question to offer: Is it necessary for a community to be *alive?* Is it necessary for a body to have a head, and for that head to hold brains? Is it necessary for human beings to be *conscious?* Modern communist philosophy exalts muscle over brain, and the "proletariat" over a so-called "aristocratic elite." In effect, what it encourages is stupidity with the purpose of gaining mass control by a false "elite" of self-centered, cloddish bullies. Tara Mata's concept of crowd management was essentially no different from that of Marx, Engel, and Lenin. Cooperative communities can succeed only if greater, not less, awareness is encouraged. The concept of God symbolizes, if nothing else, the need of every human being to aspire to the highest potential he can imagine for himself.

What do people think it *means* to be spiritual? Do they imagine it to be a matter of telling long strings of beads and mumbling incessant prayers? What kind of tasteless pudding do they think the masters have invited mankind to ingest? Do people want ideals without challenges? or safe platitudes that merely fall flat, like an eggless soufflé, the wisdom sucked out of them for fear of giving offense? Do they want popular acclaim without integrity, and principles so bland that no one even notices they exist? If you want to "people" such a wasteland with cactuses, go to your Nietzsches, your Sartres, your biologists who claim life is meaningless because they've worked out a handful of mere evolutionary mechanisms! An intentional community with no higher goal than economic security is not what I've proposed in these pages. Nor is it what I have struggled, suffered, and even risked my life to achieve. My dream at fifteen remains unchanged after sixty years. I am no longer young, but in spirit I am younger than ever, secure in a way that I see leads to inner freedom, happiness, inspiration, and the richest possible sense of meaning. If your own quest is for something else, then ignore this book. Warn your friends not to read it. Pretended solutions, however, that skirt the question of spirituality are sodas without the fizz; lemonades without the lemon; books without a light for reading.

Yes, I believe that if a community would find meaning in life, and not a sleeping pill slugged down with a glass of water, people have no choice but to be spiritual! The only thing I concede—in fact, insist upon—is that spirituality not be lumped with *religiosity.*

Man is a spiritual being. Of this I am certain. If he rejects the higher reality of his being, which would inspire him to highest achievements, he is a walking, eating corpse, incapable of bringing life to this planet, and able only to procreate other corpses like himself.

One of the most important aspects of Ananda, and a fitting note on which to close this book, is music. I have noticed, as have many Ananda members, that those who have become involved in our music, played it, sung it in our choirs, listened to it at home and at work, have understood *in their hearts* what Ananda is all about. To convey this understanding by words alone would be impossible.

Man consists essentially of sound vibrations condensed from the music of Creation. Without music, life itself would cease to be. Communities can succeed only if every member seeks his own center, not in outer consensus, but in himself. It is from this center that he should reach out to touch others. From within, finally, and in attunement with the inner Song of Creation, comes the harmony that enables people to work together in a spirit of *true* harmony.

Therefore Yogananda said, "Seclusion is the price of greatness."

We must listen to the voice of God in our souls. Inner communion with Him will put us in touch with our conscience. To walk with others in lock-step togetherness is to become at last a mere lemming, plunging to destruction because one has failed to develop awareness, lives oblivious to present realities, and ends in the gray oblivion of death. To stride through life in company with others, singing joyfully, is to become the hero, or heroine, that God has ever intended us to be.

Afterword

It's strange that something I have puzzled over for fifty years should suddenly come clear to me now, simply because it was someone else who asked me the question. It has happened to me often, however: I've pondered something for years, but only when the same question was put to me by someone else did I suddenly know the solution.

In this case, it was something my Guru said to me at least twice, and perhaps three times: "After I am gone, the monks must live in separate colonies from the women renunciates." Later I discovered he had not said this to the women, who were in fact running things. Why, I asked myself, would he say something so important to the future of his work only to me? Granted, I was in charge of the monks, but my responsibility at the time spread no further than that. In later years, my concern for finding a separate piece of property on Mount Washington was even turned against me by Mrinalini Mata who wrote the other directors in support of my ouster from SRF, "I always felt that Kriyananda's desire to find a separate property was because he wanted to get the monks out from under Daya Mata's control."

Why did Master tell me, but not Daya Mata? My puzzlement regarding Master's words was increased by the fact that Señor Cuaron, our center leader and representative in Mexico, told me once during a visit, "Master said to me yesterday, 'I see you in a building down on the corner of the property on Mount Washington.'" This was where San Rafael Avenue meets Rome Drive. Here, in later years, the monks' ashram was constructed.

Why, I asked myself, had Master insisted to me so strongly that the monks must live altogether separately from the women, then not tell anyone else, especially the women in charge, that this was his wish? And why would he then tell Mr. Cuaron he saw him in another building on the Mount Washington property, a building which he must have known would be the monks' ashram?

A friend recently put this question to me, motivating me to put it to Master in meditation. Instantly the answer came: "Because I wanted you to think of yourself as working separately from the women directors! You could never have done the work you have done, except independently of them."

One naturally wonders why he didn't simply come out and tell me so. It was necessary, however, that the karmic pattern follow its own course. I often found in his guidance that he gave only subtle hints of his deeper meaning. My service to him would not have worked out as it did, had I known his intentions from the start. I am grateful, though, for what he did state clearly at the time. I might have lacked the courage to think as independently as I did, had it not been for those words of his to me.

About the Author

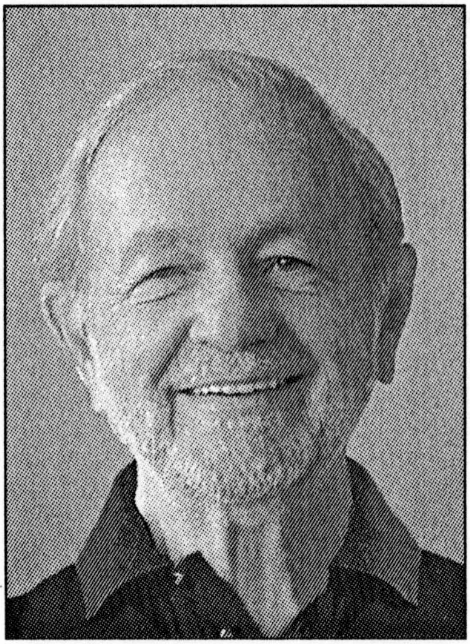

J. Donald Walters was born in Romania of American parents. He was schooled in Switzerland and England until the outbreak of World War II, when his family settled in America. There, his dissatisfaction with the schooling inspired him, years later, to develop a new system which he called Education for Life, out of which are evolving a growing number of Living Wisdom schools.

In 1948, after reading *Autobiography of a Yogi* by Paramhansa Yogananda, Walters traveled to California, where Yogananda accepted him as a disciple. *A Place Called Ananda* describes his early years of discipleship; his experience as head monk in Self-Realization Fellowship (SRF); his crisis of conscience when, following his master's death, he tried to abide by his instructions. Eventually he was expelled from SRF, under circumstances that at first seemed tragic to him, but that in fact released him to fulfill his own guru-given task and his own boyhood dream (which Yogananda shared) of founding cooperative spiritual communities.

Walters has authored some seventy books, and composed over 300 works of music, all of them written to inspire in others a higher vision of life. His major work is described in this book: the creation of the world-renowned communities known as Ananda.

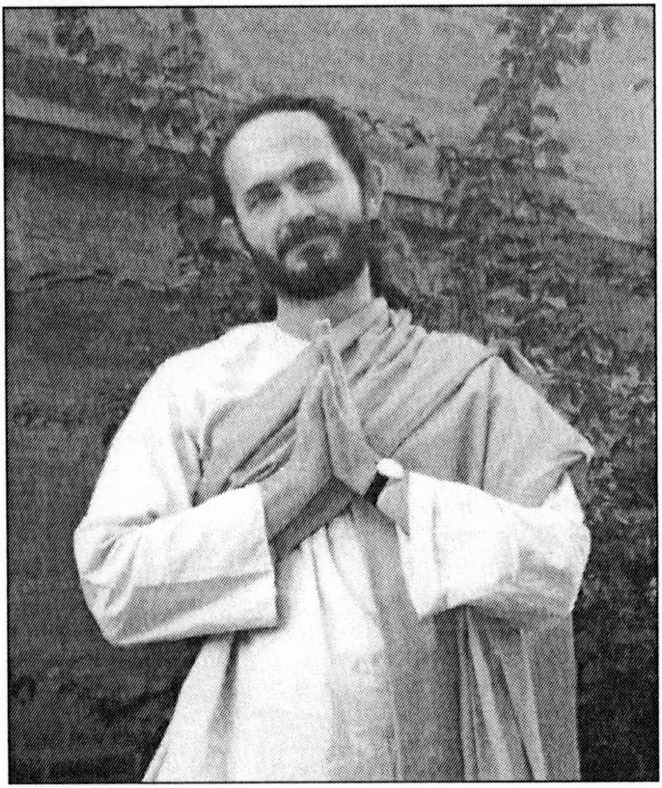

Patiala, India in 1959. I offer the traditional Indian greeting "namaste," which means, "My soul bows to your soul."

9 781565 891586